METROPOLITAN COLLEGE OF N.
LIBRARY, 12TH FLOOR
431 CANAL STREET
NEW YORK, NY 10013

BECOMING BUREAUCRATS

AMERICAN GOVERNANCE: POLITICS, POLICY, AND PUBLIC LAW

Series Editors:
Richard Valelly, Pamela Brandwein,
Marie Gottschalk, Christopher Howard

A complete list of books in the series
is available from the publisher

BECOMING BUREAUCRATS

Socialization at the Front Lines of Government Service

Zachary W. Oberfield

PENN

UNIVERSITY OF PENNSYLVANIA PRESS

PHILADELPHIA

Copyright © 2014 University of Pennsylvania Press

All rights reserved. Except for brief quotations used for purposes of review or scholarly citation, none of this book may be reproduced in any form by any means without written permission from the publisher.

Published by
University of Pennsylvania Press
Philadelphia, Pennsylvania 19104-4112
upenn.edu/pennpress

Printed in the United States of America
on acid-free paper

1 3 5 7 9 10 8 6 4 2

Library of Congress Cataloging-in-Publication Data
Oberfield, Zachary W.
Becoming bureaucrats : socialization at the front lines of government service / Zachary W. Oberfield. — 1st ed.
p. cm. — (American governance : politics, policy, and public law)
Includes bibliographical references and index.
ISBN 978-0-8122-4616-2 (hardcover : alk. paper)
1. Civil service—Training of. 2. Government employees—Training of. 3. Bureaucrats—Training of. 4. Police—Attitudes. 5. Social workers—Attitudes. 6. Organizational sociology. I. Title. II. Series: American governance.
JF1601.O24 2014
305.9'35173—dc23
2014003054

CONTENTS

Chapter 1. Bureaucratic Socialization — 1

Chapter 2. Dispositions and Institutions — 22

Chapter 3. The Long View: How Veteran Workers See Their Worlds — 39

Chapter 4. Entry: An In-Depth Account — 56

Chapter 5. In the Service of Others? Motivation, Altruism, and Egoism — 87

Chapter 6. Bureaucratic Identity: Rules and Loyalty — 113

Chapter 7. Attitudes: Social Problems, Race, and Deservingness — 140

Chapter 8. Change and Continuity at Government's Front Lines — 164

Appendix A. Research Design — 179

Appendix B. Recruitment and Job Requirements — 199

Appendix C. Measurement and Analysis — 201

Notes — 211
Bibliography — 217
Index — 231
Acknowledgments — 235

CHAPTER 1

Bureaucratic Socialization

Though it has more than four letters, "bureaucrat" is a bad word.[1] It evokes Kafkaesque paperwork and government workers who are out of touch, rule-obsessed, and heartless. Despite the word's cultural resonance, and its usefulness as a rhetorical device (Safire 1978), the myth bears little resemblance to reality: public-sector workers aren't the alienated, rigid lot of our imagination. In fact, there is considerable variation in bureaucratic thought and behavior across governments and inside particular agencies (Brehm and Gates 1997; DeHart-Davis 2007; Goodsell 2004; O'Leary 2010). Some bureaucrats are unpleasant, rule-focused, and motivated by a pension; others are friendly, comfortable bending the rules, and driven by a strong sense of public service.

Despite a growing scholarly recognition that actual bureaucrats don't resemble the bureaucrats of public imagination, we have little understanding about what explains this variation. In part this is because we know little about bureaucratic socialization—the process by which public-sector entrants develop the knowledge, attitudes, and behaviors necessary to function as bureaucrats.[2] To what extent do factors outside the organization shape who a bureaucrat becomes? To what extent does working in a bureaucracy cultivate particular tendencies?

Answering these questions is important because elected officials and public managers delegate responsibility to bureaucracies for implementing a wide range of services. In the abstract, this relationship is simple and evokes the efficiency of a vending machine: elected officials insert money and make selections, and bureaucrats do as they're told (Kettl 2002). In reality, the process is exceedingly complicated (Bardach 1977; Pressman and Wildavsky 1984; Riccucci et al. 2004). One of the chief complications is that bureaucrats have considerable discretion (Lipsky 1980). Elected officials pass legislation, and public managers instruct workers about how to accomplish their goals. Nonetheless, it is bureaucrats who decide what the rules mean and how they are applied in practice. Therefore, understanding public policy requires studying who bureaucrats are and how they are "made."

On a more practical level, understanding bureaucratic socialization is necessary for building responsive, accountable public workforces. If bureaucrats are mostly shaped by pre- and extraorganizational influences, then policymakers, public managers, and scholars should be primarily concerned with recruitment and self-selection. If bureaucratic thought and action are mostly a function of intraorganizational experiences, we must understand how newcomers are affected by the social forces that they encounter. As this discussion suggests, there are two basic explanations for bureaucratic socialization: the dispositional and institutional perspectives.

The dispositional perspective emphasizes the role that individuals and extraorganizational influences play in how entrants develop (Cheek and Piercy 2001; Griffin and Ruiz 1999; Kuhlman 1976; Zimbardo 2004). According to this view, the attitudes and experiences that workers bring with them into their organizations affect how they think and act as organization members; therefore, at the macro level, the character of an organization would depend upon patterns of self-selection and recruitment. Politically, the dispositional perspective resonates with arguments about the primacy of individual self-sufficiency and responsibility. As such, it is frequently invoked after the misdeeds of a particular public worker or group of workers are made public. For example, consider Abu Ghraib.

During the Iraq War, coalition forces overtook Abu Ghraib, a prison that had been used by Saddam Hussein, and began using it to detain common criminals and suspected insurgents. Military Police (MPs) were charged with running the prison, and by most accounts, they did a bad job. An internal Army investigation reported numerous instances in which the MPs abused prisoners and revealed the existence of pictures, which were subsequently released to the public, that showed them posing happily with dead bodies and humiliating prisoners (Hersh 2004). The pictures shocked the U.S. public and created a public relations firestorm for the Bush administration. In response, the administration sought to portray the MPs as rogues and to argue that they were not representative of other troops or the broader war effort (Reid 2009; Shermer 2007). In doing so, they made a classic dispositional argument—they sought to direct attention and culpability to a few "bad apples."

In contrast, the institutional perspective points to the intraorganizational systems, processes, and dynamics that shape how bureaucrats see themselves and act (Griffin and Ruiz 1999; Hall 1977; Merton 1940; Skolnick 1966; Zimbardo 2004).

From this perspective, individuals internalize the views embedded in the organizations that they enter. For example, Barnett (1999, 7) argues that bureaucracies are not just aggregations of the people who enter them. Rather, they are "orienting machines" and incubators of "ethical claims." As such, the character of a bureaucracy and the thoughts and actions of individual bureaucrats depend upon internal social forces like culture and management.

This line of argument also has considerable public traction: during bureaucratic crises, media outlets and academics that are critical of a political body or government agency tend to invoke the institutional perspective. For example, in response to the Bush administration's dispositional argument about the Abu Ghraib MPs, critics countered that the abuses emerged due to the prison's social dynamics, the lack of oversight by the armed forces, and improper training (Gourevitch and Morris 2008; Hersh 2004; Shermer 2007).

To a certain extent these two perspectives set out explanations that are too simplistic and self-contained—it is a truism that organizational psychology and behavior result from a combination of dispositional and institutional influences (O'Reilly, Chatman, and Caldwell 1991; Saks and Ashforth 1997; Zimbardo 2004). Nonetheless, many studies essentially end there, arguing that "it's both." In other words, they recognize the importance of dispositions and institutions but make little effort to specify how much each matters. For instance, Kaufman's (1960) *The Forest Ranger* suggests that rangers' preferences and behavior are shaped by job experiences and the organization's efforts to "preform" their decisions during training. However, the book also notes that the department depends heavily on recruitment and self-selection. Men with a "love of the woods" are encouraged to join the ranks, while others are advised to spend their lives "in some other way" (Kaufman 1960, 162). Thus, via a mixture of recruitment and training, Kaufman argues that the Forest Service is able to create a workforce that thinks and acts as the organization desires. Though his account is commendably holistic, the extent to which entering characteristics matter, compared to institutional forces like training, remains opaque.

Though most accounts of bureaucratic behavior highlight the importance of dispositions and institutions, those that stake out a position on their relative importance tend to side with the latter (Arendt 1963; Barnett 1999; Kelman and Hamilton 1990; Lipsky 1980; H. Simon 1947, 1997; Zimbardo 2004). For example, in Herbert Simon's pathbreaking book *Administrative Behavior* (1997, 18), he argues, "One does not live for months or years in a particular position in an organization, exposed to some streams of communication, shielded from others, without the most profound effects upon what one knows, believes, attends to, hopes, wishes, emphasizes, fears, and proposes." Michael Herzfeld (1993) agrees with Simon that something changes in people when they enter organizations. Although Simon doesn't specify whether exposure to an organization is positive or negative, Herzfeld (1993, 1) argues that after being put behind a desk bureaucrats become "humorless automatons."

Ralph Hummel (1982, 2) echoes Herzfeld but ups the ante by arguing that "bureaucracy gives birth to a new species of inhuman beings. People's social relations are being converted into control relations. Their norms and beliefs concerning human ends are torn from them and replaced with skills affirming the ascendancy of technical means, whether of administration or production. Psychologically, the new personality type is that of the rationalistic expert, incapable of emotion and devoid of will." Accounts like these are compelling because they align with modern narratives about how good-intentioned public servants become burned-out bureaucrats. The problem, however, is that many institutional accounts rely more on myth than data. Those that do examine personnel data tend to look at organizations and people at a single moment in time. In other words, there are precious few studies that employ longitudinal research to show how individual public bureaucrats are socialized into their organizations over time.[3]

As such, we are left with somewhat muddy accounts, which don't specify how much one set of factors matter, and studies that suggest support for the institutional perspective, but rely upon conventional wisdom or cross-sectional research. To bring some clarity to our understanding of bureaucratic socialization, this book studies two sets of street-level bureaucrats, police officers and welfare caseworkers, as they enter their organizations and become insiders. By understanding where they start and tracking how they develop psychologically, the book shows how newcomers become bureaucrats.

Although the psychological development of bureaucrats is an important outcome in its own right, this book is motivated by an interest in bureaucratic behavior. Thus, at the outset, it is crucial to discuss the relationship between bureaucratic thought and action.

Bureaucratic Behavior and the Logic of Appropriateness

As scholars have looked inside organizations to study what drives bureaucratic behavior, they have discovered a surprisingly complicated story (Barnard 1938; Brehm and Gates 1997; Crozier 1964; Downs 1967; Golden 2000; Kaufman 1960; Soss, Fording, and Schram 2011a; Weick 1995; J. Wilson 1989). As rational choice and principal-agent accounts would expect, bureaucratic actors appear to be motivated, at least in part, by satisfying their personal interests. For instance, Golden (2000) examines the bureaucratic response to the Reagan administration in the early 1980s. Though much of Reagan's agenda conflicted with the values and goals held by bureaucrats, they were responsive to the incoming administration's policy directives. In part, she argues, this responsiveness was driven by the desire to maintain and advance their careers. In this way, her account squares with a basic understanding that elected officials are powerful principals who have considerable leverage over unelected agents.

However, while acknowledging that there are times when bureaucrats act as principal-agent theory would expect, elected officials and public managers cannot always or perfectly structure the incentives of lower-level bureaucrats. In part, this is because public principals are disadvantaged in making effective use of incentives compared to their private-sector colleagues (Rainey 2003; J. Wilson 1989). For example, rewarding employees monetarily is typically not as feasible in the public sector as it is in the private. In addition, public agents are different from private agents because they are often asked to be responsive to multiple principals. Because these principals may have competing ideologies and political interests, it isn't always clear to whom public agents answer and what they should do.

Perhaps as a result, many accounts suggest that bureaucratic behavior is driven by identities and motivations that are difficult to formalize, legislate, and incentivize (Brehm and Gates 1997; Brewer and Selden 1998; Maynard-Moody and Musheno 2003; Portillo 2008; Sandfort, Kalil, and Gottschalk 1999; Schram et al. 2009; Selden, Brudney, and Kellough 1998). For example, the representative bureaucracy literature indicates that bureaucrats use their racial and gender identities to guide their actions on the job. One study in the literature, for instance, shows that bureaucrats in the Farmers Home Administration who identify as minority representatives are more likely to make loan decisions favoring minority applicants (Selden, Brudney, and Kellough 1998). Similarly, the public service motivation literature shows that bureaucrats who are motivated by protecting the public interest are more likely to act as whistle-blowers when they observe waste and fraud in government (Brewer and Selden 1998).

As these accounts suggest, it would be a mistake to assume that bureaucratic behavior can be understood by studying incentives and rules alone. However, it would be equally foolish to assume that bureaucrats do not act purposefully or that their attitudes and identities are divorced from their interests. As such, this book argues that bureaucratic behavior follows a logic of appropriateness (LOA). This decision-making theory, developed by James March and Johan Olsen (March

1994, March and Olsen 2006), suggests that organizational behavior is associated with the norms that individuals develop about what constitutes appropriate, exemplary behavior. Specifically, it theorizes that as bureaucrats make decisions on the job they go through something of a mental checklist. In roughly sequential order they ask themselves who they are as members of an organization, what kind of situation they are facing, and what people like themselves should do in a situation like the one they are facing. Thus, the theory suggests that behavior is largely a question of situation recognition and identity determination. Although this process may sound onerous and unnatural in the abstract, in practice it is second nature. In other words, like Bourdieu's habitus, norms of appropriateness are learned, internalized, and forgotten (Desmond 2007). Thus, bureaucrats can take appropriate, efficient action even when they face complicated situations.

Seeing bureaucratic behavior as driven by a LOA does not ignore the importance of preferences or consequences; rather, this framework portrays personal interest as one factor that may contribute to an actor's perceptions of what is appropriate. For example, in some situations bureaucrats may recognize that it is appropriate for them to minimize the amount of work they are required to do. However, in other situations they may do more work than is required because they understand it is proper for someone like them. As these examples show, LOA is useful because it provides a theoretical framework for understanding decision making. More specifically, it points to two outcomes that are thought to be important predictors of behavior, identities, and attitudes. However, the LOA is a general decision-making theory and does not put forward a holistic view of bureaucratic psychology. Therefore, the next section constructs a framework for organizing how bureaucrats understand themselves, their organizations, and the people with whom they interact.

Bureaucratic Personality

Weber's *The Theory of Social and Economic Organization* (1947) was one of the first works to consider the psychology of bureaucracy. In his account, he compared the various types of legitimacy—rational, traditional, and charismatic—that form the backbone of social authority. Rational types, which include bureaucracy, are perceived as legitimate due to their adherence to objectivity and rules. Inside organizations, Weber argued, rules create a spirit of "formalistic impersonality" among administrative staff. This spirit minimizes the messy affective characteristics of human interaction, like anger and fondness, and cultivates precision, stability, and reliability. Impersonal bureaucrats, according to this view, are unattached to the people they process, apply rules neutrally, and treat like cases alike. Though Weber viewed rational legitimacy positively, he was cognizant that impersonality could create its own problems. Previewing the concerns of later scholars, Weber worried that formalization, the perfection of legal procedures, could degenerate into formalism, excessive concern with process (Allinson 1984; Herzfeld 1993; Hummel 1982; Scott 2003).

Scholars around the middle of the twentieth century, reckoning with the growth of organizational life, picked up on Weber's concerns and argued that bureaucracy caused pathological psychological responses in workers. Most famously, Merton (1940) argued that the social contexts and structural bases of bureaucracy exert constant pressure on individuals to be methodical, prudent, and disciplined. Though these characteristics are positive and desirable in the abstract, in practice they are harmful. Specifically, he argued that bureaucracy foments "trained incapacity" (inability to respond to change), "occupational psychosis" (discomfort with change), and "professional deformation" (an unraveling of professional norms). In short, bureaucracies condition bureaucrats to develop "bureaucratic personalities" that emphasize the rules and process over justice and outcomes.

This view was echoed by many others. For example, Whyte's *The Organization Man* (1956) charted the existence of individuals who lived their lives as subjects, literally and psychologically, of their organizations. The pressures of organization life, in his account, negatively impact the thinking and behavior of organization members. In much the same way, Argyris (1957) expected "inevitable conflict" between mentally healthy people, who question things and want to take initiative, and their organizations, which favor passivity and subordination. The result of this conflict, he predicted, was frustration and an unhealthy concern with the parts of the organization as opposed to the whole. Similarly, Thompson (1961) emphasized the insecurity of the individual, in relation to the organization, and the individual's need to control his or her work life. He argued that the anxiety that results creates "bureaupathology": aloofness, resistance to change, and a ritualistic devotion to routine.

Although many of these midcentury works were about organizations generally, over time the concerns about bureaucracy's effects on people became predominantly associated with public organizations (Goodsell 2004). These organizations, with their massive workforces, seemingly endless rules and regulations, and policymaking monopolies, came to be seen as the organizations most likely to create "bureaucratic" workers. In effect, the stone-faced indifference of workers in the Department of Motor Vehicles became a cautionary tale about what public organizations could do to people.

Despite these concerns, as James Wilson (1989) argues, there has never been much empirical evidence supporting the bureaucratic personality hypothesis. For example, one early study showed that government employees were quite flexible in following bureaucratic rules and procedures (Blau 1955)—they appeared to interpret freely and use their discretion readily. Another showed that career federal civil servants, at the GS-14 level and higher, were not the alienated, dispossessed lot predicted by Merton (Warner 1963); rather, bureaucrats were, on average, idealistic and "strongly oriented toward achievement" (J. Wilson 1989, 69). Another examination compared men who worked in hierarchical organizations (including public and nonprofit organizations) with those that do not (Kohn 1971). It found that bureaucrats were more intellectually flexible, open to new experiences, and self-directed than men who worked in nonbureaucratic workplaces. More recent works continue to cast doubt on the bureaucratic personality thesis. For example, an analysis of the views of public and private managers found that public managers favored fewer rules than their private counterparts (Bozeman and Rainey 1998). In addition, studies have shown that there is significant heterogeneity inside public organizations vis-à-vis risk propensity, nonconformity, and rule breaking (Brehm and Gates 1997; DeHart-Davis 2007; O'Leary 2010).

In addition to these critiques, a body of research has developed suggesting that individuals, including public-sector bureaucrats, have multiple identities and that they enact different selves at different moments (Ellemers, Spears, and Doosje 2002; T. Lee 2009; March and Olsen 2006; Maynard-Moody and Musheno 2003; Scott 2003). From this perspective, bureaucrats should not be understood as static. Rather, as they interact with one another and the public, they understand and perform different selves.

Research like this has rightly discredited the bureaucratic personality thesis. It seems clear that many of the concerns articulated by early organizational observers have not come to pass. However, there are two reasons not to take the critique too far. First, scholarship has also revealed that there are important psychological commonalities among specific groups of employees (Bachman et al. 2000; Becker and Connor 2005; Chappell and Lanza-Kaduce 2010; Downs 1967; Kappeler, Sluder, and Alpert 1998; Lipsky 1980; Rubinstein 1973; Skolnick 1966; Van Maanen 1975; Watkins-Hayes 2009; J. Wilson 1989). In fact, research shows relatively high levels of personality homogeneity within particular organizations and industries (Schneider et al. 1998). Findings like this may help explain why forest rangers (Kaufman 1960) and police officers (Skolnick 1966) share similar sensibilities about who they are as officials and how they should act in their official capacities. This is not to imply that all employees in an organization think exactly alike. Rather, the point is that there may be important, distinct patterns of thought and behavior inside bureaucracies.

Second, even if bureaucrats have a store of identities from which to choose (Ellemers et al. 2002), and even if particular identities aren't static, it is important not to portray identity as too fluid. Rather, as Brubaker and Cooper (2000) argue, implicit in the identity concept is an understanding that who people are, or who they project themselves as socially, is relatively consistent over time. From their perspective, it would be psychologically disorienting if people adopted radically different selves at different times. In fact, their argument is buttressed by longitudinal personality studies that show strong patterns of psychological continuity over the life course (Costa and McCrae 1994; De Fruyt et al. 2006; Hampson and Goldberg 2006). If this is true generally, we might also expect it to be true within bureaucracies. In other words, though bureaucrats' identities may evolve over time, and though they may choose to be different people in different situations, we might also expect that there are durable patterns of psychological and behavioral continuity at the individual level over time. In fact, historical studies of individual bureaucrats support this expectation (Caro 1975; Carpenter 2001). Thus, it is important to take a balanced view of identity change and selection—bureaucrats may choose different selves in different moments, and their notions of self may evolve over time. However, they might not experience massive identity change over time or choose radically different selves at different moments.

As such, one of this book's arguments is that personality, the psychological tendencies people have (in terms of self-concept, habits, and attitudes) and the processes they use to integrate new experiences (Costa and McCrae 1994), remains a useful concept for understanding bureaucratic behavior. However, "bureaucratic personality" should not be understood as deterministic, static, or negative. Also, bureaucrats should not be assumed to be more rule-focused or rigid than nonbureaucrats. Instead, the term "bureaucratic personality" should identify key psychological dimensions that are relevant for organizational life and investigate the extent to which there is variation among a particular bureaucratic population. Also, like general personality definitions, it should allow for stability or change over time (Costa and McCrae 1994).

Thus, this book defines bureaucratic personality as the psychological tendencies and structures that bureaucrats use to make sense of themselves and their work. As discussed in the prior section, March and Olsen's (2006) LOA theory directs attention to bureaucrats' identities and perceptions. In addition, there is a strong consensus that motivation and behavior are closely related (Barnard 1938; Brewer and Selden 1998; Brewer, Selden, and Facer 2000; Crewson 1997; Downs 1967; Golden 2000; Houston 2000; Moynihan and Pandey 2007; Perry 1996, 1997, 2000; Perry et al. 2008; Perry and Wise 1990; Rainey and Steinbauer 1999; Vandenabeele 2007; Weber 1947). Thus, the concept of bureaucratic personality proposed here includes three general components: bureaucratic identities, attitudes, and motivations. Figure 1.1 graphically depicts bureaucratic personality and its constituent parts. As this diagram shows, bureaucrats' identities, attitudes, and motivations are conceived of as distinct but not independent: they refer to discrete psychological phenomena but have the potential to interact with one another. For example, bureaucratic identities can be understood as behaviorally consequential on their own but also may be influenced by, or influence, motivation.

This rendering of bureaucratic personality is useful because it is powerful and parsimonious. Though it includes only three parts, these are psychological phenomenon that many studies suggest are important drivers of bureaucratic behavior. It is also general: it can be used for investigating bureaucratic thought and behavior across a wide array of bureaucrats and bureaucracies. Finally, the framework is inclusive: its three main components are broad enough to cover most of the myriad components of bureaucratic psychology. For instance, outcomes like commitment (Steinhaus and Perry 1996) and role orientation (Saks and Ashforth 1997), could fit under motivation and bureaucratic identity, respectively.

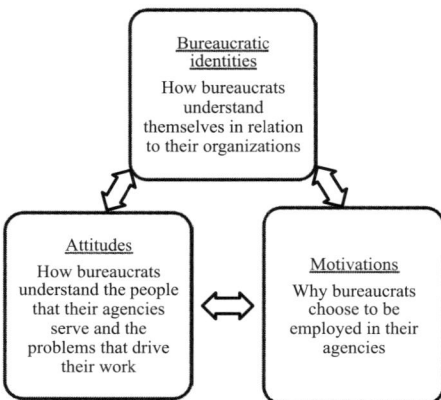

Figure 1.1. Bureaucratic Personality

But what precisely is meant by motivation, bureaucratic identity, and attitudes? Which components of these outcomes are examined in this study? It is to these questions that we turn next.

Motivation

Motivation is the internal psychological force that guides and compels behavior (Perry and Hondeghem 2008). Over the years, there have been various efforts to categorize and understand bureaucratic motivation (Downs 1967; Golden 2000; D. Katz and Kahn 1966). For example, Weber (1947) argued that subordinate behavior was based on custom, affection, material interest, and idealism. He implied that organizations that rely on material interest only are likely to be unstable. Similarly, Barnard (1938, 143) noted that subordinate cooperation depended upon tangible incentives and persuasion but that material rewards "unaided by other motives . . . constitute weak incentives."

In recent years, many public administration scholars have focused on the concept of public service motivation (PSM) (Brewer and Selden 1998; Brewer, Selden, and Facer 2000; Crewson 1997; Houston 2000; Moynihan and Pandey 2007; Perry 1996, 1997, 2000; Perry et al. 2008; Perry and Wise 1990; Rainey and Steinbauer 1999; Vandenabeele 2007). This concept has various meanings but generally refers to a cluster of "motives associated with serving the public good" (Perry and Hondeghem 2008, 3). As such, PSM research highlights the "service side" of public-sector work. Though research suggests that public workers are more devoted to service than their private-sector colleagues (Crewson 1997; Houston 2000), it would be a mistake to assume that all public workers are driven by PSM. Indeed, studies suggest that bureaucrats may also be motivated by rewards like job security, a pension, and the power inherent in a government position (Barnard 1938; Golden 2000; Perry and Hondeghem 2008; Perry and Wise 1990; Weber 1947).

To develop a broad picture of what drives public workers, this book examines altruistic and egoistic motivations. Altruistic motives, including PSM, refer to a subjective concern to help or serve other people (Piliavin and Charng 1990). Although altruism was perceived as an illusion or disguised self-interest for many years, researchers from various fields have coalesced around the view that altruism is real, inherent in human nature, and necessary for social functioning (Koehler and Rainey 2008; Piliavin and Charng 1990). Though people obviously are concerned with their own interests, empirical studies show that they use their resources to contribute to things that do not directly benefit them and that they sacrifice their interests for others. In contrast, motivations that are driven by self-advancement, or the satisfaction of a personal desire, are defined as egoistic. There is no shortage of examples of public workers motivated by egoistic rewards. For instance, Brehm and Gates (1997) showed that, across a variety of bureaucratic settings, the decision to work, shirk, or sabotage was predominantly driven by solidary preferences—the desire to make or maintain personal relationships with coworkers. Perhaps few actions or individuals are driven purely by altruism or egoism; nonetheless, as a conceptual device this dichotomy is useful for categorizing different motivations and investigating them empirically.

Bureaucratic Identity

Identities are the perceptions that people have about themselves and the personas that they project when they interact socially (Abdelal et al. 2009; Brubaker and Cooper 2000; Ellemers, Spears, and Doosje 2002; Goffman 1959). Identities are useful because they serve as guides for prospective behavior and help people make sense of actions taken in the past. In particular, this book is concerned with what it refers to as "bureaucratic identities"—the understandings that bureaucrats have about themselves as organization members and the ways that they project themselves as they do their work.[4] These identities are crucial for understanding bureaucratic behavior because, as organization members take action, they must reckon with who they are as organization members and how someone like them would act in a situation like the one they are facing (March 1994).

Within the realm of bureaucratic identities, there are many possible outcomes worthy of study. This book focuses on bureaucrats' rule-following identities—their understandings of themselves vis-à-vis their organization's rules. Rules are authoritative guides of behavior, and by many accounts, they are the lifeblood of bureaucracy: they standardize action, enable accountability, and permit a relatively easy interchange of personnel. As such, it is essential to understand how bureaucrats situate themselves in relation to the rules. Although bureaucracies prize rule following and impersonality in theory, in practice bureaucrats must learn to balance rule following and responsiveness (Lipsky 1980). To manage these competing expectations, bureaucrats develop rule-following identities that they use as guides as they interact with the public and their coworkers (Maynard-Moody and Musheno 2003). By asking entrants about how they see themselves in relation to the rules, and tracking these identities over two years, this book demonstrates how entrants construct their rule-following identities.

In addition to studying rule-following identities, this book charts the development of entrant loyalty—the level of allegiance individuals have toward their organization. Loyalty isn't an identity per se because it envisions a division between the organization and the self. Nonetheless, the two concepts are related because loyalty captures the extent to which an individual identifies with, and feels connected to, his or her organization. Loyalty is also important for behavioral reasons: it has been linked to absenteeism, effectiveness, and general performance (Downs 1967; S. Lee and Olshfski 2002; Wanous 1992). Because organizations understand that all behavior cannot be contractually mandated, they try to encourage loyalty among employees and cultivate employees who will act as strong organization citizens (Bardach and Kagan 1982; Dessler 1999).

Attitudes

The third set of outcomes under the bureaucratic personality umbrella is bureaucrats' attitudes—their summary evaluations about an idea, group, or thing (Ajzen 2001). According to the LOA framework, bureaucrats' attitudes are important because they are useful for classifying the people and situations that they face. This is an important point because some works have portrayed attitudes and situations as alternative explanations for bureaucratic behavior. For instance, in assessing studies about the beliefs and behaviors of welfare caseworkers, James Wilson (1989, 53) argues, "In short, the imperatives of the situation more than the attitudes of the worker shape the way tasks are performed in welfare offices." Similarly, Worden (1989) compares "situational" and "attitudinal" explanations for police behavior. This approach is flawed, I argue, because it portrays situations as objective realities rather than moments to be interpreted by a human observer. Seeing bureaucratic behavior in this latter way, the LOA suggests that bureaucrats use their attitudes to assess, categorize, and respond to situations.[5]

Because this book studies street-level bureaucracies, it focuses on bureaucrats' attitudes about the people whom their agencies serve and the social problems that they encounter in their work. One of street-level bureaucrats' main tasks is people categorization: welfare caseworkers divide their caseloads into types of recipients (Sandfort, Kalil, and Gottschalk 1999; Small and Lerner 2008); homicide investigators differentiate between "citizens" and "criminals" (D. Simon 1993); police patrolmen categorize deservingness and suspiciousness based on physical appearance, social status, and employment (Conlon 2004); and public defenders arrange better plea deals for criminal suspects who they see as "hardworking" or "nice" (Heumann 1981).

As these examples show, as street-level bureaucrats categorize people, they make determinations about which traits or individuals are deserving of public aid. These determinations rely, to some extent, on street-level bureaucrats' perceptions of which groups an individual belongs to and the group's moral reputation (Soss, Fording, and Schram 2011a). When an individual is seen as a member of a group, and that group has a positive moral reputation, the bureaucrat may act favorably toward the individual. Conversely, if an individual is classified as a member of a group that has a negative moral reputation, the bureaucrat may take punitive action against the individual.

One of the key determinants of a group's moral reputation is the extent to which its members are seen as responsible for the problems that they encounter. Because street-level bureaucrats interact repeatedly with low-income populations, and manage the problems associated with poverty and criminality, this book focuses on bureaucrats' attitudes about the causes of these problems. Also, because race is an important component of deservingness calculations (Gilens 1999; Thompson and Bobo 2011), it explores bureaucrats' attitudes about race, racism, and racial inequality.

Entrants and Bureaucratic Socialization

Thus far this chapter has argued that bureaucratic behavior is driven by a LOA—as bureaucrats interact with people and situations, they are guided by their understandings of who they are as public officials, who they are interacting with, and what they should do in particular situations. Because the LOA framework doesn't set forth a holistic portrait of bureaucratic psychology, the chapter assembles a revised bureaucratic personality framework that includes bureaucrats' motivations, identities, and attitudes. Though many prior studies have examined these or similar psychological outcomes (Aberbach and Rockman 2000; Chetkovich 1997; DeHart-Davis 2007; Golden 2000; D. Katz and Kahn 1966; Lipsky 1980; Maynard-Moody and Musheno 2003; Merton 1940; Perry 1997; Portillo 2012; Prottas 1979; Sandfort 2000; Sandfort, Kalil, and Gottschalk 1999), most rely upon cross-sectional research designs that take a snapshot of a group of experienced workers at a particular moment in time.[6] These studies are useful for describing psychological patterns among bureaucrats, but they cannot account for self-selection effects or explain changes over time. As such, we have little understanding about how bureaucrats develop their bureaucratic personalities.

Though there has been relatively little attention paid to socialization in the various public affairs literatures (public administration, political science, and public policy), there has been considerable research on the topic by business scholars and psychologists in the organizational socialization (OS) literature (Jones 1986; Morrison 2002; Saks and Ashforth 1997; Saks, Uggerslev, and Fassina 2007; Van Maanen and Schein 1979; Wanberg 2012b; Wanous 1992). This literature will be helpful in guiding this book's analysis. In addition, the book contributes to the OS literature in three ways. First, although some works in the literature focus on public workers, the majority examine private-sector entrants. Because public and nonpublic organizations differ in important ways (Bozeman 2004; Meier and O'Toole 2011; Perry and Rainey 1988), this book contributes a new account of public-sector entry. Second, few OS works examine the types of psychological outcomes set forth in the bureaucratic personality framework. Rather, they typically focus on outcomes such as employee satisfaction and turnover. Thus, this book makes a contribution by focusing on a wider array of psychological outcomes.

Third, there is disagreement in the OS literature about the length of socialization. Some argue that it is an ongoing process throughout one's career (Wanous 1992, 194), while others imply that the initial "breaking in" period is the "most persuasive" part of socialization (Van Maanen 1975, 207). In practice, most OS studies focus on an entrant's first six months to a year inside his or her organization (Allinson 1984; Cooper-Thomas and Anderson 2006; Morrison 2002; Saks and Ashforth 1997; Wanous 1992). This book takes a longer time frame and follows entrants during their first two years on the job. As such, it shows how entrants develop after their first six months.

Although the period studied here is longer than those examined in most organizational socialization studies, it obviously is not the entirety of entrants' careers. Though this initial period is generally understood as an important time in employees' career trajectories (Wanous 1992), the book does not make any assumptions about how entrants develop after two years. It does, however, compare newcomers' and veterans' bureaucratic personalities (the focus of Chapter 3). As such, it is able to make some observations about how entrants compared to veterans at entry and over the two years of the study.

Street-Level Bureaucrats

By studying bureaucratic socialization, this book contributes to our general understanding of bureaucratic psychology. However, because this book examines two particular types of street-level bureaucrats, police officers and welfare caseworkers,[7] it is important to justify these cases.[8] Street-level bureaucrats are a useful group to study because, in one important respect, they are typical: they encounter the classic administrative struggle over decisional latitude (Bardach and Kagan 1982; Blau 1955; Crozier 1964; G. Huber 2007; J. Huber and Shipan 2002; Lipsky 1980; Taylor 1983). Bureaucrats tend to want more latitude, or discretion, and public managers, executives, and elected officials typically want them to have less. In an effort to control the decisions of lower-level workers, organization leaders develop rules and protocols (Evans and Harris 2004). However, as they go about their work, bureaucrats invariably come across situations in which the rules cannot or, they believe, should not be followed (Maynard-Moody and Musheno 2003). As such, in all bureaucracies there is an ongoing tension between upper- and lower-level workers about decisional latitude.

Street-level bureaucrats come face-to-face with this tension every day. They are powerful because they operate outside the immediate views of their supervisors and oversee a massive number of cases (making monitoring difficult). However, they exist in "rule-saturated" environments in which there is a protocol, and accompanying paperwork, for nearly every action that they take (Maynard-Moody and Musheno 2003). As such, they are in many ways typical of all lower-level bureaucrats: they are constrained by rules but possess discretion.

In other ways, of course, street-level bureaucrats aren't typical of all bureaucrats. In particular, they differ from many government workers by meeting face-to-face with the public on a regular basis. These face-to-face interactions have the potential to generate emotional volatility that is absent, perhaps, in the work life of a federal policy analyst whose job is centered on research and report writing. Although this distinguishes street-level bureaucrats in some ways, it also makes them an important case to examine: as Lipsky (1980) notes, street-level bureaucrats are the face of government. Some citizens vote and contact their elected officials, but, on a day-to-day basis, street-level bureaucrats are the government actors whom the public interacts with and observes. As a result, street-level bureaucrats are symbolic of government's authority, reach, and morality (Theobald and Haider-Markel 2009)—a corrupt police officer or public defense lawyer may be taken as indicative of a corrupt legal system.

The symbolic importance of street-level bureaucrats may be even greater for disadvantaged groups, like racial minorities and low-income groups, who are less likely to participate in traditional politics (voting, contacting elected officials, etc.) but are more likely to experience the coercive power of the government (Wacquant 2009). Because vulnerable citizens may learn particular political lessons when they interact with government (Bruch, Ferree, and Soss 2010; Soss 2000; Weaver and Lerman 2010), street-level bureaucrats are an important class of workers to study.

Research Design

To study bureaucratic socialization, this book analyzes longitudinal data gathered from 2006 to 2008 in a large U.S. city. These data were collected using two main research methods: in-depth interviews and pen-and-paper surveys.[9] Complementing these methods, I also arranged for a period of "observant participation" (Wacquant 2004)—during the first year of the study I trained and was employed as a welfare caseworker. The goal of this experience was to get a firsthand understanding of the process of becoming a bureaucrat. Using these three methods, I was able to gather qualitative and quantitative data. Analyzing a variety of data types is relatively unique in the bureaucracy and public administration literatures and enables this book to rigorously chart population-wide trends while "digging down" to deeply understand the experiences of individuals.

To protect the identities of the people who participated in this study, I do not name the city where these workers were employed. Focusing on a single geographical area has the potential to raise concerns about generalizability because there is some variation in the welfare and criminal justice policies enacted by states and cities across the United States. Also, each city has a unique history and demographic characteristics. Despite these concerns, there are good reasons to think that the book's research location is not likely to skew its findings. First, according to a variety of demographic metrics, the city is not significantly different from other large cities. For instance, according to the Bureau of Justice Statistics, from 1985 through 2008 the research city had a roughly average violent crime rate compared with other large cities. As the national rate rose and fell, so did the research city's rate. Also, the poverty rates in the state and city were close to the national rates throughout the study, as estimated by the Current Population Survey. In addition, the city's nonwhite community was disproportionately poor, which reflected national trends.

Also, the welfare and police departments in the city are not radically different from those in other large cities. Though the police department has suffered its share of scandals, and particular cases have garnered national attention, this is also true of other large cities. Also, the department has been ordered to take up particular reforms—including community policing (Glaser and Denhardt 2010)—in sync with departments in other cities. The welfare department also mirrors those in other large cities—its main task is eligibility determination, while work training and job placement services are performed by nonprofit or for-profit contractors (Lurie 2006).

Thus, the city in which this research took place is demographically similar to many other large U.S. cities. Also, from a policy perspective, the city is neither a leader nor a laggard. Therefore, though there are obviously ways that the city and its history are unique, it does not appear to be an outlier in these respects. As such, it serves as a useful site for research.

The book's research design is also useful because entrants into these two groups were expected to develop somewhat differently. In the policing literature, socialization is frequently depicted as strong (Chappell and Lanza-Kaduce 2010; Gallo 2001; Kappeler, Sluder, and Alpert 1998; Macvean and Cox 2012; Rubinstein 1973; Van Maanen 1974, 1975; Wilkins and Williams 2008). For example, Kappeler, Sluder, and Alpert (1998, 84) argue that police socialization leads to "an ideology and shared culture that breeds unprecedented conformity to the traditional police norms and values"; Chappell and Lanza-Kaduce (2010, 189) portray entrants as "young and impressionable" and, therefore, easy to mold to "accept the organizational culture." Gallo (2001, 15) writes that police academies are places that turn "reasonably normal young men and women into cops." In part, police socialization is expected to be strong because of the danger inherent in the job. To survive, observers agree, police officers develop strong bonds with other police and closely watch out for one another's well-being. In addition, police officers work odd hours and deal with fundamentally different occupational dilemmas than do other civilians. As a result, outside of work police officers develop strong social networks with other police whom they come to see as family.

Although less is known about the process of becoming a welfare caseworker, it seems likely to be less intense. In part this is because welfare work is conducted during regular work hours and lacks the physical danger inherent in police work. As a result, caseworkers work a normal nine-to-five schedule and describe the office as, in some respects, a typical workplace (see Chapter 3). Because their work and workplace are more normal, they would seem less likely to need to band together for their well-being or to get their work completed. Also, the culture of welfare offices is typically described negatively: caseworkers are considerably burdened by clients, paperwork, and supervisors (Goodsell 1984; Lurie 2006; Watkins-Hayes 2009). Perhaps as a result, studies suggest there is a give-and-take between entrants and established welfare office cultures (Riccucci 2005; Sandfort 2000) whereas police socialization is typically portrayed as a one-way street.

Though this research design has important limitations,[10] it is generally useful for exploring bureaucratic socialization. It provides qualitative and quantitative data that enable the drawing of a detailed portrait of entry. The two cases are similar in many ways (and therefore comparable) but also are expected to differ in terms of the intensity of entry. By examining what is common and distinct about these cases, the book is able to develop a general understanding of bureaucratic development.

Summary and Chapter Road Map

Though we have some understanding of how bureaucrats think and act, we know relatively little about how they are socialized into their agencies. In particular, it isn't clear how they develop their bureaucratic personalities—the psychological tendencies and structures that bureaucrats use to make sense of themselves and their work. These structures are important because bureaucrats use them to decide how to act in particular instances. Thus, without a strong understanding of bureaucratic socialization we cannot understand the actions of individual bureaucrats. Also, at the macro level, we are limited in explaining how public organizations function and change. This book contributes by exploring how two sets of street-level bureaucrats, police officers and welfare caseworkers, develop during their first two years on the job. Though they do not represent all bureaucrats, this case study's findings provide in-depth insight into a process that is important across government. As such, it generates evidence that will be helpful for theory and practice.

Chapter 2 delves into the animating conflict at the heart of this book—the competing hypotheses drawn from the dispositional and institutional perspectives. The dispositional perspective expects that bureaucrats will remain tied to their entering views, motives, and selves. As such, entrants' bureaucratic personalities are expected to minimally change during entry. In contrast, the institutional perspective expects considerable change over the course of entry as entrants encounter their organization, undergo training, and gain a new peer group. The chapter explores these divergent perspectives as well as the concepts and theories that undergird them. In addition, the chapter reviews accumulated evidence in support of each perspective and discusses how these perspectives are examined in the book's empirical chapters.

Chapter 3 begins the book's empirical analysis by exploring the bureaucratic personalities of experienced workers in each of these two organizations. It relies on a literature review of prior studies, analysis of survey data, and interviews that I conducted with experienced workers in the research city. The chapter shows that, though all veteran organization members don't see the world in exactly the same way, in each organization there are patterns of thought that unite experienced workers. As such, it helps us understand the organizations that entrants joined and provides clues about how they might develop.

Drawing from interviews, surveys, and my own work inside the welfare agency, Chapter 4 creates a detailed portrait of newcomers' experiences during entry. In particular, it highlights the scenes that they entered on their first official days inside their organizations and some of the messages sent to them during training. It also includes a description of how entrants described interactions with peers, veterans, and supervisors after graduating from training and beginning work. As such, this chapter serves as a backdrop for understanding what entrants experienced and how they developed.

Chapter 5 examines entrants' motivations over the course of their first two years. It begins by describing what motivated entrants to seek out their work and why they remained in their organizations. It shows that police and caseworker entrants began their careers with different motives. Police tended to be motivated by altruistic desires like providing protection to people and keeping order in the streets. Most welfare caseworkers, in contrast, chose their work primarily for the benefits. However, the chapter also shows that below these general trends there were a variety of altruistic and egoistic motives that drove entrants. The chapter's statistical analysis shows modest change over the two years for both groups. It also shows that the strongest and most consistent predictors of entrants' motivations at each time were the motivations that they articulated at entry.

Continuing the inquiry, Chapter 6 focuses on entrants' bureaucratic identities. In particular, it studies entrants' understandings of themselves in relation to their organization's rules and the level of loyalty that they felt toward the organization. It shows that at the outset of training there were differences between the two populations: police entrants were more devoted to a by-the-book approach to the rules than caseworkers and were considerably more loyal to their department. Over time there was change and stability. Police loyalty stayed high, caseworker loyalty stayed low, but police rule following diminished considerably. As a result, by the end of the study, fewer than half of all police indicated that they take a by-the-book approach to policing. Though the chapter shows evidence of modest change, again the strongest predictors of entrants' bureaucratic identities at each stage were their entering bureaucratic identities.

Chapter 7 shifts to the final component of bureaucratic personality: entrants' attitudes. In particular, it asks about their views about deservingness, racism, and the causes of social problems like poverty and criminality. Like Chapters 5 and 6, the chapter shows a mix of change and continuity. Both groups shifted somewhat over the course of entry away from structural views about the causes of poverty and criminality. Instead, they came to see these problems as related to an individual's choices and character. However, again, the changes were modest. Also, as in prior chapters, the strongest and most consistent predictors of entrants' views at each time were their entering attitudes.

The conclusion, Chapter 8, brings together the book's empirical findings and discusses their theoretical and practical implications. Because entrants remained connected to their entering views, and only modestly changed their bureaucratic personalities over the course of the study, the chapter argues that bureaucratic development is best understood as differential continuity. At entry there was some variation across individuals within each group. During development the group shifted in a particular direction, but individuals remained strongly connected to where they began. Thus, from a practical perspective, the chapter shows that it is crucial for organizations to know what recruits and entrants think prior to entry. Bureaucracies may be able to shape entrants' views somewhat during development, but fundamentally remaking them seems unlikely. From a theoretical perspective, the chapter argues that bureaucratic socialization is less intense than typically understood. In fact, the evidence here suggests that entrants form most of their bureaucratic personalities prior to organizational entry. Thus, most of the work of organizational replication and maintenance may depend upon recruitment and self-selection. The chapter closes with a call for further socialization research so that we can build a more general understanding of how public-sector entrants are (and aren't) shaped by the bureaucracies that they enter.

CHAPTER 2

Dispositions and Institutions

In his study of police officer development, Van Maanen (1974, 84) quotes a police chief as saying, "The day the new recruit walks through the doors of the police academy he leaves society behind him to enter a profession that does more than give him a job, it defines who he is. For all the years he remains, closed into the sphere of its rituals . . . he will be a cop."[1] Desmond (2006), in his study of wildland firefighting, argues that firefighters are drawn to their work, and feel comfortable doing it, because they view themselves as "country competent"—skilled in dealing with and surviving in the natural world. This identity drives their choice of careers as well as their actions as they confront towering, volatile forest fires.

Although neither author takes a one-dimensional approach to bureaucratic psychology and behavior, these examples highlight the general expectations of the institutional and dispositional perspectives. The police chief expects that the institutional influences inside the walls of the police academy have a swift and meaningful effect on entrants. Desmond indicates that understanding wildland firefighters requires attention to who they were before they entered the organization. To a certain extent, of course, the institutional and dispositional perspectives are extreme: it is a truism that bureaucratic psychology and behavior result from a mix of personal and organizational factors (O'Reilly, Chatman, and Caldwell 1991; Saks and Ashforth 1997; Schneider 1987; Zimbardo 2004). Unfortunately, many academic accounts essentially stop there, arguing "it's both." Those that go further, and take a more definitive position, tend to emphasize the institutional perspective and the importance of situations. However, these works often rely on cross-sectional research designs that cannot account for self-selection. Because we have few rigorous, longitudinal accounts of socialization, it is unclear whether bureaucratic behavior and psychology are shaped equally by each set of influences, or predominantly by institutional factors.

This book contributes by following two sets of bureaucratic entrants and evaluating how the dispositional and institutional perspectives explain their development. In service of that goal, this chapter discusses the reasons why we might expect change and continuity during entry. In other words, this chapter presents concepts and theories from psychology, sociology, and political science that may help explain why bureaucrats develop as they do. As readers will see, there are no absolutes here: each section shows that development is likely to be a process shaped by institutions and dispositions. Nevertheless, the two perspectives are useful as they differ considerably in what they portray as the driving force behind bureaucratic socialization. In addition, the chapter discusses empirical evidence supporting each view to illustrate how dispositional and institutional factors may matter. Finally, the chapter outlines how each perspective will be analyzed in the book's empirical chapters.

The Dispositional Perspective and Continuity

As discussed in Chapter 1, the dispositional perspective is a powerful, popular way of explaining the thinking and actions of government workers. This perspective need not imply psychological intractability or institutional impotence, but it does expect that the psychological characteristics that entrants bring with them to their organizations will be the most salient factors in their development. As such, the perspective expects a reasonably high level of continuity during the course of an entrant's career. However, it is important to note that there are different types of psychological continuity (Caspi and Roberts 2001). Absolute continuity refers to the stability of a particular trait or attribute, at the level of the individual, over time. For example, to examine absolute continuity a bureaucratic psychology study could administer a Big Five personality examination to a group of enlisting soldiers and then administer a second examination ten years later. Exploring how much each individual diverged from his or her initial score, in each of the five personality areas, would reveal a measure of absolute continuity. In contrast, differential continuity refers to the continuity of an individual relative to a group. Keeping with the prior example, analysis may show that on the first examination there was a roughly normal distribution of extraversion among enlisting soldiers. Examining differential continuity would entail studying the extent to which soldiers remained in a particular place along the extraversion distribution, relative to the group, over time.

Whether absolute or differential, the dispositional perspective expects high levels of continuity during organizational socialization. As such, it suggests that an organization's character depends heavily on the people whom it attracts, selects, and retains (Schneider 1987). This section explores this expectation from a conceptual standpoint and discusses the reasons why such continuity might occur. In essence, this section argues that basic psychological characteristics, like personality and habitus, are formed early in life and are likely to remain stable during organizational socialization. If these are the psychological foundations upon which bureaucratic personalities are erected, it would seem unlikely that entrants would radically change after entry.

Personality

One of the concepts that undergirds the dispositional perspective is personality—a core idea used by psychologists to explain human psychology and behavior. Though there are varied definitions, personality is generally understood as the psychological tendencies that people have and the processes they use to integrate new experiences (Costa and McCrae 1994). In the psychology literature there is a range of views about the plasticity of personality over the life course (Caspi and Roberts 2001; Heatherton and Weinberger 1994; Roberts, Walton, and Viechtbauer 2006). Nonetheless, some degree of psychological continuity is inherent in the concept—how people think and act today is expected to be somewhat consistent with how they think and act tomorrow. Since time is inherent in the idea of personality, it is important to note that psychologists treat it with nuance: based on a solid block of longitudinal research, personality is understood as relatively durable over time but certainly not intractable (Costa and McCrae 1994; De Fruyt et al. 2006; Hampson and Goldberg 2006).

In explaining this continuity, researchers are increasingly turning to genetics (Caspi and Roberts 2001; Riemann, Angleitner, and Strelau 1997). Studies that have examined change and continuity among monozygotic and dizygotic twins suggest that between 50 and 80 percent of phenotypic stability may be associated with genetic factors. Theoretically, people's genes shape a variety of physiological and neural processes, which in turn shape the personalities that they demonstrate. Although there is considerable support for the view that genetics has an effect on personality, psychologists are generally careful not to take the argument to biological determinism. In other words, while acknowledging that genetic influences may play an important stabilizing role, they also highlight the crucial role that environments can play in shaping personality and development (Caspi and Roberts 2001; Shonkoff and Phillips 2000).

Although environments clearly matter a great deal, there are two important qualifying points from the perspective of bureaucratic socialization. First, even though environments are important, they may have a stabilizing influence if individuals remain in largely similar social settings throughout life. For example, if people choose organizations with cultures that are consonant with their existing sensibilities or values (Wright and Pandey 2008), or in which they have existing personal connections (Conlon 2004), they may not change much as a result of this contact. Thus, recognizing the importance of environment does not necessarily strengthen institutional arguments about bureaucratic development.

Second, it is important to consider the role of age vis-à-vis environmental influences. For many years psychologists have contended that age is a key factor in personality development. In the nineteenth century, William James argued that character is "set like plaster" around the age of thirty (Heatherton and Weinberger 1994, 21). Although the metaphor implies an intractability that scholars today reject, across a variety of literatures and research programs there is evidence that younger people are more impressionable and that psychological consistency increases with age (Caspi and Roberts 2001; Costa and McCrae 1994; Elder 1998; Inglehart 1981; Jennings 1990; Visser and Krosnick 1998).[2] Thus, by the time individuals are old enough to enter a workplace, many of their psychological tendencies are likely to be fairly set. They may encounter powerful social forces inside their organizations but, due to their ages, use established psychological processes to navigate through them.

In sum, personality research suggests that we should expect relatively little psychological change during organization entry. If personalities are the foundations upon which bureaucratic personalities are built, we would expect bureaucratic personality continuity during entry. To assess this expectation, the book's empirical chapters compare the bureaucratic personalities that entrants demonstrated at entry with those that they expressed throughout the two years of the study.

Habitus

Another concept that undergirds the dispositional perspective is habitus. This idea, drawn from sociology, refers to the constellation of unconscious factors that guide human action. More specifically, a habitus is a system of "durable, transposable dispositions" that informs and animates action (Bourdieu 1990, 53). For Bourdieu, a habitus is imprinted on individuals early in life and, as such, is "second nature":

it structures thought and behavior without feeling oppressive or foreign. In fact, the habitus concept overlaps considerably with March and Olsen's logic of appropriateness theory (discussed in Chapter 1)—it gives people an automatic recognition of what is inside and outside the realm of acceptable action. In other words, habitus is "internalized and forgotten socialization" (Desmond 2007, 12) that shapes the scripts that people use and their sense of the possible, acceptable, and proper. A habitus is historical in the sense that it carries along past understanding and practice (perhaps from prior generations) through patterns of social and familial interaction. Since it is embedded in individuals "in the form of schemes of perception, thought and action," it "guarantee[s] the 'correctness' of practices and their constancy over time, more reliably than all formal rules and explicit norms" (Bourdieu 1990, 54). From the perspective of this project, the habitus concept would help explain the continuity expected by the dispositional perspective—individuals would enter their organizations with a habitus that is defined early in life and, in all likelihood, maintain it throughout their time inside their organizations.

Though the concept generally supports the dispositional perspective, it is important to note that Desmond (2006) argues that a habitus can be "general" or "specific." A general habitus is formed early in life and informs behavior across a large segment of society; a specific habitus is acquired later in life, through education, training, and organizational contact, and, as such, pertains to the views and actions of a smaller group. This distinction raises an interesting question: How much do a general and specific habitus relate? In other words, is the development of a specific habitus a relatively small tweaking of an established pattern of thought and action, or is it a more substantial change? From a recruiting standpoint, since organizations are interested in creating good person-organization fits (O'Reilly, Chatman, and Caldwell 1991; Zhang and Gowan 2012), they would seem to be likely to select entrants who share their specific habitus (or in whom a specific habitus isn't difficult to cultivate). Similarly, from a self-selection standpoint, if outsiders understand an organization's character, they would seem likely to choose employers that fit their specific habitus.

Since organizations and individuals have incentives to make the finding of one another as painless as possible, it is generally expected that the development of a specific habitus requires relatively little individual change. In fact, the idea of a specific habitus may reinforce the dispositional perspective by suggesting that there are deep social-psychological patterns that explain bureaucratic socialization: people do not randomly choose their professions but are guided there as they seek work that is consonant with their personal mores. After arriving in their organizations, entrants may need to adjust somewhat to create a specific habitus. However, from this perspective it would be surprising if this adjustment required radical change. Therefore, the general and specific habitus concepts suggest that bureaucratic socialization is likely to be strongly influenced by entrants' preorganizational dispositions.

Accumulated Evidence

So far in this section I have argued that a newcomer's personality and habitus are likely to remain stable during organization entry. If an entrant's bureaucratic personality is connected to these deeper psychological characteristics, we would not expect much psychological change during entry. This section pivots to discuss empirical evidence that supports this expectation. Again, it is important to note that there are no absolutes here: the evidence in total suggests that dispositions and institutions matter. Nonetheless, dispositions are often undervalued by social scientific accounts of bureaucratic psychology and behavior (Hummel 1982; H. Simon 1997; J. Wilson 1989; Zimbardo 2004). Therefore, this section presents evidence from two public administration literatures—representative bureaucracy and public service motivation—that, to at least some degree, supports the dispositional perspective.

Representative Bureaucracy

The representative bureaucracy literature explores how variation in descriptive and substantive representation is related to agency performance and citizens' experiences with government (Keiser et al. 2002; Meier 1993; Theobald and Haider-Markel 2009). In particular, the literature has an abiding interest in how the sex and race identities held by workers shape organizational performance. The literature's general expectation is that bureaucracies that include workers who look like the populations that they serve will tend to be more responsive than those that don't (Grissom and Keiser 2011). To test this proposition, scholars have studied a variety of public-sector employees like teachers, welfare caseworkers, and police officers. For instance, Meier (1993) examines the effect that Hispanic teachers and administrators have on the academic standing and success of Hispanic students. His findings show that Hispanic students have more academic success, and receive fewer disciplinary actions, when they are taught by Hispanic teachers. As such, he argues that Hispanic teachers may actively represent the interests of Hispanic students.

In fact, this finding is one of many that show a positive relationship between the representativeness of bureaucrats and a variety of public-sector outcomes. Explaining this relationship has led scholars to consider the dispositional and institutional elements of representativeness. In essence, the literature suggests that institutional environments set the conditions that permit for the expression of workers' dispositions. For example, representativeness depends upon institutional factors like the amount of discretion that bureaucrats have and the extent to which their work relates to their identities (Keiser et al. 2002). However, representativeness also depends upon workers remaining connected to their preorganizational identities. For instance, Hispanic teachers are more likely to act as representatives of Hispanic students if an institutional condition is satisfied: they work in schools with a critical mass of Hispanic educators (Meier 1993). However, implicit in this account is a more basic assumption: Hispanic educators will act as representatives under this institutional condition because they remain connected to their ethnic identities. As such, this literature, to at least some extent, lends empirical support to the expectations drawn from the dispositional perspective.

Public Service Motivation

For many years scholars have been interested in the motives that galvanize bureaucratic work. The resulting scholarship shows that bureaucratic behavior is determined by a combination of factors including self-interest, custom, affective ties, and idealism (Argyris 1993; Barnard 1938; Brehm and Gates 1997; March 1994; Selden, Brudney, and Kellough 1998; Weber 1947). One of the most important concepts to emerge from such inquiries is public service motivation (PSM)—the cluster of "motives associated with serving the public good" (Perry and Vandenabeele 2008, 3). Although not all public work is idealistically motivated, scholars have shown that public workers tend to value public service more than private-sector workers (Crewson 1997; Houston 2000).

The best explanation for PSM to date directs attention to employees' background characteristics. For instance, one study examines the relationship between PSM and five sets of preorganizational correlates: parental socialization, religious socialization, professional identification, political ideology, and individual demographic characteristics (Perry 1997). The findings show that individuals are more likely to be motivated by public service if they have a closer relationship with

God, have parents who value public service, and achieve more education. The study concludes that formative experiences affect workplace motivations. Other studies reinforce this view by showing that education, training, and particular life events are associated with motivation (Perry 2000); education is related to motivation (Moynihan and Pandey 2007); age and education are associated with motivation (Houston 2000); and the motivations of public service award winners are related to family socialization, religious activity, and volunteer experiences (Perry et al. 2008).

Recently the literature has moved toward a more rigorous examination of the institutional components of PSM (Moynihan and Pandey 2007; Wright, Moynihan, and Pandey 2012). However, currently the strongest explanation for PSM is variation in sociohistorical antecedents. As such, the literature supports the expectations drawn from the dispositional perspective.

Summary

Two concepts—personality and habitus—explain why we might expect continuity during bureaucratic development. Personality, research suggests, is influenced by genetics and early-life environmental experiences. An individual's general habitus is learned early in life, internalized, and then forgotten. A person may develop a "specific habitus" later in life, as a result of organizational contact, but one's general and specific habituses are expected to be similar. Thus, though they have different explanations for continuity, and neither implies total inertia, both concepts suggest that we should expect psychological stability throughout bureaucratic socialization. As such, the dispositional perspective predicts that entrants will remain connected to their entering bureaucratic personalities throughout their development.

The section also discussed some of the empirical evidence that supports the expectations drawn from this perspective. Although little evidence suggests that dispositions are all that matter, there is empirical support for the dispositional perspective. Now the focus of the chapter shifts to a consideration of why we might expect bureaucratic socialization to be a time in which newcomers undergo considerable change.

The Institutional Perspective

In his book *Eyewitness to a Genocide*, Michael Barnett (1999) describes the ineffectual response of the United Nations (UN) to the humanitarian crisis in Rwanda in 1994. Despite having real-time knowledge about the unfolding disaster, UN bureaucrats acted with indifference. In this way, his book is similar to other accounts that criticize bureaucratic inertia or incompetence in the face of some crisis (Woodward 1995). What makes Barnett's account different is that he is also judging his own response—during the year of the genocide he was a political officer with the U.S. mission to the UN. As the crisis unfolded, Barnett, like others in the organization, argued the typical UN line—the organization shouldn't commit peacekeeping troops unless there was a peace to keep. As an "insider" in New York, he saw the critiques of outsiders as idealistic and unknowing. However, after leaving the organization and returning to academia, he analyzed his own view again and saw its defects: if the UN, fifty years after the Nazi Holocaust, couldn't act to protect innocent people from genocide, what was the organization's purpose?

By highlighting the evolution of his own views, Barnett provides a striking example of the institutional perspective on bureaucratic psychology and behavior:

> The UN was not a totalizing institution that transformed fairly independent-minded diplomats and international civil servants into bloodless bureaucrats, but it did profoundly influence how they looked at and acted upon the world. Government officials and UN staff came to know Rwanda as members of bureaucracies; the bureaucratic culture situated and defined their knowledge, informed their goals and desires, shaped what constituted appropriate and inappropriate behavior, distinguished acceptable from unacceptable consequences, and helped to determine right from wrong. Bureaucracy is not only a structure; it is also a process. Bureaucracies are orienting machines. They have the capacity to channel action and to transform individual into collective conscience. The existing stock of knowledge, the understanding of what constitutes proper means and ends, and the symbolic significance of events were organizationally situated. (Barnett 1999, 7)

Across the social sciences there is support for this basic view (Arendt 1963; Hummel 1982; Kelman and Hamilton 1990; Lipsky 1980; H. Simon 1997). In effect, this position is rooted in a Weberian expectation that working in a bureaucracy changes people in fundamental ways. Such accounts also implicitly invoke social identity theory—as individuals move from "out-group" to "in-group," they adopt the in-group as a reference for social comparison and take on its views as their own (Wood 2000). Since March and Olsen's (2006) logic of appropriateness theorizes that identities and perceptions influence behavior, the institutional perspective has major implications for our understanding of bureaucratic functioning and individual decision making.

This section investigates this perspective and discusses two reasons why organizations may shape individuals: the rational systems and natural systems perspectives. Though the reasons behind these perspectives differ, they are united by the basic expectation that entrants will adopt new views as a result of contact with the social forces inside their organizations. As in the prior section, there are no absolutes here: to use Barnett's (1999) language, the institutional perspective doesn't portray organizations as "totalizing institution[s]" that take blank slates and transform them into "bloodless bureaucrats." However, institutional accounts differ from dispositional accounts in emphasis: they conceive of organization stimuli as explaining a sizeable amount of the variation in organizational thought and behavior. In addition to developing the conceptual underpinnings of the institutional perspective, this section provides examples of empirical work that support its basic premise.

Rational Systems Perspective

One of the most enduring approaches to understanding organizations is the rational systems (RS) perspective (Scott 2003). This perspective, articulated by Max Weber (1947), Herbert Simon (1947), and Charles Barnard (1938), and elaborated by more recent scholars like James Wilson (1989), conceives of organizations as mechanical systems of hierarchy. As such, it is believed that organizations can be internally manipulated to achieve desired ends. For instance, Wilson begins his book by comparing failing schools, armies, and prisons with similar, successful organizations. He argues that the typical explanation for success—"it's not the organization that's important, it's the people in it" (Wilson 1989, 24)—is incomplete. In his view, an organization's people are deeply influenced by the situations in which they operate and the leaders who guide them. In essence, he argues that organizations succeed when they are run well.

As this example shows, scholars in the RS perspective see organizations as discrete entities that pursue specific goals using formal processes (Scott 2003, 27). Although this definition may seem obvious, it is important to consider its implications. Unlike the open systems perspective, which conceives of organizations as porous and embedded in an environment, the RS perspective takes a rather narrow view of the organization: understanding why an organization succeeds or fails requires looking inside the organization itself. In other words, the RS perspective directs attention inward as opposed to outward. For instance, an RS approach to education might explain success and failure by pointing to the leadership exercised by a school's principal and the systems used to monitor and regulate the actions of teachers. Less important, from this perspective, are the neighborhood in which the school is located and the state's teacher recruitment and training system.

The RS perspective also expects that organizations have specific goals. In other words, organizations are understood as relatively united in the pursuit of discrete objectives. To take a simple example, a fire department has the goal of protecting property and individuals from fire. The RS perspective would expect that people within the department, including dispatchers, emergency medical technicians, managers, and firefighters, share these basic goals.

Finally, the RS perspective emphasizes the importance of formalization—the standardization of practices, policies, rules, and roles (Hall, Johnson, and Haas 1967). In particular, it expects that formalization shapes how organization members think about their roles, make decisions, and communicate. An appreciation of formalization directs attention to the "official" mechanisms used by organization leaders to shape thought and compel behavior. For example, an RS approach to understanding the behavior of Internal Revenue Service auditors would study how auditors are trained, managers communicate goals to auditors, and managers monitor and respond to the actions of auditors. These mechanisms are, relative to informal organizational influences like culture (discussed below), under the control of the organization and its leaders. As such, they are understood as important instruments that organizations can use to shape the thoughts and actions of lower-level employees.

As this section makes clear, the RS perspective highlights a number of reasons why organizations may be expected to shape the views and actions of its members. It places individuals in hierarchical systems that define their goals, superiors, and roles and exposes them to formalization. In doing so, it communicates essential information to employees about how they should think and act. It also sends signals about the organization's values. As such, the RS perspective offers a potential explanation for how organizations shape individuals.

Natural Systems Perspective

A second reason to expect that organizations may shape entrants directs attention to the informal parts of the organization. Whereas the RS perspective sees organizations as discrete, unified entities, the natural systems (NS) perspective conceives of organizations as more porous and disjointed. From this perspective, "organizations are collectivities whose participants are pursuing multiple interests, both disparate and common, but who recognize the value of perpetuating the organization as an important resource. The informal structure of relations that develops among participants is more influential in guiding the behavior of participants than is the formal structure" (Scott 2003, 28).

As this definition implies, the NS perspective questions the assumption that organization members share a discrete goal. Rather, within and across levels of an organization, members may hold different goals. For example, sergeants in an urban police force may want to increase the number of tickets given for "quality-of-life" crimes, like graffiti, whereas patrol officers prefer to use their time focusing on crimes that they perceive as more serious, like robberies. Sacrificing the assumption of goal uniformity is problematic for the RS perspective: if organization members are not unified in the pursuit of a single goal, how can organizations achieve their desired ends? In other words, internal goal divergence brings up the possibility that one part of an organization can be unaligned or, even worse, working at cross-purposes with another part.

A second component of the NS perspective, and another way that it critiques the RS perspective, is its questioning of the importance of an organization's formal tools. For instance, the NS perspective challenges the notion that formal tactics—like training, monitoring, and communication—are most important for unifying the goals and actions of lower-level workers. Rather, the NS perspective draws attention to the importance of informal influences like norms, cultures, and peers (Argyris 1993; Downs 1967). Although these informal influences are not found on any organization charts, they create an organization's internal social climate. In this way, they orient organization members to what is appropriate behavior and, perhaps, establish perspectives about how they should think and act. For example, in trying to understand how a school, army, or prison operates, NS scholars may highlight the importance of an organization's culture. From this perspective, training and leadership affect an organization's culture, but so do a host of less organizationally controlled factors.

As this example shows, the NS perspective does not portray formalization as unimportant or formalization and informalization as mutually exclusive. Rather, there is considerable interest in understanding the interplay between these two areas and gauging the extent to which organization leaders can shape informal outcomes (Bass and Avolio 1994). Whether they succeed in this regard is up for debate. The key point is that, compared to the RS perspective, scholars in this tradition highlight the prominence of the informal components of organizational life.

Accumulated Evidence

So far this section has outlined two perspectives that undergird the institutional perspective and help explain why bureaucratic development may shape the thoughts and actions of newcomers. To illustrate this process, we turn to the organizational socialization and street-level bureaucracy literatures. Again, there are no absolutes here: the evidence in this section highlights the important role played by institutions but does not imply that dispositions are unimportant. Nonetheless, these literatures are important to review because of the prominent role that they give to institutional factors.

Organizational Socialization Literature

Across a variety of disciplines, scholars have been interested in understanding organizational socialization—how newcomers develop the knowledge, attitudes, and behaviors needed to function as organization members (Louis 1980; Saks and Ashforth 1997; Wanberg 2012b; Wanous 1992). Taken as a whole, the literature points to an array of dispositional and institutional factors that shape socialization. To illustrate the effect of institutional influences, this section highlights two formal organizational forces that appear to affect newcomers' thoughts and actions: training and supervision.

Many works in the organizational socialization literature point to the importance of training[3]—the period during which new organization members are taught about the organization and their roles in it (Saks and Ashforth 1997). As they begin work, training is the first formal contact that employees have with their organizations. The structure of training appears to affect entrants' experiences and development. For instance, Jones (1986) showed that when business organizations use institutionalized tactics (entrants are trained together in a group), entrants were more likely to develop passive identities that promote the organization's status quo. When organizations used individualized tactics (entrants are trained individually), he found that entrants were more likely to adopt identities that questioned the status quo and promoted innovation.[4]

As this work shows, training appears to be important because it helps newcomers make sense of their place in their organizations. As organizations set about instructing entrants about the organization and how they fit into it, entrants may experience some anxiety and surprise (Louis 1980). Training is thought to influence entrants by reducing uncertainty and enabling them to feel more comfortable in their organizations (Saks 1996). One of the key social forces that entrants come into contact with during training is instructors. These organization members are tasked with giving newcomers the information and skills necessary to function as effective insiders. Because they are chosen by organization leaders, they are an important formal tool that organizations may be able to use to imprint newcomers with desired goals and values (Chappell and Lanza-Kaduce 2010).

In addition to training, organizations may be able to shape workers' experiences, views, and actions using another formal tool: management. Management, which includes supervision and leadership, is the approach used by organization leaders to maintain and advance their organizations using planning, motivation, and communication (Rainey 2003). There is considerable evidence that management matters—how leaders govern their organizations affects individual- and group-level perceptions and performance (Ingraham, Joyce, and Donahue 2003; Lowe, Kroeck, and Sivasubramaniam 1996; Moynihan 2007; Oberfield 2012). As might be expected, management also matters for organizational socialization. For example, the information provided by superiors to entrants appears to be one of the most important factors in shaping the success of entrant socialization (Ostroff and Kozlowski 1992; Saks and Ashforth 1997). Managers may be important due to their symbolic status. As official representatives of the organization, their words and actions are imbued with considerable symbolic authority. For example, by emphasizing what they will monitor, and how seriously they will do it, managers may communicate the organization's values to newcomers (Riccucci et al. 2004).

Street-Level Bureaucracy Literature

The street-level bureaucracy literature also demonstrates the potency of the institutional perspective. In particular, this literature highlights the importance of an organization's culture—"the unwritten rules, mores, customs, codes, values and outlooks" (Chemerinsky 2000, 559). Culture is a potentially powerful influence because it has can shape entrants' views about their organization's goals and how they should act to achieve them. As they enter their organizations, newcomers are confronted by an established culture that specifies how tasks are accomplished, how members of the public are treated, and how followers are managed. There are different accounts about how entrants respond to and interact with their organizations' existing cultures. Some work suggests that existing cultures have a strong, unidirectional effect on entrants (Kappeler, Sluder, and Alpert 1998). Other work suggests that the relationship is more of a dialectic: entrants are shaped by and shape the cultures that they enter (Sandfort 2000). Whatever the relationship, there is general support for the notion that an organization's culture imprints at least some attitudes and patterns of behavior on members.

Coworkers are another important focus of the street-level bureaucracy literature. In effect, two sets of coworkers are thought to shape the experiences of entrants, peers and veterans. Peers, or fellow entrants, may have an impact on entering workers because they provide an immediate social context for sensemaking (Evan 1963; Morrison 2002). For example, a newcomer's peers can offer complementary or competing responses to training experiences and, thereby, challenge or reinforce a newcomer's developing views. Also, there is evidence that the actions of individuals, once they end training and begin their work as insiders, are shaped by peers. One study shows that, across a variety of street-level bureaucracies, behavior was driven more strongly by solidary preferences—the social connections among workers—than by supervision (Brehm and Gates 1997).

Whereas a newcomer's peers are collaborators in the sensemaking process, experienced organization members, or veterans, are established insiders. Although contact with veterans is not part of official training in all organizations, in many organizations veterans serve as informal guides for entrants (Ellwanger 2010; Prottas 1979). As newcomers arrive in their workplaces following training, they enter, to at least some extent, a new social context. In this new milieu, veterans use stories to convey information about the organization, the people whom entrants will encounter, and their understanding of their role as organization members. Veterans tell rookies about "what it's really like out there" and that training has not prepared them for it (Van Maanen 1974). Rookies, to at least some extent, are thought to use the model that veterans portray to construct their organizational realities. As such, there is general support for the expectation that veterans play a role in shaping the views and behavior of entrants.

Summary

This section has discussed the RS and NS perspectives—two approaches to understanding organizations that undergird the institutional perspective on bureaucratic socialization. Though they offer different explanations for why organizations matter, they are connected by the expectation that the social dynamics individuals encounter inside organizations will shape how they think and act. However, it is important not to overstate the case: neither perspective ignores dispositions or implies that entrants completely change. Nonetheless, each devotes considerable explanatory power to institutional factors like culture, training, and peers. As such, they lend support to the expectation that entrants' bureaucratic personalities are developed as a result of contact with their organizations. The section also discussed some of the empirical evidence that supports this expectation.

Empirical Analysis

The final part of this chapter discusses how the dispositional and institutional perspectives are analyzed in Chapters 5 to 7. To begin, each chapter presents qualitative evidence from interviews conducted throughout the study. These data are useful for presenting entrants' views and experiences in their own words and providing an initial sense about how their views evolved or remained static during entry. To more rigorously assess these competing perspectives, each chapter then analyzes entrants' survey responses. First, each chapter examines the trends in group-level responses—levels of agreement and standard deviation for each question—over time. Second, the chapters discuss an analysis of how individuals altered their responses to each question over the course of the study.

The empirical chapters also include a discussion of a statistical analysis of entrants' survey responses. The first goal of the analysis was to explain variation in entrants' views, using multivariate or bivariate models, throughout the study. To examine the dispositional perspective, postentry analyses included entrants' first responses as independent variables. As such, the chapters show how much respondents' views remained connected to their entering views. In addition, the analysis included extraorganizational demographic characteristics, like age, race, and class experiences, that are thought to be important predictors of entrants' views.[5] To examine the institutional perspective, the analysis included a variety of organizational variables as independent variables.[6] Based on the RS perspective, there are three formal organization influences that are analyzed in subsequent chapters: training, monitoring, and supervisors. Based on the NS perspective, the book charts the effect of three informal influences on entrants: culture, peers, and veterans.

The second goal of the statistical analysis was to explore the likelihood that entrants would adopt new views. As such, the empirical chapters report findings from an analysis of individual-level change data (calculated by taking the difference between newcomers' entering and subsequent responses). This analysis investigated how dispositional and institutional variables predicted entrants' likelihood of adopting different views at different times throughout the study. For example, Chapter 7 discusses the role that entrants' racial identities played in their likelihood of adopting different attitudes about the existence and harm of racism. Were whites more likely to alter their views about racism than were minorities? By answering questions like this, the analysis helps explain why some entrants adopted new views and others didn't.

Conclusion

This book studies the development of two sets of entering street-level bureaucrats. It is guided by divergent explanations: the dispositional perspective suggests that workers will largely maintain their entering views and that their views will be associated with extraorganizational factors like their ages and racial identities; the institutional perspective suggests that workers will adopt new views and that their views will be associated with organizational influences. This chapter has discussed the concepts, theories, and perspectives that explain why we might expect stability and change. In subsequent chapters this book evaluates these basic explanations to see how useful they are at explaining these cases of bureaucratic socialization.

However, in the next chapter, we take a small detour and direct our attention to the experienced workers in each of these organizations. These veteran workers were the people whom newcomers first encountered after completing training. As such, they help us understand the organizations that entrants joined and provide clues about how they might develop.

CHAPTER 3

The Long View:
How Veteran Workers See Their Worlds

As they enter bureaucracies, new public workers meet peers, are told how to think and act by instructors, and begin their work. Various ethnographic studies suggest that this process is formative for entrants (Conti 2009; Kappeler, Sluder, and Alpert 1998; Macvean and Cox 2012; Rubinstein 1973; Wanous 1992). For example, in a study of police socialization, Rubinstein (1973, 127–28) notes, "While he is learning to do his work, he is also defining for himself the nature of his place on the street, discovering the contradictions inherent in his position as a guardian of the 'public' peace and the ambiguities of being a regulator of people's conduct." Focusing on two street-level bureaucracies, this book explores this process during newcomers' first two years on the job. Its main goal is to assess how well the dispositional and institutional perspectives explain bureaucratic socialization. To achieve this goal, it is important to understand how newcomers' bureaucratic personalities compare to those held by experienced workers in each organization. This chapter facilitates such a comparison by exploring the views held by veteran police officers and welfare caseworkers. The data presented here are drawn from prior studies and surveys of experienced workers in these two fields. In addition, the chapter includes data from in-depth interviews with eleven experienced workers in the research city.

To some extent, this endeavor is fraught with difficulty: in Chapter 1, I argued against a deterministic and one-dimensional view of bureaucratic personality; research suggests that across government and inside particular agencies there is variation in bureaucratic thought and action (Balch 1972; Brown 1988; DeHart-Davis 2007; Muir 1977; O'Leary 2010; Worden 1995); and public workers' views may vary over the course of their careers (McElroy, Morrow, and Wardlow 1999). Despite these concerns, it is important not to take the point too far: Chapter 1 also shows that there are distinct patterns of thought within organizations and occupations. As such, it is worth trying to develop an understanding of the views of experienced workers in each of these fields.

As readers will notice, there are some areas in which experienced workers seem to share similar views and other areas where there are significant differences. Thus, it is important to note that the book takes a consciously nondeterministic posture: it does not expect that all entrants are destined to think alike. Similarly, it does not assert that the views articulated in this chapter are representative of the views of all experienced workers in these two organizations. Rather, this chapter's findings can be interpreted as establishing some rough outlines about how experienced workers in these organizations think. In doing so, it will give readers a sense of the people whom entrants encountered after entry. In addition, the chapter enables a comparison of newcomers' and veterans' bureaucratic personalities. Did entrants report similar views to the ones held by veterans at entry? Did their views grow closer over time? By comparing the findings of this chapter with the findings of subsequent chapters, we can begin to answer these questions.

Experienced Police Officers

Bureaucratic Identity

Interviews with veteran police and a review of the U.S. policing literature suggest that there are discernible police identity patterns (Chappell and Lanza-Kaduce 2010; Conti 2009; Gallo 2001; Muir 1977; Rubinstein 1973; Skolnick 1966; Worden 1995). In particular, most police appear to see themselves and act as legitimate, authoritative actors who represent the legal and moral authority of the state (Alpert and Dunham 2004). In other words, police are relatively comfortable exercising power and understand their role to include the upholding of traditional social or moral norms and the punishing of deviance. For example, Michael, an African American officer whom I interviewed, commented, "Now today you have young people hollering at the old people and that's not right. I didn't grow up that way. If your grandfather tells you to come in the house you have to go in the house. Especially if it's curfew time and he's trying to save you from getting [a] write up for truancy or curfew. He's trying to tell you right, not wrong." In instances like this, Michael indicated a willingness to engage with young people to reinforce the morally proper behavior.

As Michael's comments show, some police appear to see the scope of their job quite broadly. Nonetheless, there were few indications in my interviews or in the police literature that police see themselves as all-powerful (Muir 1977). Indeed, national survey data suggest that most police acknowledge that there are limits to what they can do, especially regarding the use of force (Weisburd et al. 2001). Perhaps as a result, police see their power as versatile: they know that they can't rely solely upon coercion, and, in interacting with the public, they indicate wearing a variety of "hats" (Martin 1999; Muir 1977). For example, Calvin, a black officer interviewed for this book, noted, "Actually being a police officer is almost like being a psychiatrist. Or having more than one job. Different aspects of it dealing with everyday people one day you may have to be a landlord, the next day you may have to be a child care provider, the next day you may be a plumber or an electrician or a mechanic. It goes from one end to another."

Another recurring theme in the police literature is emotional detachment (Bakker and Heuven 2006; Martin 1999; Muir 1977; Rubinstein 1973; Van Maanen 1974). Part of being an effective police officer is the effective management of one's feelings. For some police this may mean sporadic or conditional detachment in response to particularly difficult situations; for others it may mean a more general dispassion or "flatness." Reflecting this latter approach, one veteran officer commented, "The only way you survive on this job is to grow calluses. You put on a shell the beginning of every shift and take it off when you get home. When I'm working, I'm as hard as stone 'cause I gotta be, it's my only defense" (Van Maanen 1974, 98). Though some officers may adopt this approach, research suggests that police do make exceptions and allow themselves to feel emotionally connected to members of the public (Maynard-Moody and Musheno 2003). In fact, these moments appear to be important to police because they remind them about why they chose their work and rekindle the idea that they have some efficacy. Though these moments may be important for maintaining morale and motivation, in the general course of their jobs it may be too emotionally taxing for police to engage or invest in many people or situations.

As noted in Chapter 1, rule following is an important component of bureaucratic identity. Situating one's self in regards to the rules presents something of a challenge for police: they report wanting to treat people equally and be responsive to particular situations. On the one hand, police are loath to be seen as prejudiced, and a national survey of officers suggests that they generally believe that they treat people equally (Weisburd et al. 2001). However, police also do not want to see themselves as automatons or "mere administrators"; for many police the chance to help someone who needs and deserves it was a motivating factor for joining the police (Raganella and White 2004). Perhaps in response to this tension, studies show that police behavior is situation-dependent (Brown 1988; Muir 1977; Rubinstein 1973; Terrill and Mastrofski 2002; Terrill and Reisig 2003; Worden 1989).

Most of the veteran officers interviewed for this book indicated that this case-by-case style typified their approach to policing. For example, Calvin said, "A lot of times you basically have to pick and choose your battles when you're interacting with people. . . . Believe it or not, it's case by case." Maria, a Hispanic officer, echoed this view, saying, "Every situation has to be treated differently." Helen, a white officer who had been on the force for over a decade, noted going by "gut" and "circumstance," while Frances, a black officer with less time on the force, made a distinction between traffic stops, which are "by the book," and other situations in which everyone has to be treated "a little differently."

In effect, officers appear to see their authority as context- and person-dependent. For instance, Rubinstein (1973, 163) writes that when officers approach unruly crowds on the street, their actions "depend a good deal on their response to him." Maria, the younger Hispanic officer whom I interviewed, noted, "You give me respect, I'll give you respect." Similarly, Calvin commented, "Half the time it's normally how a person . . . come[s] off to me or how they approach me."

Although police may describe themselves as going case by case, few studies suggest that they see themselves as untethered, rogue agents. They may not welcome additional rules and regulations (Weisburd et al. 2001), but they recognize that they are to some extent bound by the law. As such, police appear to understand that in some areas or situations they have discretion while in other situations they do not. For example, throughout interviews for this book, experienced police noted that in cases of shoplifting, even if they believed that the accused was doing it for meritorious reasons (like hunger), they were constrained by the desires of the shop owners. If police officers wanted to give suspects a break but the shop owners wanted them arrested, it was out of their hands.

Finally, it is important to discuss police officer loyalty—the level of allegiance officers have toward their departments. Although there is clearly variation across departments and individuals, in general police appear to be relatively loyal to their departments (Chappell and Lanza-Kaduce 2010). Police work is, for many officers, all-encompassing: they are friends with other police and identify as a police officer on and off the job. Brown (1988, 83) notes that police culture "demands of a patrolman unstinting loyalty to his fellow officers, and receives, in return, protection and honor." However, survey data suggest that loyalty to one another—the "blue code of silence" (Skolnick 2002)—is a bit different than traditionally understood. Though they articulate high levels of loyalty to their departments and fellow officers, most police downplayed the importance of the "code of silence" and saw whistle-blowing, even in the face of possible retribution, as worthwhile (Weisburd et al. 2001).

Motivation

The motivation of police is a long-standing interest to scholars and practitioners. One classic study that examined police entrants showed that newcomers begin their careers motivated to work hard to gain desired outcomes; however, over the course of the study (approximately thirty months), levels of motivation fell considerably (Van Maanen 1975). Behind their general motivation to work hard or shirk, what specific motives drive them? In the literature there is evidence that police are motivated by egoistic and altruistic rewards. For example, some studies show that police officers are strongly motivated by solidary rewards—rewards from interacting in a social environment (Brehm and Gates 1997; Gaines, Van Tubergen, and Paiva 1984). These studies suggest the importance of egoism since police are motivated primarily by the satisfaction of their own need to interact socially. In addition, because many police come from lower- or middle-class families, officers may be driven by the stable pay and security of police work. Similarly, some officers appear to be oriented toward gaining personal pleasure from their work, like the job's excitement, as opposed to helping or sacrificing for others (Teahan 1975).

On the altruistic side, many police report being motivated by a desire to help people (Raganella and White 2004). These officers see policing as collaborative, not coercive, and understand their work as "giving back." However, the meaning of "giving back" or "helping" is somewhat unclear. Studies suggest that initially police are motivated by somewhat grand desires, like helping people turn their lives around or changing how the police are perceived by the public (Gallo 2001). Over time, they may adopt more practical, less romantic notions of helping. For instance, police may come to recognize that they have the power to help some people but can't save an entire neighborhood (Muir 1977).

The experienced officers interviewed for this book reported altruistic and egoistic motivations. For instance, Helen indicated being motivated by helping people solve their problems and letting them vent. Similarly, Michael noted, "I decided when I was growing up that I wanted to do something good." However, others indicated egoistic motives. For example, Frances indicated a desire to "make rank" and Maria suggested that her choice was driven by need: "I was in college, community college. . . . And I had a situation where I needed money, so college, I couldn't afford paying college no more so I had filled out the application like a year ago, like a year before I got into college and it like came up you know that they wanted me to take the test and so it came up the opportunity and I was like why not?" Clearly, a range of motives drive police work, and individual police appear to have multiple motives.

Attitudes

The key attitudinal outcomes of this book are workers' views of the people whom they interact with, social problems, and deservingness. In these areas, as with other sections of this chapter, I expect that officers' views vary to some extent. Nevertheless, my goal here is to assemble some general parameters of officers' views and to detect if there are any patterns based on prior studies and my interviews with experienced police.

Across the police literature there is support for the view that police see the people in the communities that they police in binary terms: good and bad. The good people, who are deserving of their help, are respectful, law abiding, and employed. Although they may live in a troubled neighborhood, they are making a good-faith effort to improve their lives and their communities. In contrast, there are bad people who are disrespectful law breakers who aim to destabilize communities and wreak havoc. It is these people who ruin the neighborhoods for everyone else. Describing one officer's views, Muir (1977, 22) notes, "The world was divided into two camps, the builders, who 'like to see progress,' and the 'night people,' the predators, the destroyers. On the 'good' side were the 'family men,' who 'hustled,' were ambitious, had 'pride.' . . . On the other side was the enemy: the 'runners,' the 'fighters,' the 'big-mouthers,' the 'crowd-gatherers,' . . . the 'jailbirds.'" In my interviews with experienced police, I heard this perspective as well. For instance, Maria noted, "You've got your good people out there, hardworking people who are unfortunately stuck in bad areas and can't afford to move out. Then you've got the people out there who are doing illegal stuff and just give you a hard time and sometimes you don't want to deal with certain people in the community."

Another trait linked to perceptions of deservingness, according to experienced police, is honesty. Someone who comes clean and levels with police is likely to be seen as deserving. Someone who evades or dissembles is not. For instance, Frances described how she assessed people she interacted with:

> Mainly honesty. When I walk up to someone if they're honest and if I say, "License, registration and insurance." If they say, "I don't have my license on me," and I say "Ma'am do you have a license" or "Sir do you have a license?" If they say, "Yeah I got a license," but I want you to be honest because if you say, "Officer, the car [is] not registered." "I don't have no insurance," or something like that. Be honest then I can [use] my discretion you know [to do what I can] for you. If I can't do anything for you [I'll] tell you, I'm gonna have to take your vehicle. But honesty.

Another element of deservingness, which is evident in popular imagery, the police literature, and my interviews, is the deservingness of the old and the young. For example, Frances, when discussing to whom she might give a break, noted, "If they elderly. I know most of the elderly they are mainly like a fixed income. I'm not trying to give them tickets or anything . . . that's just me. Other people might. I don't do that. I don't want to put them through that." Similarly, children are seen as particularly deserving of police help and protection. Maria told me a story of giving a girl accused of shoplifting a second chance (with the permission of the shopkeeper). I asked her why she had used her discretion in this way. "Just her age and the way she would, I don't know. Sometimes we're young and dumb and I've made mistakes at that age that I know I shouldn't have. And I think that she was just young a dumb and pressured. It was just a dumb mistake she did and I felt like she could have done better." As is evident in this comment, there is a sense that there is still hope for some young people, and, as a result, the officer used her discretion to help the girl out of a jam. We also see the importance of relatability: deservingness perceptions may be determined by the extent to which police understand and connect with the experiences of members of the public.

In addition, perceptions of deservingness may be based on officers' interpretations of intent. People who did something wrong but did it for the right reasons may be seen as deserving. For example, consider Calvin's comments describing a call about shoplifting:

> I also had one twelve-year-old girl who . . . was stealing school supplies for school. Her mom didn't have the money and she needed it for school. She wouldn't tell the store security what she was doing it for and . . . I asked her, "Why you stealing this stuff?" and I'm looking and it's all

school supplies and I'm like, "You need this for school?" And she's like, "Yeah, my mom don't have the money and I don't want the other kids to make fun of me." So I went in and talked to the owner and paid for the stuff and gave it to her and let her go.

The other side of the story is undeservingness: the people whom police are unlikely to see as worthy of a break or a second chance. Across the policing literature, and my interviews with veterans, the undeserving are the lazy, difficult, dishonest, and bad. For example, a nationwide survey of police shows that nearly half of the respondents agreed that if a suspect has a "bad attitude" a police officer is more likely to arrest him or her (Weisburd et al. 2001). Similarly, people who are perceived as moral reprobates may be singled out for punishment (Rubenstein 1973). In addition, people who are physically unkempt, drug abusers, or recidivists may be seen as undeserving (Conlon 2004).

How do police officers generally understand the causes of social problems like crime, poverty, and the overlap of race and poverty? Again, this chapter does not claim that there is a single perspective on these issues. However, the police literature suggests some common themes. To begin, it is important to note that policing was historically a profession for white, middle-class men. Today there is significantly more diversity—along the lines of race and sex—but most police officers in the United States are white men (Weisburd et al. 2001). Public opinion research shows that although overt racist attitudes may have diminished in recent years, many whites still harbor significant racial resentment and hold racially charged views about a variety of public policies (Gilens 1999; G. Wilson and Nielsen 2011). In particular, whites tend to explain minority poverty and inequality in terms of choices and character. In contrast, blacks and other minorities are more likely to view racial disadvantage, and related social problems, as caused by structural issues like the economy or history. For both groups, how one understands a problem is inextricably linked to how one accounts for the problem (Thompson and Bobo 2011).

If whites tend to view social problems, especially those linked with race, through the lens of individual choices, and most police are white, it follows that most police will hold individualistic views on social problems. However, minority police may see the world differently. In other words, though the police department is often portrayed as an effective socializing agent, racial differences may persist even after training (Sun 2003; Sun and Payne 2004; Teahan 1975; Wilkins and Williams 2008). This seems like an area in which officers' views may be tied to their identities and preorganizational experiences. Supporting this notion, my interviews with experienced police revealed a mix of views about the causes of crime, poverty, and other social problems. As might be expected, this variation seemed connected to officers' racial identities. For instance, Helen, a white woman, speculated that the high rates of minority poverty resulted from minorities' unwillingness to work hard. She continued, "Black people are blaming whites saying, 'You're holding us back.' Whites say, 'You need to work like us. You don't hear Asians or Hispanics complaining.'" In contrast, most minority officers pointed to bigger, structural factors at play. For example, Maria, when asked about the high incidence of minority poverty, responded, "I would just say that history has a lot to do with that." Similarly, Frances, when asked about the causes of poverty generally, replied, "I can say like lack of schooling and lack of jobs I would think."

Summary

This section has sketched out the attitudes, identities, and motivations held by experienced police officers according to interviews with veterans in the research city and prior research. In total, we see that police are motivated by altruistic and egoistic motives, understand their jobs as discretion-laden but do not believe that they have carte blanche, are generally loyal to their departments, have a range of views about the cause of social problems, and see hardworking, honest people as deserving of help. Next we consider the identities, motivations, and attitudes held by experienced welfare caseworkers.

Experienced Welfare Caseworkers

The attitudes and identities of public welfare caseworkers have long been a point of political contestation. Conservatives historically have seen welfare workers as bleeding-heart "do gooders," while liberals have seen them as "nosy skinflints" (J. Wilson 1989, 51). Perhaps unsurprisingly, when scholars have sought to move beyond reputation and investigate what actual welfare caseworkers think, a more complex picture emerges (Prottas 1979; Riccucci et al. 2004; Watkins-Hayes 2009). Like the previous section, this section draws from prior scholarly accounts, surveys, and interviews that I conducted with experienced workers.

Bureaucratic Identity

Welfare caseworkers have a variety of general bureaucratic identities that they employ as they interact with applicants and recipients. One of these identities is that of the empathetic "social worker" who sees herself as working to help or protect vulnerable people (Cheek and Piercy 2001; Watkins-Hayes 2009). Workers who understand their jobs in this way seem to believe that they are qualitatively the same as welfare clients and, under slightly different circumstances, could be on the other side of the application desk. From this perspective, welfare casework is a helping job where workers have the chance to lessen the demands of a difficult system in order to make people's lives a little better.

Though some caseworkers may view themselves as "social workers," and perform accordingly, welfare caseworkers, like police, also have a detached, professional identity that they use. This identity is assertive and abrupt and deemphasizes emotional connection with applicants or recipients. Watkins-Hayes (2009) refers to this as the "efficiency engineering" identity and argues that, when it is employed, workers will recite policy without delay and present themselves somewhat coldly to clients. For example, she quotes one worker who embodies this identity. "By contending that the job is 'black and white' and 'like an assembly line,' Jackie stakes out a professional orientation that deemphasizes personalized advising to address the challenges facing each client and asserts a more utilitarian (and arguably time-efficient) approach to service delivery" (Watkins-Hayes 2009, 65).

In addition, many welfare caseworkers project an authoritative air that suggests personal control and decision-making power (Prottas 1979, 29–30). From this perspective, rules may be important constraints, but workers also understand, or project, that they have some flexibility for deviation or selective application of the rules. The flexibility with which caseworkers understand their jobs may explain why welfare recipients view caseworkers as powerful and, oftentimes, capricious (Soss 2000).

In my interviews with experienced caseworkers, I also detected elements of this identity. Many caseworkers appeared to understand their work as treating situations and people differently based on circumstances. For example, Terri, a black caseworker with over ten years on the job, commented, "Honestly I treat them differently. If you come to me and I see that you have the spark and the fire and the desire to want to do something then that affects me. That kind of spirit then I'm more ok, I'll go the extra mile. To give you the information. The other people I'll give you that information but it stops at what you need to know." Paula, who immigrated to the United States from the Caribbean as a teenager, echoed this view: "It depends on the client and what the need is. Basically it's on a client-[by]-client basis and some need more help than others."

Although workers may project a powerful, discretion-using identity at times, many also indicate seeing themselves as having little power, as mere cogs in a giant system. For example, in some instances workers will assert their powerlessness when pressed by applicants for leniency or speed (Prottas 1979, 29). Lipsky (1980, 149) notes that this assertion may be part of an important power play: "Denying discretion is a common way to limit responsibility. . . . Strict adherence to the rules, and refusals to make exceptions when exceptions might be made, provide workers with defenses against the possibility that they might be able to act more as clients would wish." Reflecting these findings, in a four-state survey that asked welfare caseworkers what shaped their decisions, an average of 73 percent of workers indicated seeing their decisions as "always" or "usually" based on clear rules (Lurie, Riccucci, and Meyers 2001).[1] In particular, these caseworkers saw their decisions about sanctioning and handling Medicaid and Food Stamps as rule driven.[2]

This trend was also evident in my interviews with experienced workers. Interestingly, some of the workers who described themselves as going case by case also saw themselves as powerless. For example, Paula, who reported giving help to clients when needed, also commented, "The bottom line is you don't have any power. You're there to enforce the policy. You cannot do anything more than what they allow us to do and basically that's little." Although she meant this in part to say that workers are limited in helping clients, she later also voiced concern that workers were limited in their ability to punish clients via sanctioning: "If you have a client who didn't do X, Y, and Z. We say we're gonna sanction you. But then when it gets to the next level, and it doesn't go through, it makes it look like we don't have any kind of pull. So whatever we say doesn't matter. And all the caseworkers feel that way: we don't have no control over anything [except] 'do what I say' and that's it."

Although these views seem to contradict—how can workers see themselves as having discretion and as powerless?—perhaps this indicates that they have discretion within a narrow range of options, but little real power. Alternatively, how workers understand themselves in relation to the job may depend on the context of the client or the case. When workers wish to bend the rules and make an exception they project and enact the powerful, discretion-using identity; when they do not want to make an exception they project the powerless bureaucrat.

Another possibility is that workers may actually feel that they have limited power in some situations but project authority anyways. For example, Paula, after acknowledging that the eligibility decision was not hers, discussed the language that she used with clients:

> I don't want to make any promises to the client. 'Cause the first thing the client is going to do is check. If I say, "You're gonna get your benefits on Tuesday" and on Tuesday the benefits aren't there . . . the client will call me and say ". . . Where are my benefits?" Then they hang up the phone with you and call the supervisor. "Well [my worker] told me that I'd have my benefits by Tuesday or blah blah blah." So what I say is "I'll see what I can do." Sometimes we allow partial benefits. Sometimes the system is down. You never know. It's best not to give the client any definites unless you know for sure.

It is unclear how pervasive this rationale is among experienced welfare caseworkers. Nonetheless, welfare caseworkers appear to hold and project competing views about themselves and the rules. On the one hand, they see and demonstrate themselves as treating people case by case; on the other hand, they see themselves as constrained and powerless because of the rules.

In addition, it is important to discuss caseworker loyalty. Like the police, many welfare caseworkers, especially in urban settings, operate in stressful environments that are loud, crowded, and shabby (Goodsell 1984; Watkins-Hayes 2009). However, unlike police, the welfare caseworkers whom I interviewed had very little loyalty to their agency. For example, Terri reacted with surprise at the question: "Loyalty? I have no loyalty to the [agency]." Patricia, a veteran of over twenty years, who started working as a caseworker directly after high school, commented that she felt connected to other workers in her unit or office, but no sense of allegiance to the broader organization. In my work at a welfare office I found this to be the common sentiment: the department and its leaders weren't trusted, so workers saw little purpose to being loyal.

Motivation

Prior studies suggest that welfare caseworkers are likely to be driven by altruism and egoism (Lipsky 1980; Prottas 1979; Watkins-Hayes 2009). On the altruistic side, Watkins-Hayes's (2009) "social workers" are motivated to help welfare applicants by protecting them from a system that may not be treating them well. On the egoistic side, caseworkers may be motivated by reducing the amount of work that they have or the salary and benefits that they draw from their work. Like other street-level bureaucrats, the civil service system may "deaden" their motivation and encourage "primarily selfish considerations" (Lipsky 1980, 82).

In my interviews, I sought to understand why workers had sought out casework. Initially, I found most were drawn by the job's stability and benefits. Paula told me, "When I first started to have a government job was incredible. You know you'll always have benefits. You have good benefits. As far as leaving your job or being laid off or whatever? It wasn't going to happen because of job security." Terri, who was working in a different state office, indicated that she was encouraged to take the caseworker test by a friend. "I said, 'Oh what the heck, what do I have to lose?' I had no instincts and no desire to be a caseworker. It was just opportunity presented to me and I took advantage of it." Other accounts mirrored these. Melissa, a white worker with thirty years of experience, initially found the job because she was out of work: "I was collecting unemployment compensation, I was a hippie [and] it was 1971 and I was sent to apply for a welfare job which they were doing an emergency hiring. So I got the job." Similarly, James, a white caseworker with over twenty-five years on the job, said, "I was broke . . . and [it] was uh one of the easier jobs to land." Patricia commented, "I was just looking for a government job that could give me some benefits and a steady paycheck and my dad always told us that government jobs just don't fire you arbitrarily because you have to go through a whole bunch of stuff."

When the topic turned to their current reasons for working as caseworkers, few indicated altruistic motives. Paula commented, "On the whole, it's just another job. You go in, you do your job. You know what I mean? We don't get involved in their lives, you know what I mean?" Terri echoed this, saying, "the job is not, is not so great. It's not a fulfilling job. If you feel like you're a person who really wants to make change then this isn't the job for you." In contrast with most workers, Melissa, the self-described hippie, indicated an altruistic motivation: "I still have a kind of naïve, kind of innocent approach to people. I mean there are people that are vulnerable that are needy and welfare does supply a security a safety net so I still feel it has a value. I personally don't think I've fallen into the cynical 'This is just like a bunch of bullshit.' . . . I still have a sense that what I'm doing is worth something. . . . But I am also not as naïve as I do know that people do cheat and there's a lot of fraud and bilking the system." The sympathy articulated by Melissa and the sense that the job was "worth something" were, in my interviews with experienced caseworkers, exceedingly rare.

Attitudes

The third major outcome is caseworkers' attitudes about welfare clients, poverty, and deservingness. Some have suggested that professional service providers develop disparaging views of those whom they serve (Reingold and Liu 2009). If true, we might expect that social service providers like welfare caseworkers would articulate negative views about poor people. Other studies suggest a bit more nuance. For example, welfare caseworkers may divide welfare clients into groups based on their assessments of them (Maynard-Moody and Musheno 2003; Sandfort, Kalil, and Gottschalk 1999). Some clients would be categorized as worthy and deserving of assistance, while others would not.

While these studies suggest potential leads, national survey data about the attitudes of welfare caseworkers are lacking. As a result, in describing the attitudes of welfare caseworkers toward clients, I begin by making use of a four-state survey of welfare caseworkers (Lurie, Riccucci, and Meyers 2001).[3] The survey results suggest that approximately half of welfare caseworkers see welfare as a chosen lifestyle as opposed to a result of financial difficulty. In all, 52 percent agreed that "Everyone can get off welfare if they want" and 49 percent agreed that most Temporary Assistance for Needy Families (TANF) clients "would rather be on welfare." Other questions suggest that an even greater percentage of caseworkers were skeptical of welfare clients and why they were on welfare: 74 percent agreed that clients could get a job if they wanted, 71 percent agreed that the local economy made it easy for recipients to find a job, and most workers believed that most of their caseload was on welfare due to circumstances within their control.[4] Although relatively few workers agreed that it was easy to find a job that pays enough "to support themselves and their children," workers overwhelmingly believed that it was fair to require recipients to work.

My interviews with experienced workers reflected this general view. Many workers believed that the welfare system offered real opportunities for advancement but that most recipients were not interested in taking these opportunities. Terri commented that recipients were "ignorant" because they did not take advantage of the opportunities to get off welfare. "Well I would say that you're given an opportunity to go to school. You went to school, I went to school. They have an opportunity, and they don't go to school, don't go to work, they don't want to do anything. They have so many excuses why they can't do that. So that's the difference. The difference is someone that doesn't want to change their lifestyle." James commented that "they work very hard not to tell us about the employment that they have. I think that they have a strategy that about half of our clients adopt that they find employment that won't last more than a couple months they can make a lot off of the system if they get a job and then terminate it before we can find out about it or adjust for it." Although they differed on the percentage, most of the experienced workers whom I spoke with indicated that over half of welfare clients were "coasting" or "scamming."

In addition, workers indicated that welfare recipients have "bad attitudes" that make it difficult to work with them and prevent them from finding work. For example, James declared that a welfare client is someone who "almost makes a profession out of being hostile and not listening and someone who's really needy who'll call you up rather than read a piece of paper that's right in front of her and ask you what the piece of paper says even though she could read it herself."

These selections hint that most caseworkers saw most welfare clients as undeserving. However, they did see some recipients as deserving. For example, Paula commented that some clients "really want to work but they can't for whatever reason. Those are the clients that I feel sorry for." She also viewed the elderly as deserving of assistance. Another pointed to a mother who was caring for a severely disabled child as someone who was deserving of welfare assistance. Patricia conjured up "hard worker" clients: "I would say somebody like maybe a person in their late fifties who did menial work all their lives, like hard . . . laboring jobs. Um low wage, no pension plans, no 401(k)s and those people need to have some kind of supplement to their lifestyle. They deserve it, they worked."

These accounts suggest that there is more than one category into which caseworkers can place welfare recipients. Another important qualification is that when I asked caseworkers about social problems in the abstract, as opposed to the clients and cases that they see every day, they pointed to structural, as opposed to individualistic, explanations. For example, Paula had particularly negative and individualistic views of welfare clients. However, when I asked her about the causes of poverty she said, "Lack of education. Health issues. Opportunities. Role models. Parents. Your mother and your father." When I asked her about why minorities were more likely to be poor than whites, she pointed to "history." When I asked the same question of Terri, another caseworker with negative views about welfare clients, she commented, "The majority of minority people live in inner cities and there's not a whole lot of resources put into inner cities to help minorities like education." Patricia said, "We would almost have to go back to slavery times. . . . And not to say that the educational system is the same just from one section of the city to the other. But still it's education."

Summary

As with the police, caseworkers appear to have nuanced, context-dependent views and identities. Nonetheless, there are some patterns as well. Compared with the police, there seemed to be a greater unanimity among experienced welfare caseworkers that egoistic motives were their primary reasons for staying in the job. In particular, the job's benefits and stability were a major motivation for working in welfare. In terms of identity, veteran workers indicated an array of identities: from the powerless paper-pusher to the case-by-case discretion-user. As they navigated their work lives, and chose appropriate identities, there was general agreement that experienced caseworkers saw welfare clients as lazy and gaming the system. However, when asked about macroeconomic conditions, like the existence of poverty, they tended to draw from structural theories that emphasized history and environmental factors.

Conclusion

This chapter presented an overview of the views of experienced workers in each of these fields by drawing from prior research and my own interviews with experienced workers. Since there are few nationally representative surveys of these workers and none, to my knowledge, that inquire about all the outcomes of interest in this study, it is important to see this chapter as impressionistic. As expected, the chapter shows that there are some areas with strong patterns in workers' views and other areas where it is difficult to say what experienced workers thought. Thus, what follows is a brief summary including some observations about the extent to which there appears to be clarity about workers' views.

Most police appear to see themselves as legitimate, authoritative actors who wear many hats as they interact with the public. Some may see themselves as playing a key role in upholding society's moral order. As they interact with people, many police indicate that, while they are not all-powerful rogues, they treat people and situations differently based on circumstances. This finding matches the findings of large-scale observational studies that suggest that situations strongly affect officer decision making (Terrill and Mastrofski 2002; Terrill and Reisig 2003). Police also seem to be generally loyal to their departments but may be emotionally detached from the public. In general, in the realm of identity, there appears to be a fair amount of commonality across officers.

In regard to the other two outcomes, motivation and attitudes, there appears to be less commonality. Police articulate altruistic motives, like helping or protecting people, and egoistic motives, like benefits and excitement. It is unclear whether the majority of police are primarily motivated by altruism or egoism. While there are some commonalities among officers' attitudes—like the view that those who are honest, hardworking, and young or old are deserving—there are also places where there is considerable variation. For example, although police are likely to be suspect of explanations that they perceive as evading personal responsibility for an action, at least some recognize that there are larger, structural factors that influence individual choices.

With welfare caseworkers, we see that experienced workers hold a variety of identities. Depending upon the situation, they may see themselves as compassionate "social workers" or calculating "efficiency engineers" (Watkins-Hayes 2009). Although workers may enact a powerful, case-by-case persona to clients, and occasionally feel that they manage their caseloads that way, they also appear to at least sometimes feel powerless or project powerlessness: although they may want to help a person out, or punish someone who breaks the rules, they indicate or truly feel bound by the rules. In addition, welfare caseworkers appear to have little loyalty to their department. Regarding their motivations, welfare caseworkers may have some altruistic motives but, in general, appear to be motivated by the job's pay and benefits.

Attitudinally, caseworkers see some welfare clients as deserving and others as undeserving. Like police, caseworkers saw those who are working hard or diminished by age as deserving of benefits. However, on the whole, caseworkers seem to have negative views of welfare clients whom they see as scamming the system and having bad attitudes. Nevertheless, there was broad support for the view that social problems like poverty and racism were structural and that individuals who grew up in bad neighborhoods had few opportunities.

We now have some sense about how workers inside these organizations view themselves and the problems that they encounter. Now it is time to turn back to the book's main question: how do entrants form their bureaucratic personalities? To begin to answer this question, Chapter 4 builds an in-depth portrait that shows what entrants experienced after arriving on the steps of their organizations on the first day of training.

CHAPTER 4

Entry:
An In-Depth Account

A group of welfare caseworker trainees sat nervously on the first day of training. We talked quietly among ourselves and took in the sights and sounds around us. The state office building in which we sat was modern, with clean carpeted hallways and inspirational posters about the benefits of work. Eventually two trainers walked up to the front of the room. They welcomed us and began to inform us about the day's events. About fifteen minutes into their presentation, a harried trainee rushed into the room apologizing for his lateness. The problem, he explained as he sat down at his desk, was that he had been stuck in the elevator between floors with a group of other state workers for the last twenty minutes. Laughter rippled across the room, and the trainers looked at each other and smiled knowingly. His ordeal wasn't surprising to them. As they spoke, it became clear that the good looks of the building belied some of the structural deficiencies that lay beneath, like faulty elevators, computers, and ventilation. The trainers' response to the elevator incident mirrored many of the messages that they sent us in those first few days: working for the state sounded good in theory but was difficult and thankless in reality.

As this story shows, this chapter's goal is to describe what entrants experienced after joining their organizations and beginning training.[1] It explores the messages that they received from trainers as well as how they related to their peers. Substantively, it relies upon a mix of survey and interview data as well as my experiences and observations during the year that I spent working in the welfare department. Since I did not have a comparable work experience in the police department, the chapter completes the portrait of police socialization by drawing from prior studies (Chappell and Lanza-Kaduce 2010; Conlon 2004; Conti 2009; Gallo 2001; Rubinstein 1973; Van Maanen 1974). By understanding the process of entry, we begin to see how entrants experienced their organizations. As such, this chapter serves as a bridge connecting the discussion of dispositional and institutional perspectives in Chapter 2 and the analysis of bureaucratic socialization in Chapters 5 to 7.

Training

Day One: Messages and the Scene

On day one, aspiring caseworkers and police officers arrived at a training center and joined a group of other trainees who would be their companions over the coming months. As evident in this chapter's opening anecdote, at the welfare training center the main message of the day was "that's what it means to work for the state." This statement was repeated by trainers throughout the day, often with a look of resignation or amusement. In addition to the shoddy elevators, the instructors told us that the state's benefits, commonly understood as comfortable, had eroded considerably in recent years. Working for the state also meant that we should expect a lot of paperwork and inefficiency. Trainees, still feeling optimistic, smiled along with trainers but also shook their heads and wondered what type of world they had entered.

Another message on the first day was that welfare clients were to be treated respectfully, but that there was a line between "them" and "us." They had their bathrooms and we had ours. They were to park on the street whereas we could park in the employee lot. We were told by trainers to treat clients like we would want to be treated but not as friends or allies: "you can't have too close a connection to the customers."[2] We were also informed that welfare offices could be dangerous places to work and that violence was not an atypical occurrence. But if provoked, we were instructed, "don't take it personally" because "you're representing the [agency] now. You're not you anymore."

Though I did not experience police cadets' entire first day, I was at the academy on the first day of training to administer surveys and observe some of their experiences. In general the first day had a military feel as cadets were barked at by instructors, had their hair and appearances carefully scrutinized (there were particular regulations on the length and cut of their hair as well as how their uniform looked), and were arranged in military configurations for marching. Like in the welfare office, the first day of training was spent mostly filling out forms and learning about the organization's benefit plans.

Both facilities felt institutional with prefabricated windows, worn doors, and antiquated heating and air conditioning systems. Based on appearances, the welfare training office looked better than the police academy, which featured broken blinds and holes in some of the walls. Both training facilities were adorned with posters. At the police academy one poster proclaimed "Just say no!" Another featured a group of muscular, angry-looking felons in a prison yard lifting weights. The caption read, "Every day you don't work out, they do." At the welfare training center, one poster read, "Believe in the power of work." Others, with pictures of waterfalls, sunsets, and mountains, featured inspirational narratives on "Success," "Motivation," and "Goals." Another extolled the virtues of treating clients with dignity and respect. As these posters make clear, the first day marked the beginning of bombarding trainees with organizational information and messages.

Police Academy Instructors and the Gray Area of Discretion

After their first day, police officers were divided into platoons of twenty cadets. Their training included classroom lectures, hand-to-hand combat training, firearm practice and instruction, and physical fitness education. The dominant actors for the remainder of training were instructors—experienced officers who were asked to teach cadets how to think and act as police. Like in other jurisdictions, the formal curriculum that trainers were asked to convey to cadets was focused on the technical aspects of policing. Since this information is often boring to all involved, cadets clamor for instructors to share their "war stories," and instructors are happy to comply (Chappell and Lanza-Kaduce 2010; Ellwanger 2010; Macvean and Cox 2012). These stories are thought to be an important part of the academy's "hidden curriculum" in which trainers communicate a distinction between how the job is supposed to be done and how it is done in reality. Storytelling may also be useful for cadets as it enables them to picture situations that they will encounter and begin to envision how they might act. In the language of the logic of appropriateness, stories enable cadets to anticipate future interactions with the public and who they might want to be in them (Conti 2009). In my interviews, cadets indicated that these stories were important—they portrayed some of the difficulties awaiting them and provided them with clues about how they might be handled. In addition, studies suggest that, like in the welfare department, academy trainers convey to cadets that they are "not normal anymore" (Conti 2009, 418). Rather, they are told that they are now part of an exclusive culture in which only other members of the organization, their new family, truly understand them (Chappell and Lanza-Kaduce 2010, 203).

To develop a more complete picture of the role of instructors, I asked cadets five questions about how they viewed trainers after three months in the academy (Time 2) and before graduation (Time 3). These questions inquired how much cadets agreed that they had learned a lot from academy instructors, that instructors' stories were important, that instructors paid close attention to cadet development, that communication with instructors was satisfactory, and that it was easy to ask instructors questions.[3] For each question, and at both survey times, over three-quarters of cadets agreed or strongly agreed. As such, it appears that police entrants generally thought highly of their trainers and felt that the lessons that they taught were useful.

But what specific messages did instructors send to the cadets? Prior studies and my own interviews suggest that cadets receive conflicting messages about rule following from instructors. For example, cadets are told that they should not expect or accept favorable treatment because of their status as police. Rather, they must "follow laws outside of work" and not see themselves as "special" (Chappell and Lanza-Kaduce 2010, 201). Similarly, I found that cadets were told that they should be neutral law enforcers and not show any bias or favoritism. However, they were also told that they should use their discretion and treat each situation differently. For instance, Pamela, an older black entrant, commented: "Yes I think that at the academy what they're trying to really, really, really, [laughter] put in my mind is that you have to be fair. And really not be racist or biased in any way. Not be sexist and really treat people very equally and what have you and I don't know if that's what's gonna happen on the street but that's really what they're trying to turn it into there." At the same time the cadets received messages indicating that they would have discretion and would have to learn how to use it. Instructors told them that they could not teach discretion because it was inside of them. They referred to it as a "huge gray area" where they should follow their "gut" in determining how they wanted to act. In particular, they were told to figure out what their "pet peeves" were and when to ticket and when not to.

After speaking with the academy trainer in charge of teaching "ethics and morality," I came to understand these conflicting messages as a sophisticated effort in identity shaping: instructors were telling entrants that they had discretion and attempting to standardize how cadets would use it. In other words, the instructors were recognizing that policing requires some degree of figuring it out on the fly and were trying to give entrants guidance about how they should do so. They were, as per the logic of appropriateness, trying to instill cadets with a sense of what was correct behavior as they navigated interactions with the public.

A major component of this effort was teaching entrants about what types of citizens deserved a break. For instance, David a young, white, college-educated cadet, recalled a hypothetical training scenario:

> They tell us like the crime situation and the vehicle situation. Someone speeds and they can get a ticket. They can get a ticket ok. Someone blows a stop sign, they can get a ticket. But they also want to get us thinking and tell us some situation and, say you pull this person over for an illegal right turn or whatever. And you pull them over and they say "Sorry" and say that they're two houses away. You look at their ID and they really do live two houses away. And they say they've been working all night and all day. That's like I would be, I think I would [be] doing a huge disservice if I gave them a ticket and said you broke the law, you broke the law. Goodbye [let them go]. 'Cause what's that person going to do? They're going to say, "I can't get a break." They're going to say, they're going to look at the police as being cold and heartless and that's not really what I think the police should be perceived as. And when they tell us about discretion too, they tell us don't go walking around the street with sunglasses on . . . they say like make yourself available to people. And I'm 100 percent on board with that.

Though taught as "common sense," the messages from this situation are clear: you can use your discretion with low-level offenses and you can reward someone if he or she is contrite, honest, and hardworking. Although it is unclear the extent to which instruction standardizes the use of discretion, at least some officers initially received the message that instructors sent about following and deviating from the rules.

In addition to teaching cadets about discretion and deservingness, instructors provided more general lessons about how to act. For instance, cadets were instructed that they needed to be authoritative at the scene of an incident: keep your eyes up and "show no fear." However, simultaneously they were taught that they should not try to be "Rambo," "Robocop," or "a cowboy." Rather, they should be open to individual contact and accessible to the public. Moreover, instructors told them that they were held to a higher standard and should "take the high road" even if civilians were disrespectful or violent. It is not clear to what extent these lessons were taken to heart, but Jacob, a young white cadet, commented, "If a guy walks [up to me on the street], I'm in full uniform with my stick and gun and the guy punches me square in the face and takes off. If he stops and puts his hands up and says, 'I give up,' I have no right to hit that guy. And you should never.

Because that person gave up. If you hit him, it makes you a wimp. It makes you a pussy."

As Jacob's reaction makes clear, the instructors at the police academy made a strong push to try to shape cadets' thinking about proper behavior on the street. Although some cadets seemed unaware of this, others were more conscious of the instructors' efforts. For instance, Pamela commented extensively on a video shown by instructors about how a police officer should handle violent resistance.

> Then the situation was that the driver had drugs in the car and had a warrant out for his arrest and he didn't wanna go to jail and rather than just give [up], he had a gun and then he fought the police officer and the gun discharged and the police officer did get the gun from the motorist. But they fought for like two minutes on the ground and I'm trying to put myself in that situation and I can see myself reacting in the same way that the police officer did and I never thought I would be able to see that other side and that really surprised me because that was just last week. That surprised me because just in the short period of time of me coming in the door I knew that they were going to try and brainwash me to feel that all criminals are bad and we have to just stop them and that's kind of how I felt coming in the door. Now I'm feeling like because I felt that the other day I'm like wow it's like a ton of bricks it was like wow I'm changing. . . . Because I really put myself in the police officer's position you know and it was a really powerful video to see this guy and I envisioned myself on the ground with this guy fighting for my life with this other guy who has a gun and as much as I wouldn't want to take someone's life I can really see, I can understand doing that exact same thing. I understood. So that's how I think I've changed a little bit . . . [but] I really am trying to keep myself really levelheaded and keeping an open mind and trying to understand what's going on and taking in everything and trying to stay the same if that's possible.

The police academy, as an institution, and instructors, as the main players at the institution, made an effort to shape police cadets' views and identities. By describing or showing cadets particular interactions, and how experienced police respond to them, instructors were able to communicate what it means to be police and how cadets should act when faced with similar situations.

Although cadets gave high marks to academy instructors, later in their careers some came to see the lessons of the academy as too stringent. For example, after a year on the force, Allen, a black officer, commented, "That's the thing you learned in the academy [being strict and neutral]; for the most part it's right. But when you get out to the street there's gray areas. You can do it differently once you get out on the street. You don't have to do everything you know 100 percent by the book." At the same time, another black officer, Reggie, made a similar comment. He said that the academy was useful for teaching "theory" and "principles" but that "you don't necessarily do things exactly the way they tell you to do them." Chapters 5 to 7 assess how entrants responded to training and the extent to which any lessons learned during training persisted after beginning street work.

Welfare Training Instructors

When I began surveying trainees in the welfare department, one day I received a phone call from a trainee's supervisor who was unhappy that her trainee had participated in the project's survey. After I explained the project to her, and that I had an agreement with the department, she told me that my project was a waste of time because trainees "have no beliefs yet." Though trainees would likely have taken issue with her comment, it nicely captures the organization's sense that they build caseworkers. The heavy lifting during training is done by the welfare training instructors who lead classroom instruction each day. Mirroring the situation for police, most caseworker entrants indicated learning a lot from trainers: after a year in the department, 75 percent of caseworkers agreed strongly or agreed that they had "Learned a lot from the instructors during training." But what messages did trainers convey about the job, welfare clients, and how entrants should act?

Who's Faking and Who Isn't: Tiered Deservingness

Since public assistance programs in the United States are surrounded by considerable stigma (M. Katz 2008), one of the stated goals of welfare caseworker trainers was to combat entrants' biased and negative images of welfare recipients. To do this, early in training we were shown a video about welfare clients that, according to one trainer, would break down a lot of the "nasty" things that we believed about welfare. The video showcased the stories of three hardworking, clearly deserving claimants. The message was that we, as future welfare caseworkers, needed to drop our preconceived notions about welfare recipients and accept that some were deserving.

After watching the video, we began our study of each of the welfare programs: General Assistance, Temporary Assistance for Needy Families (TANF), Food Stamps, and Medicaid.[4] As we studied them, the training instructors sought to build our understanding about each program's history, eligibility rules, and application requirements. Also, less explicitly, they were trying to build our organizational "common sense" about each program. In essence, they sought to shape our views of deservingness in program-specific ways. Using stories and aside comments, they presented us with a portrait of tiered deservingness in which some programs, and the people they served, were deserving and others were not. According to the logic of appropriateness, such information is essential because who caseworkers choose to be in a particular moment depends in part on how they categorize the people with whom they are interacting.

At the lowest rung of the deservingness ladder, according to trainers' stories, were claimants seeking General Assistance (GA), a welfare program that provided cash benefits to disabled adults without children. At the time of the study GA was overseen and funded by the state, like in other jurisdictions. In order to receive GA, claimants had to produce a doctor's note indicating a disability as well as make an application for federal disability benefits (Supplemental Security Income or Social Security Disability Insurance). In the training classroom, instructors' stories painted GA claimants as lazy and lying. For instance, one instructor told of a hobbling old man who came into the district office looking for GA. He said that he had no money left in his savings as he had not worked in two years, and the instructor indicated that he felt sympathy for him. The instructor then checked the state's computer database, which organizes information about people who work in the state (earnings, criminal incidents, Social Security receipt, etc.), and found out that the old man was not telling the truth. In fact, he had been working. When the instructor confronted the applicant, he said, "Oh, man! How'd you find out?" The story was humorous and meant to show trainees that GA claimants would lie to us, and though they might appear deserving, they were not.

A similar story indicated to trainees that GA clients would try to "dress the part" to convince workers that they were low on money even though they may not be. The trainer provided a script for what caseworkers might come to think about GA clients when he indicated that he thought to himself, "Why don't you get a job instead of working so hard to fool the system?" The other message to trainees was that GA claimants could work but chose not to; in effect, their disability claims were false and should be treated with suspicion. They may present letters from doctors indicating that they are disabled, but, the instructors noted, there are a lot of shady doctors out there who are willing to sign off on a disability form in return for a kickback.

At the next highest rung of the deservingness ladder was TANF, a cash-assistance program for adults with children created in 1996 to replace Aid to Families with Dependent Children. At the time of the study, TANF was funded by a block grant, disbursed from the federal government to the state governments and supplemented with state monies. Though the federal government paid a larger portion than the states, state and local policymakers retained significant control over the program (Schott 2012). For example, the states were responsible for, among other things, determining application rules and the size of family allotments.

The messages that instructors sent to trainees about TANF were mixed. On the one hand, TANF recipients were often portrayed as deserving and "up against it"; at other times they were depicted as undeserving people whom the state needed to move off the rolls. When portrayed as deserving, TANF mothers were struggling women who had too many kids to expect them to be very functional. One trainer was particularly sympathetic, noting that he too was a father and he could not imagine raising kids by himself—"God bless them" was the message he gave to the trainees about how he felt about such families. TANF women were also often portrayed as victims, and therefore deserving, because the men who fathered their children were often unsupportive, unreliable, and abusive. On the other hand, TANF mothers were also portrayed as "comfortable" due to the large subsidy that they received for child care. At these times instructors were keen to mention that the goal of TANF was to get these women off the program.

At the top of the welfare deservingness ladder, according to training instructors, were recipients of Food Stamps,[5] a program that provides monetary benefits that can only be used to purchase food, and elderly medical assistance (a particular type of Medicaid). At the time of the study, Food Stamps was funded and controlled by the federal government. When we learned about Food Stamps, the instructors portrayed recipients as hardworking and presented a trickle-down rationale for liberal dispensing of Food Stamps: they were good for the economy because they stimulated spending at grocery stores. As I sat in class listening to the argument, I thought that one could make the same argument about TANF or other cash-like welfare transfers that are highly liquid and rapidly injected into the economy. Food Stamps, however, were presented as different.

The other group consistently presented as deserving by the welfare instructors was the elderly, who, we were told, often have fixed incomes and were only seeking help with health care costs. In most cases, we were told the elderly were applying for a special Medicaid program jointly funded by the federal and state governments. At the time of the study, the federal government established Medicaid's goals but states determined the nature of their specific programs. As with TANF, since the federal goals were rather broad, states had a great deal of flexibility in how they designed their Medicaid programs (Center for Budget and Policy Priorities 2013). One of the key elements of the research state's Medicaid system was that it allowed applicants to spend down their resources in order to qualify for benefits. The message sent by instructors during training was that we should help the elderly understand what they needed to do to be approved for benefits.

Throughout the study, I spent considerable time trying to understand why trainers presented these four programs in the ways that they did. One explanation is that the trainers were repeating messages that they had received from state policymakers in an effort to keep the state's economy strong but not spend too many state dollars. In this way, caseworker training could be understood through the lens of state budget politics—elected officials sent messages to bureaucratic elites about the generosity with which programs should be administered (based on a particular program's budgetary implications). Bureaucratic elites then passed the message down the line. For example, the program at the lowest rung of the deservingness ladder, GA, was funded exclusively by the state. As such, perhaps state policymakers conveyed to the state's welfare department elites that they should be stringent in granting GA eligibility.

This explanation would also seem to explain why Food Stamps was presented differently than TANF. In its founding law, Congress specified that TANF dollars can be used to provide cash assistance to needy families, end welfare dependence, and promote marriage. Since these goals are rather general, states have considerable discretion about how TANF dollars are spent (Falk and Aussenberg 2012). As a result, if political elites wish to spend TANF dollars on nonassistance goals, they can do so if they successfully deter applicants or move existing recipients off of the rolls. In contrast, since the Food Stamps program does not give the states flexibility in how monies are spent, there may be little incentive for state policymakers to decrease the number of Food Stamps recipients.

Although the budget politics explanation seems plausible, it has a difficult time explaining why Medicaid, a program that is jointly funded by the federal and state governments like TANF, was consistently presented as a deserving program. Perhaps state political elites sent a message to the welfare department about keeping people off of Medicaid but it fell on deaf or defiant ears inside the department. Alternatively, perhaps Medicaid was presented differently because it was not funded through a block grant, and, as such, elites would not have much flexibility in how they spent any savings that they recouped.

Another possible explanation for the system of tiered deservingness that was presented to caseworkers is that trainers were trying to map typically held public views onto specific welfare programs. For instance, in the United States able-bodied adults have not typically been thought of as deserving of welfare assistance (Katz 2008). By defining GA recipients as able-bodied people pretending to be hurt, trainers linked a typically held view with a specific program. In contrast, able-bodied mothers have had a more complicated deservingness status—they are often pitied but not seen as deserving enough for generous federal welfare programs (Gordon 1994; Mettler 1998). Therefore, it would make sense that TANF would elicit a mixed bag of stories from instructors and a mid-level position in a system of tiered deservingness.

Although this explanation seems generally useful, it is important to note that the portrait detailed by trainers differed from public opinion polls in at least one way: within the constellation of welfare programs, one study suggests, Americans support Food Stamps the least (Cook and Barrett 1992). Nonetheless, Food Stamps recipients were presented as deserving.

How to Act: Being the Sheriff

In addition to sending signals to trainees about who deserves what, welfare instructors also indicated how we should present ourselves and act as caseworkers. In logic of appropriateness terms, they effectively defined a variety of caseworker identities from which we could choose when we were on the job. In contrast to police cadets, who were told that they had some discretion, welfare caseworker trainees were explicitly told to follow rules and regulations from the time of our entrance into the city's training facility. Trainers never mentioned that workers have discretion as they carry out their duties and instead relied upon a phrase that, it became obvious, was something of a safety blanket for workers: "policy states . . . ." This phrase indicated that policy dictates a worker's decisions. We were instructed to point to the rules for cover when clients complained or questioned our actions. According to this view, workers are neutral and objective as they manage their cases. The ideal that trainers held out for trainees was, in essence, Watkins-Hayes's (2009) efficiency engineer: operate quickly, keep your desk clean, and treat everyone the same.

A search that I conducted of the three voluminous handbooks—cash assistance (TANF and GA), Food Stamps, and medical (including Medicaid)—which together included approximately 110 chapters, and which served as a guide and training document for caseworkers, reinforced this message. The word "discretion" appeared a mere eight times in the handbooks. Other words that emphasized the workers' duties as an interpreter of policy, as opposed to mere implementer, like "questionable" and "reasonable," appeared 29 and 118 times, respectively. The department's overt approach to implementation was that workers have little discretion, so it didn't matter what was questionable or reasonable.

Despite this message, as students of welfare administration have noted, discretion is inherent in the caseworker's job (Lipsky 1980; Maynard-Moody and Musheno 2003; Prottas 1979; Sandfort 2000). Discretion may mean sliding a disfavored client's case to the bottom of a caseworker's pile of things to do, giving some people more information than others, or choosing which among the voluminous, and sometimes contradictory, rules to follow. Whatever it means in practice, in the abstract discretion gives caseworkers power. With it, they have some control over who gets what and when.

In line with this reality, at times during training we were told that we had some latitude for decision making. For instance, during training one instructor commented that "a lot of this job is interpretation" of the rules. Just as instructors articulated a hierarchy of deservingness, they suggested that different types of clients should be dealt with differently. On the day when we learned about Medicaid for the elderly, one instructor reminded us that this is a time to "be a caseworker," which meant go out of your way to help them get eligible. He said, "You might not believe me, but I took care of my elderly." He meant that elderly Medicaid applicants might not understand the rules, or might be close to eligibility but not understand how to become eligible. His underlying message was that they were deserving and that we should use our discretion to help them.

Another area in which trainees were given the message that they had some latitude was regarding good-cause exemptions. In most states, receipt of TANF required compliance with employment and training regulations. Caseworkers, however, could sometimes exempt claimants from participation in the programs for "good cause." The agency defined good cause as "circumstances beyond the household member's control." Since this definition depends on a worker's views about which aspects of life are possible to control, instructors aimed to clarify how trainees should act. One trainer indicated that he didn't think that claimants should be granted good cause if they quit their job because "you want them to be self-sufficient, right?" In a training exercise, a claimant who woke up late and missed her bus was considered as not having good cause while a client with limited English proficiency, who didn't understand the rules, was. In another situation a trainee asked an instructor if good cause could be granted for moving and changing addresses and therefore not getting mail about an employment and training program. The instructor responded, "Could be, I'm liberal."

Trainers also indicated to trainees how to use their discretion in beginning an investigation into a client suspected of fraud. Though caseworkers in the city rarely went into the neighborhoods in which they worked in their official capacity, some offices had inspectors who caseworkers could ask to investigate a client suspected of fraud. Generally this investigation consisted of an inspector driving to a claimant's stated address and talking to the claimant and her neighbors. But it was not clear to trainees when we should start an investigation. When asked, instructors indicated that when claimants frequently change their addresses, or often indicated a change in the household's members, they should be investigated. However, such decisions are inherently discretionary and, at least to some extent, tied to workers' official identities. They require them to decide what type of worker they want to be in a particular situation. Trainers appeared to give us two identity options: the sympathetic friend of the poor and the skeptical realist. As the "friend of the poor" we were told not to "be the sheriff" and that "it's not your money"; the feeling toward the clients at these times was "these people are poor and need all the help they can get."

At other times trainees were told that they *should* be the sheriff. For instance, one of the tasks that trainees were instructed about was inquiring into claimants' "management," a term that meant checking to see how people with no resources and income were managing prior to applying for welfare. Inherent in the idea of management is a skepticism about the stories caseworkers hear from recipients: since people need some income to live, the expectation is that, prior to applying for welfare, applicants had some form of income.[6] Trainees were informed to bring a dubious eye to claimants' applications, which typically indicated no forms of income, to ascertain how they were "managing."[7] When workers had determined how claimants were managing prior to their welfare applications, the next goal was to understand why this prior source of income was no longer available. If we were satisfied with applicants' accounts of why this source of income was ending, we were to inform them about how to complete the application so that it would "make sense" in the eyes of a supervisor or quality control reviewer. In a typical scenario a client would, after "coming clean" about prior income, indicate on the application that the support was ending or no longer possible. Usually this claim would be verified with a letter from the person from whom they were receiving the support. Since these forms of support are often informal, and sometimes illegal, providing documentation puts applicants in a difficult position. Nonetheless, this was one area in which we were told that we should "be the sheriff" and make sure applicants weren't hiding ongoing sources of income.

Depersonalize

In Chapter 3 we saw that some experienced caseworkers indicated using a detached, efficient persona as they interacted with clients. Although we cannot say for sure how they developed this identity, during welfare training instructors conveyed that depersonalizing was an important aspect of the job. For instance, one instructor told trainees not to ask too much about clients during interviews because "you don't want to know their stories." He presented this as an argument for greater efficiency: hearing why a claimant lost her job does not matter and will only slow you down in processing her case.

Similarly, many training documents said, "The agency will verify . . ." This phrasing created some confusion because it was not clear to trainees who in the agency would verify a particular item. When queried about this phrasing, a trainer said, "You said 'yes' when they offered you the job, so you're the agency!" By seeing themselves as "the agency," trainers seemed to indicate, it would be easier to depersonalize and enforce department rules. For instance, when a claimant was upset about a rule or a caseworker's decision, trainers indicated that we could defuse the situation by blaming the state's rules. In one training exercise I was doing a mock interview of a client in front of the other trainees with the trainers watching. When the trainee playing a claimant asked me why she had to go to an employment training class, I responded "those are the rules, it's mandatory." In the follow-up discussion, the trainer indicated that this phrase was "great." He continued, "Always blame the agency not yourself. There's no such thing as 'I' now, only the agency you work for."

Instructors also indicated the requisite level of compassion that trainees should show to clients. The trainees were told "not to take work home" with you, that "you don't have to be compassionate," and that you should "leave your conscience at the door." One trainer indicated that when she began her job she was caring too much and actually gave clients her home phone number. Quickly her work-life balance spiraled out of control as she received calls from clients at all hours of the day. She said that one of the lessons that she had to learn was that "you can't help everyone out."

But trainers also said that trainees should not be nasty to clients, should care about clients somewhat, and should help people in their neighborhoods to understand the system and, when possible, get on welfare. One trainer reminded trainees that, but for a downturn in the economy, it could be us on the other side of the welfare desk. Another trainer said to trainees, "They tell you that you have to be a caseworker not a social worker but what's the difference really? You can't just shuffle papers, at least I can't."

Managing Your Load

Another lesson taught during training was how to manage a caseload. One of the first tricks of the trade that instructors suggested was to deal with complainer clients first. This lesson was based on the simple logic that complaints travel uphill fast and can cause trouble with superiors. One trainer said that if claimants "make enough noise they get what they want." Another said that he had learned from welfare claimants not to be passive when he is in a waiting room because "the squeaky wheel gets the oil."

Another important message about caseload management was that, as workers, we should never make promises to the claimants. We were told that one of the most common questions we would get would be "when am I going to get my check?" Echoing Paula's reported practice (in Chapter 3), instructors indicated that trainees should always answer vaguely because many things along the bureaucratic chain from application to check issuing can go wrong. If you make a promise, we were told, you are putting yourself on the line and are likely to get a complaint if the promise is not kept. Instead we were told to keep details to ourselves and to provide only vague assurances like "it should be there by Friday."

Finally, trainees were instructed about the basic mechanics of interviewing clients including body language, tone of voice, and facial expression. In essence, the instructors told trainees to find a middle ground between aggressive and passive; workers should not threaten the clients, but they also should not lose control of the interview since, we were told, "you are the authorities now."

Informal Training: The Influence of Police Cadets

Trainers, the above section suggests, send a variety of messages to entrants during the training period. However, the relationships that trainees form with their peers also have the potential to shape their views of their jobs and their behavior (Brehm and Gates 1997; Morrison 2002). For instance, peer entrants may help newcomers digest and make sense of the messages that they receive in formal training. In this way, they may minimize or magnify the power of the messages sent by the organization.

In the policing literature, there is evidence that peers play an important role in how entrants experience the academy (Conti 2009). Early in socialization, trainers convey to entrants that their experiences will be painful and, in some respects, degrading. Those who persist will become police and those who thrive will become leaders of police. Cadets with military training are featured as examples of those who have persisted in the face of pain and may be given leadership roles. Since rewards and punishments are doled out to the group, peers begin to evaluate and critique one another. Some are held up as exemplary in one form or another while others become examples of "what not to do." As a result, peer interactions may be an important way that police learn how to act on the streets.

Since I was able to survey the police cadets at two extra times during their official training at the academy, I sought to understand how cadets assessed their new peer group. On the surveys that I administered while cadets were at the academy, I asked them how much they agreed with three questions: "I have developed some good relationships with other cadets," "I have learned from other cadets,"[8] and "In general I am impressed by the caliber of the other cadets." After three months of training (Time 2) and after six months of training (Time 3), over 90 percent indicated having good relationships with other cadets. At these times over 70 percent indicated having learned from other cadets and around 60 percent indicated being impressed with other cadets.

As is evident, cadets had a largely favorable view of other cadets. However, there is clearly some variation as well across these questions. Unfortunately, since no interviews were conducted at these times, it is not possible to provide qualitative evidence about what peer interactions meant substantively for cadets. However, in the following chapters I will explore the extent to which variation in cadets' views of other cadets explains variation in the bureaucratic personalities that they developed.

Workplace Influences

After about six months of full-time training, trainees in both groups graduated and were official city workers. For welfare caseworkers there was very little ceremonial pomp—on the final day of training, they passed out generic certificates of completion. To me, at least, it felt anticlimactic. One day you report to training and the next you report to your district and receive the first part of your caseload. For the police, there were many more rituals. In the final days at the academy, officers received their weapons and protective devices; at graduation they received their badges. Interviews suggested that cadets imbued these rituals with great meaning. For instance, Phillip, a white cadet with military experience, commented, "When I get that badge . . . I'm gonna feel proud and feel like a cop." Also, police graduation featured organizational elites and elected officials who welcomed the new police to the force and thanked them for their service. After graduation, both sets of workers were "on the street" meeting with the public and acting as government officials. This section begins by discussing two workplace influences at that time: supervisors and veterans. It then examines the effect of other rookies and organization culture.

Welfare Training Supervisors: "This Is Not Social Work"

Police officers and welfare caseworkers entered different workplaces. The police were assigned to districts where they orbited central offices while spending most of their time on the streets, out of the direct view of department superiors. Welfare caseworkers, upon finishing training, were also assigned to districts but were tethered closely to their offices and the ever-present eyes of their training supervisors. Supervisors served as a bridge from training to real casework. During some days of classroom training, these supervisors sat in the back listening in to the instructors and chiming in occasionally. Upon graduating, these training supervisors became a constant fixture in trainees' work lives: they were needed to review case decisions, answer questions, and deal with uncooperative clients. After nearly six months in the office, 70 percent of workers indicated that they were strongly influenced by their training supervisors.

Substantively, caseworker entrants indicated that their training supervisors were influential for two reasons: they monitored their work and instructed them on how to manage their cases. As organization newcomers, they were relatively isolated from the rest of the organization. In fact, new caseworkers were purposefully shielded from what the trainers indicated was the nefarious influence of longtime workers. Thus, their main point of contact was with their training supervisors who checked much of their work and who were needed before they could take action on a client's case. This oversight was repeatedly pointed to in interviews as a key influence of training supervisors. For example, Mary, a college-educated black caseworker, said that her training supervisor had an influence on her "mainly because . . . she's the type of supervisor that requires verification for all things so I've become the type of worker that requires verification for all things. [laughter] You know what I'm saying?"

Similarly, Evelyn, an older caseworker entrant, indicated that initially she was being too lenient with claimants by letting them have more time to submit verification and not demanding proof of all assertions. As a result, she was getting taken advantage of by claimants until her supervisor suggested that she reform her caseload management. "She has taught me that you can be lenient and they'll get over on you [trick you] and you'll never dig out or you can go by policy and go by nothing like, 'Do I like you?' or, 'Do I want you to get this?' and it's all about what do I have to do to get this job get done. The ones that I let go always came back and bit me." Mary recounted a similar experience with her supervisor. The client in the case was supposed to send some signed papers back to her, but the papers never arrived. After the deadline had passed, one of the client's friends called saying that the client was away in another state because she had to take care of a sick aunt. Mary decided that she would give the client another few days to get the paperwork to her. Then she went to talk to her supervisor, who upbraided her and instructed her to close the case. Mary learned that "I'm always giving people the benefit of the doubt . . . I can't keep doing that."

My experience corroborates these workers' stories. Superiors who oversaw me tended to perceive me as naïve to the claimant's tricks and too forgiving. At one point, when I had accepted an application that was deemed questionable, one training supervisor told me that "this is not social work, this is determining financial eligibility. You question everything and you accept nothing." Another time a training supervisor said, "You have to be firm or they'll walk all over you. It's not personal don't make it personal. It has to be a job for you." To "stay above water," supervisors advised that I "take action"; in practice, this meant if a claimant was late in getting me verification I should not wait a day or two but should begin the process of closing the case. Their point, which I ultimately came to accept, was that claimants will often not respond to requests that they provide verification unless they believe that their caseworker is willing to close their case.

After six months working in their offices, caseworker trainees had achieved a full caseload (approximately 750 active cases) and were transferred out of their training units. Only one survey respondent at Time 5 indicated that she was still in a unit headed by her training supervisor. In general, caseworkers were unimpressed with their new supervisors and indicated that they had little influence on them: only 31 percent of workers indicated that their new supervisors influenced them at Time 5 (down from 70 percent at Time 4). Whereas 26 percent of workers indicated that they turned to their supervisors first with questions at Time 4, at Time 5 only 13 percent did.

Terrell, a caseworker fresh out of college, indicated that he really only thought about his supervisor when he knew she would be reviewing a case, which sounded like a relatively rare occurrence. In his answer he pointed to the continued relevance of his training supervisor. "[My new supervisor] has a small role because I think my training supe, she had a large role in the type of worker that I am. Just because she's the one that molded us and taught us how to work. And now, mainly it's just, it's just mainly the basics as long as I get the stuff to her in time, like but you know I really haven't changed much as a worker. My supervisor stresses about the work; I don't stress about the work. I just do whatever is on the agenda for the day and then go home." Others were even more blunt. At Time 5, when asked if their nontraining supervisor affected their work, one worker responded, "None, not at all. [Not one] iota"; another said, "She doesn't." As workers made it clear that their new supervisor had little influence over them, many indicated a reverence for their training supervisors. For instance, one entrant noted, "I've become a very good investigator being under my training supe. Yes, I find all kinds of things. She was rough." Another concurred looking back on her training supervisor: "I think that she taught me well to make me do well at what I'm doing . . . even though she drove me crazy, a lot of people didn't have the expertise and help that we had but she definitely taught me what I need to know so that I could be efficient at my job."

In addition to the effect of supervisors, I sought to understand how much entrants were monitored by the department. Though there is some overlap with supervision, because supervisors were responsible for certain aspects of monitoring, it is also distinct: much of the monitoring was done by district leaders above the rank of supervisor. In fact, due to the increasingly computerized nature of their work, some monitoring was conducted by remote organizational overseers.[9] To determine how much entrants perceived being monitored, I divided caseworkers' actions into six categories—taking reapplications, periodic case reviews, computer database management, face-to-face interviewing, phone interviewing, and explaining client financial management—and asked them how much they were monitored in each. On balance, they reported feeling more monitored on easily tracked actions, like reapplications and computer processing, and less monitored on client interactions, like phone calls or face-to-face interviews.

Sergeants

After academy graduation, police officer entrants began a significantly different supervisory relationship. They were assigned to a district where they had rotating sergeants who were their supervisors. But as they merged their "book learning" from the academy with "actual policing" on the streets, their sergeants were not their main guides. Instead, their workplace training was entrusted to the experienced officers with whom rookies were assigned to patrol for their first three months on the job. In fact, their sergeants back at the district appear to have been more notable for their absence than their presence because they did not often have direct knowledge of how officers were conducting themselves. This development reflects findings from other police studies (Butterfield, Edwards, and Woodall 2005; Conlon 2004; Van Maanen 1974). For instance, Rubinstein's classic study (1973, 56) notes that the sergeant "is not a military leader; he is a foreman whose men are scattered over many city blocks. His men rarely work in his direct sight and he needs their goodwill, just as they need his protection and advice to get the job done properly." He shows that supervisors have a tenuous ability to oversee their men and rely on camaraderie and a "give and take" with patrolmen to achieve desired results. "Perhaps supervisors would like to have the authority people attribute to their rank, but they do not" (Rubinstein 1973, 450).

Recent reforms, like Compstat in New York City, have mandated a statistics-based approach to police management and given police sergeants enhanced resources for monitoring frontline police (D. Smith and Bratton 2001). However, these new tools have come with new paperwork and computing demands. Thus, although they are intended to give sergeants greater authority over their frontline police, there are indications that sergeants are still largely in the dark about many aspects of their officers' behavior (Butterfield, Edwards, and Woodall 2005). Indeed, the new officers in this study reported relationships with their supervisors that mimic the patterns described by other studies. Whereas 70 percent of welfare trainees indicated that their training supervisors were influential at Time 4, only 55 percent of police indicated that they were strongly influenced by their supervisors; this figure dropped to 40 percent at Time 5.

Illustrating new police officers' feelings about their superiors, one officer indicated that he went to the sergeant only when he couldn't handle something himself. Another said that "you don't really want to go to them. I go to my fellow officers before I go to my supervisor." One officer recalled feeling "pretty autonomous" out on the street—a sentiment that few recently minted welfare caseworkers felt. Another officer, when asked how much his sergeant influenced the type of worker he was, responded, "Not too much. I mean obviously if he asks for something like truants I'm going to find what he asks for." In contrast, Carl, a young white officer, indicated having a new sergeant, with relatively little time on the force, who was trying to get the officers in his district to crack down on what he considered minor infractions.

> Like my sergeant is new, he's a new sergeant. He's been a cop for like ten years. So I'll come into roll call and he'll be like, "If you see anybody consuming alcohol in public or peeing on the street or something like that lock them up and I'll take the paperwork." Okay sergeant [said sarcastically]. I'd never lock somebody up for that stupid shit. Like I'll stop them maybe run them for warrants and make sure they don't have a gun on them, but I would never arrest somebody even though technically it's against the law and technically you should be arrested for that. But I would never do that. . . . I mean he's like a supervisor in any other job and you don't want to fuck up 'cause you don't want them on your back. But I've pretty much stayed out of trouble and he doesn't affect how I do my job. He likes doing those little stupid arrests for shit and he wants us to do 'em, but I won't do 'em.

In addition to being supervised by sergeants, police, like caseworkers, were monitored by the department. Again there was some overlap with supervision because the sergeants collected some of the information upon which police were monitored. Nonetheless, I sought to understand how much police felt monitored on seven typical actions: making arrests, writing tickets, walking or driving a beat, keeping up with paperwork, interacting with civilians face-to-face, using a weapon, and issuing warnings. As with the caseworkers, there was variation in monitoring across tasks. For actions in which there was no written record, like walking or driving the beat or issuing warnings, entrants felt generally less monitored. However, in making arrests, doing paperwork, or using weapons, newcomers perceived themselves as being more closely monitored.

Old-Timers
Police Veterans

Following academy training, veterans may have the biggest influence on police officers (Ellwanger 2010). As new officers arrive in the district the veterans are the first people who they meet. Using stories, myths, and folklore, veterans attempt to shape rookies' views of their district, the people who they will encounter, and their understanding of their role as police. Veterans tell rookies about "real police work" and that the academy has not prepared them for it. In effect, veteran police attempt to take what cadets learned at the academy about appropriate conduct and shape it into something that they would deem more realistic (Rubenstein 1973).

I asked the rookies in this study how important veterans were for them in shaping their thinking and behavior. At Time 4, 73 percent of police officers indicated that they were influenced strongly by veterans; 63 percent indicated that they turned to veteran officers first when they had a question. In part this may be because the police department encouraged contact with veterans and saw them as a crucial resource for new officers. Entrants were paired with a variety of veterans during their first few months on the job, and it was with these officers that they first saw how the job was actually done. Perhaps as a result, new officers pointed to veterans as an important resource. John, a white officer who had served in the military, commented that veterans know "fifty times as much as I do 'cause I've only been out there for a day. Other officers, if one officer doesn't know, I guarantee that the next officer that you call he'll know what to do." Similarly, Allen, a young black officer, noted that veterans were constantly correcting him and showing him new ways to handle situations:

> They'll tell me: "You can do this different" or "Don't do it that way, do it this way." . . . They know the type of people and they know the community and they know how the community is gonna react to the way you act . . . it's helpful. . . . A lot of times let's say you're approaching some guys on a corner—they'll give you a better way to approach them then just running up there and telling them to put their hands up and telling everyone: "Let's see those hands." There's a lot of more cool, calm, and collected ways to approach it so you don't overreact. Because they're only gonna feed off of how you act.

When asked what role veterans played in figuring out how to do the job, Denise, an older black officer, indicated that they played a big part: "When you're working with [senior] partner . . . you pretty much follow their lead you know in the very beginning—not sitting back—but you're, you know, soaking in everything that's being done."

Being paired with veterans on a rotating basis, rather than a single training veteran, was also useful to entrants. For instance, David, a younger white officer, commented,

> When I first hit the district you get a chance to work with pretty much every cop not every one but pretty much a lot of them. And you pick good and bad things up from them. You know I think back to that first month when I was with a partner and it's like look at the jobs that they responded to and what they do and you look at the little things that they say sometimes help you out. So you keep the good and the bad and I think that at that point it gets really individual because each person will take different things from different officers.

Though most rookies initially saw veterans as an important resource, many indicated becoming disenchanted with veterans by the end of their second year (Time 5). Whereas 73 percent indicated that they were influenced by veterans at Time 4, at Time 5 this figure dropped to 44 percent. At Time 4, 63 percent indicated that they turned first to veterans when they had a question; at Time 5 this figure dropped to 55 percent.

Time 5 interviews suggest that this change resulted from a feeling that some veterans were "lazy" or "mailing it in." For instance, one officer noted that the old guys were not as aggressive in pursuing arrests and fighting crime generally. Mark, an older officer entrant, when asked how much veteran officers influenced the type of officer he was, commented, "It depends. . . . Some of them yes, they're very still willing to help you. And there's others just biding their time. And when they're just biding their time? Forget it. They're not gonna help you do nothing. But others are still active and, yeah, they'll help you." Henry made a similar observation about some veteran police: "Then you have your older cops who feel like they've been screwed by the department in some way and they don't do anything. That's like any job. They can't do anything to you if you're not doing anything, you know, because it's very hard to get fired as a cop. You don't have to do anything you just have to show up for work everyday and you don't have to do anything but some people are content with doing that."

Welfare Caseworker Veterans

In the welfare department, new caseworkers received a different message about experienced workers: avoid them at all costs. The agency facilitated this by grouping new workers initially in a unit with other new workers. Training instructors and supervisors reinforced the message by telling new workers that veterans were bitter and should be ignored. The reasoning behind this attempted separation was that department elites saw veterans as having bad attitudes about the job and not following new procedures properly. The hope was that by isolating new workers from veterans, they would remain positive about their work and look to their training supervisors and computer messages for procedural information. To some extent, the agency succeeded in creating a wall between new workers and veterans. Whereas 73 percent of police entrants felt that veterans had influenced their work at Time 4, only 16 percent of new caseworkers said that they were influenced by veterans at that time. At Time 5 this figure dropped to 6 percent.

In other ways, the agency's effort to isolate new workers seemed bound for failure. Veterans, as the numerically dominant group in each office, played a strong role in shaping that district's culture and conveying it to newcomers. New workers initially indicated some resistance and negative feelings about the office culture (discussed further below), but these tended to dissipate over time as workers took on and accepted aspects of the organization's common thinking. Be it through lunch groups, drop-by conversations, or working together, new caseworkers eventually came into contact with veterans.

In addition to entering a veteran-regulated culture, the department's plan may have been futile because, six months after the completion of formal training, trainee units were broken up and trainees were dispersed throughout the city. The trainees lost their training supervisors, assumed the status of a veteran, and were placed in units with other veterans. As they entered new roles and districts, they indicated looking to fellow veterans for guidance. For instance, one worker who switched offices and entered a new unit by Time 5 commented, "I picked up most of what I know about [the new job] just from my unit members." Another stayed in the same district but took on a new role. As she figured out how to do the job, she drew on what other veterans were saying to clients. At Time 5, 80 percent of entrants indicated that they turned first to their units when they had a question. By this time, of course, their units were composed of other veterans.

Rookies

The two sets of workers who participated in this project reported significantly different types of relationships with their entering colleagues. For new caseworkers, initially cordoned off from their district's experienced workers, and with a training supervisor who was often busy, fellow caseworker trainees were an important sounding board for questions. For newly minted police officers, guided by organization veterans, fellow rookies played less of a role. At Time 4, 45 percent of caseworker trainees indicated that they were influenced by other new workers in their unit. In comparison, only 18 percent of police officers indicated that they were influenced by fellow rookies. Of caseworker trainees, 53 percent noted that they turned to other new workers first when they had a question, compared with 5 percent of new police officers.

These responses were corroborated in interviews. Caseworkers indicated that they frequently asked questions of one another about how to handle a particular problem with a claimant or computer issue. In part, this reliance upon one another seemed to be facilitated by strong affective ties between trainees. For instance, when I asked Mary about her trainee unit, she responded, "I think we were the best because we had a level of friendship that was good. We were willing to help each other we were not like, 'It's all about me and I have to do better than you.' There was no competition and if it was it was friendly. And that helped us because we helped each other. We made our unit our family away from home." In my interviews with the police, few indicated such levels of camaraderie among rookies.

At Time 5, after caseworker trainees had been split up from their fellow trainees, there was a sharp decline in the number who indicated that they were influenced by them: 6 percent of caseworkers indicated that other new workers influenced them, and none indicated that they turned to workers they were trained with when they had a question. As indicated above, this may have occurred because at this time initial training units had been split up and entrants were in units with experienced workers. Rookie police again indicated that fellow rookies had a limited influence on them at Time 5. In all, 14 percent indicated that fellow rookies influenced their work and 4 percent indicated that they turned to other rookies first when they had a question.

Culture

Dueling Emails

An organization's culture—"the unwritten rules, mores, customs, codes, values and outlooks" (Chemerinsky 2000, 559)—has the potential to influence how workers think about and do their jobs (J. Wilson 1989). The welfare office culture is often portrayed as toxic: run-down facilities both reflect and contribute to the low morale exhibited by workers, who feel harried and, often, angry (Goodsell

1984). Interviews with caseworkers corroborated these findings. For instance, caseworkers reported that their office's cultures were "negative" and made them hard places to work. Janet, a black entrant in her thirties, described her office's culture as "ghetto," and, she was quick to add, she was talking about the workers not the clients.

Another theme that emerged was that welfare culture was "female" and "black." Workers who did not fit into those categories, like me, were therefore at a disadvantage. For instance, Deborah, a black caseworker, commented,

> The majority of the people who work there feel like it's a job that only a women will handle, only black women can handle. They feel like a white man working there is just pretending, he's just he's not gonna be there that long. It's gonna be too much for him and he's just gonna leave . . . it's not a job for a man. He's not gonna understand the job and he's not gonna know how to deal with the clients. . . . I think that they think that men can't relate to the situations that the people are in when they come in.

She went on to say that, of course, not all welfare clients were women, but the perception nonetheless was that men generally, and white men in particular, would have a difficult time understanding the patterns, actions, and subtexts of the office. Similarly, Evelyn told me that as a white man, without a history of welfare receipt, I was at a disadvantage as a welfare caseworker: "You were so naïve . . . you were innocent to people and their lies. You understand what I'm saying? Their shenanigans . . . because you're not of my race and you didn't deal with it. And I think it's not as common to come in contact with somebody that was dealing with it for you. Especially with your education level, it puts you in a different class of people."[10]

Another theme of the city's welfare culture was feeling abandoned by managers who, workers perceived, were always siding with clients when there was a conflict. Most caseworkers indicated having low levels of job satisfaction, and the job tended to be seen as a last resort or as a launching pad to a better career. At Time 4, 33 percent of caseworkers indicated that the district's culture influenced them; at Time 5 this figure dropped to 20 percent. In an effort to understand how personally connected they felt to their organization, I asked welfare entrants how much they agreed with the statement "My [caseworker] job is an important part of who I am." At Time 1, 26 percent of workers agreed strongly or agreed with the statement. At Time 4 this figure dropped slightly to 25 percent, and at Time 5 it dropped to 7 percent.

At one point during my employment, a song that captured the culture of the welfare office was emailed from worker to worker in the department. The song's file name was "A Song for Employees Suffering Mistreatment." The file began with an introduction by Ray, an African American male. It is unlikely that Ray's daughter was employed in the welfare office, but the song clearly struck a chord with many workers.

> [Speaking] Hi, my name is Ray and [yesterday] my daughter called me because she was stressed out because of things that were going on on her job that she felt were quite unfair. Being quite disturbed, she called for comfort and I didn't really know what to tell her because we have to deal with so much mess in our society. So I was led to write this song just for her. To just give her some encouragement while dealing with stress and pressures on her job. And I figured I'd put it on the internet for all employees under stress to help you better deal with what you're going through on your job. Here's how the song goes.
>
> [Singing] Oh, I'm about to whip somebody's ass.
> Oh, oh, oh, I'm about to whip somebody's ass.
> Oh, if you don't leave me alone,
> You're gonna have to send me home,
> 'Cause I'm about to whip somebody's ass.
>
> [Speaking] Now you might not be able to sing that out loud, but you can hum it to yourself and you know what the words are. And let it give you some strength to get through the next few moments on your job. Alright? Stay strong. Peace.

As the song was forwarded around the office, one could hear its playing followed by laughter or nods of agreement. In my view, the song resounded with workers because they too often felt frustrated by their jobs and unheard by management. Though many were unhappy with their work, most caseworkers could ill afford to lose their jobs. In short, they felt stuck in a frustrating job that paid better than jobs they could find elsewhere.

Although the culture of the welfare office was usually viewed negatively, there was some variation across the city. Some entrants were placed in district offices that had reputations for being good places to work: supervisors were generally supportive, paperwork was organized and logical, and there was a feeling of camaraderie shared among the workers. As a result, perhaps workers' views of their office's culture will help explain some of the variation in the views that they developed.

If the culture of the welfare office was perceived as mostly negative by entrants, the culture of the police department was an effective contrast: although there was some disagreement, police were generally proud of their jobs and organization. Like experienced officers (Butterfield, Edwards, and Woodall 2005; Chappell and Lanza-Kaduce 2010), many of the police entrants reported a dichotomous view of the world featuring "good guys" and "bad guys." Being a police officer meant being a part of a fraternity of the good guys who look after each other and do the right thing. On the other side were criminals and the people who sought to diminish police power by creating liberal laws and treating criminals with kids' gloves.

To understand the effect of police culture, I asked police entrants how much they viewed the department's culture as influencing them. At Times 2 and 3, I asked how much they agreed with the statement "Just being around the academy environment has had an effect on me." At Times 4 and 5, I asked them how much they agreed that "the district environment has had an effect on me." At both times during training, over 80 percent agreed that the academy had had an effect on them. As they graduated and began work, only 50 percent agreed that the district had affected them (Time 4); by Time 5 fewer than 40 percent agreed that the district affected them. Although this figure reflects a decline, it is double the percentage of welfare caseworkers who agreed with this statement at Time 5.

After corresponding with one officer by email, I was added to his email distribution list. One email that he sent, a much-forwarded piece written for retiring police officers, captured a significant part of police culture.

> We know in the law enforcement life there is a fellowship which lasts long after the uniforms are hung up in the back of the closet. We know even if he throws them away, they will be on him with every step and breath that remains in his frame. We also know how the very bearing of the man speaks of what he was and in his heart still is.
>
> These are the burdens of the job. You will still look at people suspiciously, still see what others do not see or choose to ignore and always will look at the rest of the law enforcement world with a respect for what they do; only grown in a lifetime of knowing. Never think for one moment you are escaping from the life. You are only escaping the "job" and we are merely allowing you to leave "active" duty.

So what I wish for you is that whenever you ease into retirement, in your heart you never forget for one moment that "Blessed are the Peacemakers for they shall be called children of God," and you are still a member of the greatest fraternity the world has ever known.

Civilian Friends vs. Police Friends
Civilian Friends: Get upset if you're too busy to talk to them for a week.
Police Friends: Are glad to see you after years, and will happily carry on the same conversation you were having last time you met.

Civilian Friends: Never ask for food or alcohol.
Police Friends: Are the reason you have no food or alcohol.

Civilian Friends: Call your parents Mr. and Mrs.
Police Friends: Call your parents mom and dad.

Civilian Friends: Bail you out of jail and tell you what you did was wrong.
Police Friends: Would be sitting next to you in jail saying, "Damn . . . we screwed up . . . but man, that was fun!"

Civilian Friends: Have never seen you cry.
Police Friends: Cry with you.

Civilian Friends: Borrow your stuff for a few days then give it back.
Police Friends: Keep your stuff so long they forget it's yours.

Civilian Friends: Know a few things about you.
Police Friends: Could write a book with direct quotes from you.

Civilian Friends: Will leave you behind if that's what the crowd is doing.
Police Friends: Will kick the whole crowd's ass that left you behind.

Civilian Friends: Would knock on your door.
Police Friends: Walk right in and say, "I'm home!"

Civilian Friends: Are for a while.
Police Friends: Are for life.

Comparing the caseworker email from "Ray" to this email, we see that the cultures that entering workers experienced share some similarities and some differences. One similarity is that both cultures tended to emphasize a distinction between "us" and "them." In this configuration "we" are good, play by social rules, and are underappreciated while "they" break rules, are bad, and are pampered in an unjust society. However, for the police the "us" is the police fraternity, which is pitted against civilian society and suspicious individuals. For welfare caseworkers, the "us" is lower-level workers and the "them" are the department managers. Aside from the emails, the two cultures differed in that welfare workers saw the job as a last resort, and perhaps as a result, not particularly important to them. In contrast, police embraced their work as a big part of their identities. In the chapters that follow, I examine the extent to which entrants' experiences with their organization cultures were associated with the views that they developed.

Conclusion

This chapter has discussed the experiences that newcomers had as they entered their organizations and began training. Throughout, entrants encountered people who tried to put their marks on how they would act as officials of the state. As March and Olsen's logic of appropriateness theory would predict, doing so required implicit and explicit identity and attitude instruction — entrants were given an identity quiver and told to choose how to act based on whom they were interacting with. For both groups, instructors were their first points of organizational contact. These experienced organization members taught entrants about rules and regulations, but also sent informal messages (often using stories) about the kinds of people entrants would interact with on the streets and who they could be. After six months of training, both groups graduated and began interacting with the public. They also encountered the people who would continue their training. Welfare caseworkers were placed in training units with other entrants and headed by a training supervisor. Police officers were entrusted to the care of department veterans who showed them the ropes and inducted them into the police culture.

Taken as a whole, the chapter has illustrated a variety of institutional influences that may have shaped the bureaucratic personalities that entrants developed. Some of these influences seem potent while others do not; some influences appear to matter early in development while others seem important later in the process. However, missing from much of this discussion is the dispositional perspective — the influences from outside the organization that may have drawn entrants to their work, shaped their thinking prior to entry, and colored their experiences during entry. To explore the relative influence of these different sets of factors, the chapters that follow examine how entrants changed over the course of the study, and which factors explained variation in their views. To begin, Chapter 5 directs our attention to entrants' motivations and asks these questions: Why did they choose this type of work? Why did they stay? What explains their motives at different points during development?

CHAPTER 5

In the Service of Others?
Motivation, Altruism, and Egoism

After he had worked for two years inside the welfare department, I asked Terrell what was driving him to stay in his job. Without missing a beat he responded, "I would say that it really is just to have a job and have income come in. You know what really? I just go to work and do what I'm guided to do to get through the day. I'm not really big on serving the clients 'cause a lot of it is BS. But right now my main motivation for being there is really just an income." As readers will recall from Chapter 3, this motivation closely matches those articulated by experienced caseworkers. What explains these motivations? Did Terrell feel that way at entry, or is he an example of a burned-out bureaucrat?

This chapter aims to answer questions like these by tracing and exploring workers' motivations—the internal psychological forces that guide and compel their behavior (Perry and Hondeghem 2008). Motivation matters in public service, perhaps even more than in the private sector, because public managers are relatively constrained in their ability to reward and punish behavior (Rainey 2003; J. Wilson 1989). As a result, there has long been interest in understanding what exactly motivates public work. In recent years there has been growing attention to public service motivation. This concept has various meanings, but generally refers to the service side of motivation or, put another way, altruistic motives (Perry and Vandenabeele 2008). Though public workers appear to have high levels of this type of motivation compared to their private-sector counterparts (Crewson 1997; Houston 2000), it would be misleading to see them as motivated solely by service—bureaucrats also appear to be driven by a desire for the stability, benefits, and the social standing conferred by a government position (Golden 2000; Perry and Hondegheim 2008). Therefore, motivation is conceived of as a spectrum ranging from altruism, a subjective concern to help or serve other people, to egoism, a desire to help oneself or satisfy a personal desire. Like all people, bureaucrats are probably driven by various motives and may not fit neatly into categories like "altruist" and "egoist." Also, their motives may evolve over the course of their careers based on various influences and life changes.

To explore these possibilities, this chapter tracks entrants' motivations during their first two years on the job. Each section begins by discussing entrants' responses to interview questions about their motives. Following that, it presents descriptive findings from survey data. Since the survey data are readily quantifiable, each section concludes with a statistical analysis of workers' motivations. In short, the findings here show that police officers and welfare caseworkers entered their organizations with different motivations. Police were more motivated by the chance to give back whereas many caseworkers simply needed a steady job. The chapter shows that both groups, though differing in why they sought out public work, remained strongly connected to their entering motivations.

Police Officers' Motivations

Interviews

When I first spoke with police entrants, they were just beginning their academy training. At that time, I detected a mixture of altruism and egoism. Many cadets voiced altruistic motives like wanting to give back to society at large or their neighborhoods in particular. For example, David commented, "Me as a person, I wanted to get into this because I really wanted to protect people. That's my thing . . . I wanted to provide people with the same protection that I've felt growing up." Carl indicated that his power was limited, but that he felt he could help out in particular situations:

> I'm real fascinated by police work, by everything about it. Police officers' position in society, you know, you can really affect problems and just being in situations like the situations you'll be called to handle it's really like no other job. The whole point of your job is to go in and resolve the situation that most people, most sane people, in society think they'll want to get out of it. Tense situations, anything from car accidents to robberies to murder and all this kind of stuff and all these things that go on in society and most people try to avoid, you get in there and try to have a positive influence on it and whatever and it's really amazing. It's this hands on job

where you can be out there, it's cliché to say making a difference, but I feel like in a ways you do. Maybe an individual officer doesn't make a big impact on an entire city, but you definitely affect the people that you come into contact with on a day-to-day basis.

Another theme that emerged in my interviews was the desire to improve relations between the police and residents and, thereby, the image of police in the city. This motivation seemed particularly important to minority cadets. For example, Denise, a black cadet, revealed,

> Long term my goal is to work with at-risk youth and I'm still not 100 percent sure what capacity I'll serve—whether through [community service organization] or what avenue—but this is an excellent foot in the door in that direction. . . . As far as what aspects of policing appeals to me with at-risk youth, just the idea of community policing and [partnering] with individuals in the community as opposed to, I know with myself, I look at police officers, or used to look at police officers, not so much as them versus us, because I was not on the illegal end of the spectrum, but you don't necessarily feel that there is that partnership. . . . The opportunity to create better relations between the department and the community with regard to youth is something that appeals to me.

Another minority cadet, Pamela, indicated an explicit interest in improving relations between blacks in the city and the police department. "It seems to me that minorities are just treated differently than maybe whites by law enforcement, and I'm just thinking that maybe with more minorities being in law enforcement, maybe it wouldn't be so much injustice toward minorities."

Although minorities seemed generally more interested in improving relations between city residents and police, some white cadets articulated a similar desire. For example, David indicated being motivated to enhance the public's image of the police: "And it's like, it's no secret that a lot of [city] police officers get, they've been given a bad rap pretty much. You always hear about, on the news, you hear about cops just beating, excessive uses of force, all sort of stuff like that. I'm thinking that if I get in there, possibly I can make a difference. I want police to be perceived in a different way." As this quotation shows, there were some similarities between the motives of minority and white cadets. However, it is also important to note a difference in the frames that they used to understand residents' perceptions: the minority cadets seemed to believe that there were important differences in how minorities were treated; in contrast, the white cadets saw it as an image problem.

Some cadets indicated a mix of egoism and altruism. For instance, Phillip, a military veteran, noted, "I just love being out in the dirt doing the hard work and being real physical, so I figured hey if you're not going to stay in the military for a living next best thing is to be a cop and make a difference doing it." Clearly he was drawn by the physical aspects of the work, but he also indicated an interest in improving society. Another cadet indicated that policing was attractive because it was always "in demand," so there would be job security, but also because he wanted to "help" people.

Finally, some cadets seemed solely motivated by satisfying their own interests and getting a job that was exciting and secure. For instance, Mark commented, "I was driving a truck and it was the same routine everyday and being a police officer it's different, and you don't know what's gonna happen everyday, you don't know what you're doing everyday." Many of the cadets who came to the police from the military were drawn by the department's policy of granting ex–military members extra points on their entrance exams. Henry was in a special operations unit in a branch of the armed services for a few years. When he got out, he realized that he "was eligible for the points—I got the ten points on the test—and a lot of my background on the military could be used, you know SWAT . . . so I figured why not use it? . . . I knew I could get in pretty easily and I had training in that area of police enforcement."

It wasn't surprising to find that another motivation for many cadets was family: prior studies suggest important familial connections in police recruitment (Raganella and White 2004). My interviews with cadets who had families on the force often revealed a link between police motivation and identity. In effect, family ties pushed cadets to consider policing at an early age and taught them to "think like police" prior to entering the organization. For example, Jacob commented,

> Um, I always wanted to be a cop. My dad's a cop, his dad's a cop, my dad's brother's a cop. I just grew up with that mentality, and you pay attention to it. And you say to yourself maybe it's something I'm interested in, and you check it out and you just realize that it's already a part of you, you already think like a cop because it's all you've known, is how to think like one. . . . You just look at things differently. Like, when your friends say he's going to pick up a case of—or whatever, you just look, you act, you think more cautious, you think more on the safer side than you would. It's not a bad thing, just different.

As this quote makes clear, family can play an important role in police recruitment and development. Thus, at least some entrants joining police departments arrive with significant knowledge and experience about what it means to be a police officer. Depending on how widespread this phenomenon is, it may diminish the importance of postentry socialization.

After completing training and spending significant time on the streets, I again asked interviewees about their motivation for being a police officer. Overall, there was a mix of altruism and egoism, matching the motivations of veteran officers (in Chapter 3). Although police were cognizant that they could not reach everyone, many indicated an interest in helping individuals and making a difference in their lives. When I asked Mark about his motivation, he said, "I like doing good for people, it's the times when you see their expressions that you feel like you did something good for them and made them happy. . . . You help that old person that really still cares. Or you help that kid that looks up to you and says, 'Look the police officer's helping me.' That's what motivates me to do my work." Robert, a white officer under the age of twenty-five, said,

> You gotta believe that there's people out there that want your help and need your help and they need people out there that are willing to do it. So that's basically what it is . . . you come across some people where you just want to say screw it and just turn your back, but there's still people out there that do respect you and that do appreciate you and they need you. . . . If you're not in it to, you know, help people out, there's no reason—it's the not the greatest amount of money you're not just doing it for the money. There's a lot of jobs out there that are a lot less dangerous and you could make a lot more money.

Of course, not all entrants solely indicated the importance of service. For example, Isaiah began laughing when I asked him about his motivation at Time 5: "Retirement basically, retirement. It's a good [job] but these people can get on your nerves." However, he also said he liked the job because he had the chance to "do a lot of good" and "help a lot of people."

In addition to those who voiced altruistic or mixed motives after entry, many officers indicated purely egoistic motivations. The key theme for these officers was getting overtime pay and making money. Phillip initially indicated that he was drawn by the physicality of police work and the chance to "make a difference." After two years on the force he commented that he was motivated by "just basically working with any good partner that I can and making like good arrests and get overtime and make money for my family and me.... Each arrest we get ... is court time and when we get court time we're guaranteed overtime. And overtime is money, which is money for our families." Jacob, the officer quoted above who came from a family of police officers, had a similar trajectory. Initially he indicated some altruistic motives—at Time 1 he said that "being a police officer is ... about paying attention and helping." After a year in the department (Time 4), he had grown frustrated and felt impotent:

> It pretty much sucks. You're out there, you bust your ass, and you, you don't see any change. It never changes. It's the same problem over and over again. You don't really think you're doing any good, and every once in awhile, every once in a very rare moon, you actually do something good for someone where they are appreciative of it. You lock people up, it's not always a good thing for that person. It's a good thing because you get a bad guy off the street, but it doesn't always solve something. But every once in awhile you do something good for someone and I was expecting to do that more often.

Perhaps as a result, when I asked him about his motivation at Time 5, he reported an egoistic goal, making a good impression on superiors. "Well, I like to impress the bosses. Like when they say, 'We need this' I like to go out and get it for them as quickly as possible. That's what I like to do."

Surveys

To develop a broader portrait of motivation at each time, I used survey questions to ask entrants how much they were motivated by eight motivations: protecting law abiding citizens, the job's excitement, keeping order in the streets, getting/keeping a job with good benefits, influences from family, making sure that people are treated fairly and equitably, getting/keeping a respected job, and the power that the police have.[1] They answered these questions by choosing a response on a five-point scale from "not at all" to "a lot." According to the altruism and egoism division, protection, keeping order, and treating people fairly and equitably are conceived of as altruistic; excitement, benefits, respect, and power are seen as egoistic.[2] Figure 5.1 charts police entrants' answers to these questions over their first two years inside their organization.

This figure shows strong trends of continuity over the first two years of their

In the Service of Others?   93

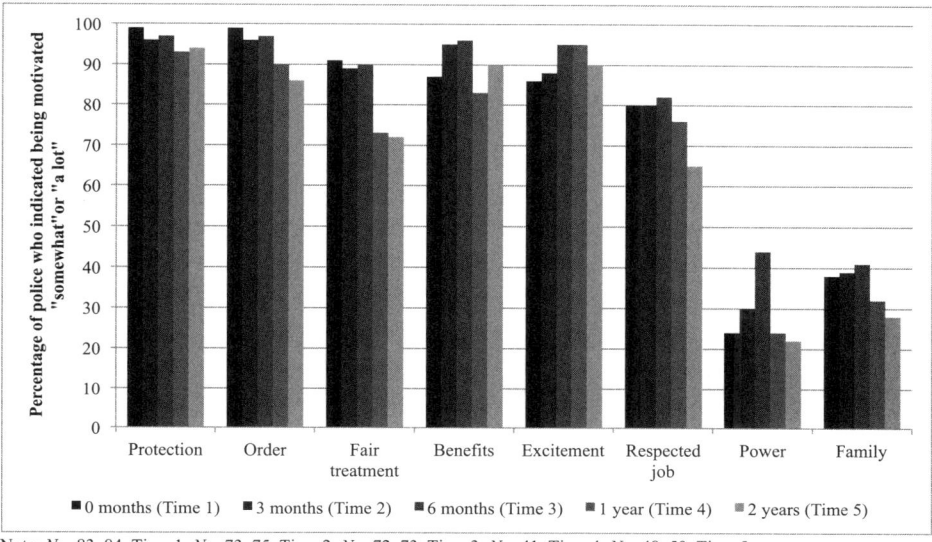

Note: $N = 83–84$, Time 1; $N = 73–75$, Time 2; $N = 72–73$, Time 3; $N = 41$, Time 4; $N = 48–50$, Time 5.

Figure 5.1. Police Motivation

careers, but some change as well. In terms of altruism, we see that over 70 percent of police were motivated by each altruistic motive at each time. Although all three dropped somewhat from Time 1 to Time 5, fair treatment dropped the most. On the right side of the chart we see that three of the four egoistic motives (benefits, excitement, and respect) remained high, and the allure of the benefits may have grown over time. Power was not a strong motive at most times. However, it did rise in importance at the end of the academy. Finally, on the right side of the chart we see that around a third of officers were motivated by family influences at each time. After beginning work, this motivation appeared to decline.

Since these scalar questions do not ask officers to rank their motivations, I also requested that they choose a primary motive. Figure 5.2 presents data on their most important motivations at each time. In examining altruism (left side) and egoism (right side), we see significant variation in this figure. In four of the five times, including Times 1 and 5, the most prevalent primary motivation for police was protecting others. However, as the percentage of police who were motivated by altruistic motives dropped, the percentage of those motivated primarily by benefits and excitement, two egoistic motivations, increased. When aggregated into altruistic or egoistic, the percentage of entrants indicating an altruistic

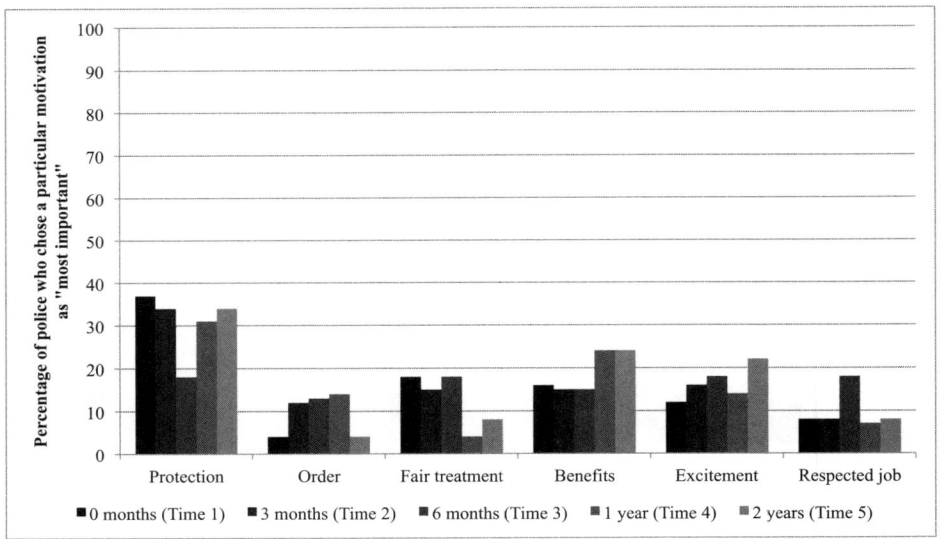

Note: $N = 73$, Time 1; $N = 61$, Time 2; $N = 40$, Time 3; $N = 29$, Time 4; $N = 50$, Time 5. "Power" and "family" are not included in this figure because they never represented more than 7 percent of respondents' top motivations.

Figure 5.2. Police Motivation: Primary

primary motive was 60 percent at Time 1; by the end of the academy (Time 3) this had dropped to 49 percent, and by the end of two years it had dropped to 46 percent. In contrast, the percentage of entrants indicating an egoistic primary motive rose from 40 percent at Time 1 to 54 percent at Time 5.[3]

In addition, it is important to consider the spread of officers' motivations throughout the study to determine whether they moved closer together, as the institutional perspective would expect, or diverged/remained static, as the dispositional perspective would expect. To do this, I examined the standard deviations of the population's responses to each motivation question over time. This analysis revealed that in seven of the eight questions, there was an increase or no change in the standard deviation from Time 1 to Time 5. The only motivation question in which the spread narrowed over time was excitement.

Thus far the survey data have been used to examine entrants' motivation responses and to make initial comments about change and continuity. Though useful for understanding population-wide trends, the above analysis is limited in explaining individual-level change because, due to nonresponse or attrition, the group of respondents was somewhat different at each time.[4] Therefore, I conducted a cross tabulation of entrants' top motivations after dividing their entering and subsequent primary motives into altruistic and egoistic. In this way, I was able to analyze whether individuals adopted new primary motives during entry. This analysis showed that at each time at least 68 percent of police entrants had the same general class of motivation (altruistic or egoistic) that they reported at Time 1.

Continuing the individual-level analysis, I calculated the absolute value of the difference between each officer's entering and subsequent motivations. Figure 5.3 charts the mean change in officers' motivations in scalar points; since the figure shows absolute values, each bar indicates total change, not change toward a particular position.[5] This figure shows general consistency: by the end of the study the largest mean change, family influences, was below 25 percent (1 scalar point). At Time 1 the mean response to the family motivation question was 2.9 (neutral) on the 5-point scale; by Time 5 the mean response was 2.6 (between disagree and neutral).[6]

However, in every outcome there was some change, and with four outcomes— excitement, order, fair treatment, and respect—the amount of change grew over time. In the other five outcomes we see some change and then a leveling off or

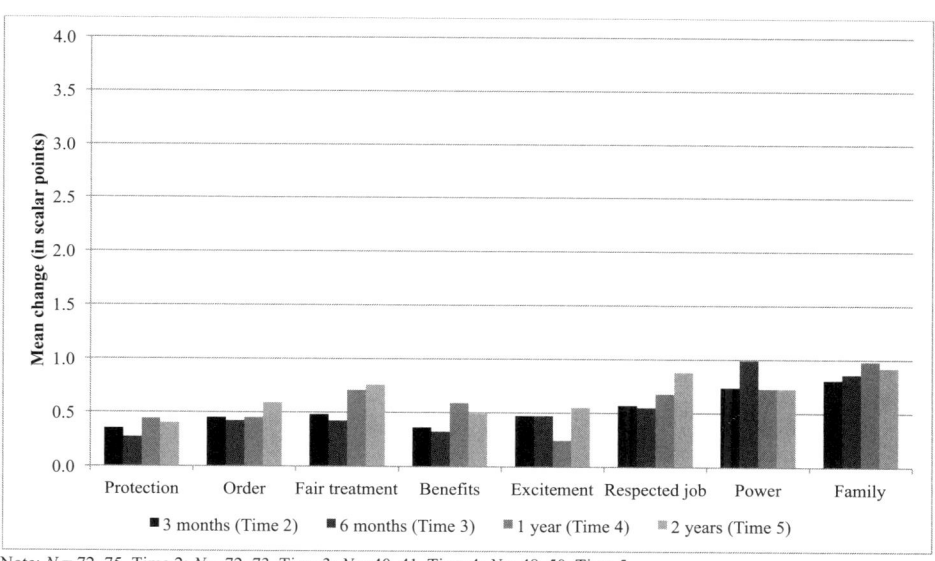

Note: $N = 72–75$, Time 2; $N = 72–73$, Time 3; $N = 40–41$, Time 4; $N = 48–50$, Time 5.

Figure 5.3. Police Motivation: Mean Individual Change

decrease in change. Taken together, there appears to be some support for the institutional perspective. However, the changes captured in the figure are modest.

Statistical Analysis

This section continues the inquiry by discussing the findings from a multivariate statistical analysis of officers' responses to survey questions.[7] Since responses to these questions were ordered and limited to a five-point spread, I used ordered probit to study the relationships between dependent and independent variables. Unfortunately, probit coefficients are difficult to interpret on their own (UCLA: Statistical Consulting Group 2013); therefore, the chapter presents the findings from odds ratio calculations. Odds ratios are the probability of a certain outcome based on variation in an independent variable, keeping all other model variables constant. An odds ratio of 1 implies that, due to an increase in an independent variable, the outcome is equally likely. An odds ratio above 1 implies that the outcome is more likely, and an odds ratio below 1 indicates that the outcome is less likely.

Initially, the analysis examined the "real-time" relationship between independent and dependent variables. For example, it analyzed whether cadets influenced by training at the time of graduation (Time 3) had different motives than those who were not. Such an analysis is useful for discussing the relationship between variables as they occurred. Second, the analysis examined the likelihood that police entrants would adopt new motivations after entry. This part of the analysis used individual-level change data (calculated by taking the difference between newcomers' entering and subsequent responses) as dependent variables.

Throughout the entirety of this study, police remained strongly connected to their entering motivations. Since police socialization is sometimes depicted as powerful and rapid, it was surprising to see that, even when controlling for institutional influences, entering motives was the most consistent predictor of police officers' motives in each wave of the study. For example, an officer who was motivated by the job's benefits at entry was more likely to be motivated by the job's benefits throughout the two years of the study. In addition to being a consistent predictor, police officers' entering motivations was by far the most powerful predictor of their subsequent motivations. Figure 5.4 presents the relationships between entering and subsequent motivation throughout entry.

This figure shows that initial motivations remained strongly tied to subsequent motivation even when controlling for a host of extraorganizational and organiza-

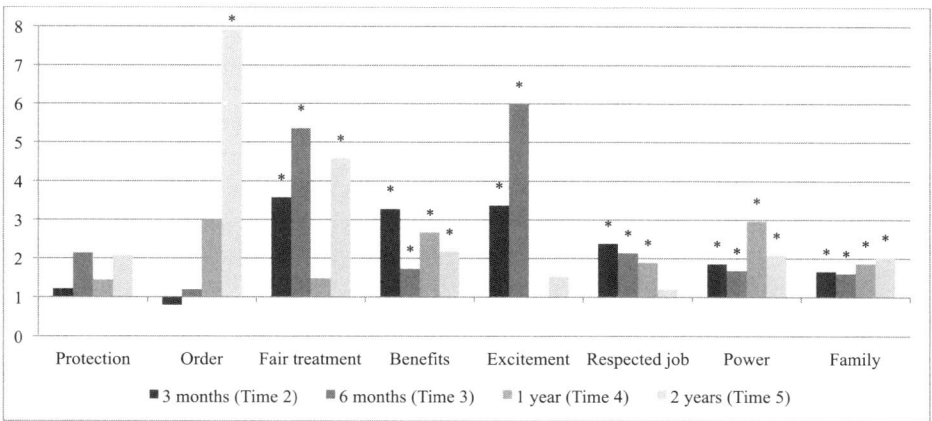

Figure 5.4. Predicting Police Motivation: Entering Motivation

tional factors. For example, a police officer who was motivated by treating the public fairly at entry was approximately 3.5 times more likely to be motivated by that outcome at the end of two years.[8] Although many of the odds ratios are big (in comparison with other predictors shown below), they are not uniform in size or trend. For instance, the size of the odds ratio for benefits is consistently larger than that for family. Also, they are trending in different directions: the relationship between entering and subsequent benefit motivation appears to be diminishing over time, while the relationship between entering and subsequent family motivation appears to be increasing.

It's also interesting to see that the relationship between entering and subsequent order motivation grows considerably at Times 4 and 5. Police who indicated being motivated by order at entry are nearly seven times more likely to be so motivated at Time 5. Finally, note that two initial motivations appear to diminish over time. Being motivated by the job's excitement or respect is a good predictor of being motivated by these outcomes at Times 2 and 3. However, by Time 5 the predictive power of these entering motivations appears to have diminished considerably and they have lost their statistical significance.

The second point emerging from the statistical analysis is that, in general, there were few strong, consistent associations between extraorganizational characteristics (i.e., education, age, preacademy family income, etc.) and entrants' motivations. For example, older cadets did not have systematically different motives throughout entry than younger cadets. However, there is one important caveat: race. Reflecting findings from Chapter 3 and interviews discussed in this chapter, there were consistent and strong differences between the motivations of minority and white police throughout the study.[9] As evident in Figure 5.5, this was particularly true for three altruistic motivations and one egoistic motivation.

Throughout the course of the study, racial minorities were generally more likely to be motivated by protecting the public, keeping order in the streets, and treating people fairly. In each of these areas, the likelihood of minorities being motivated by these outcomes grew through the end of the first year (Time 4). However, we see that this likelihood diminished somewhat at the end of the second year (Time 5). Nonetheless, even at that time minorities were approximately

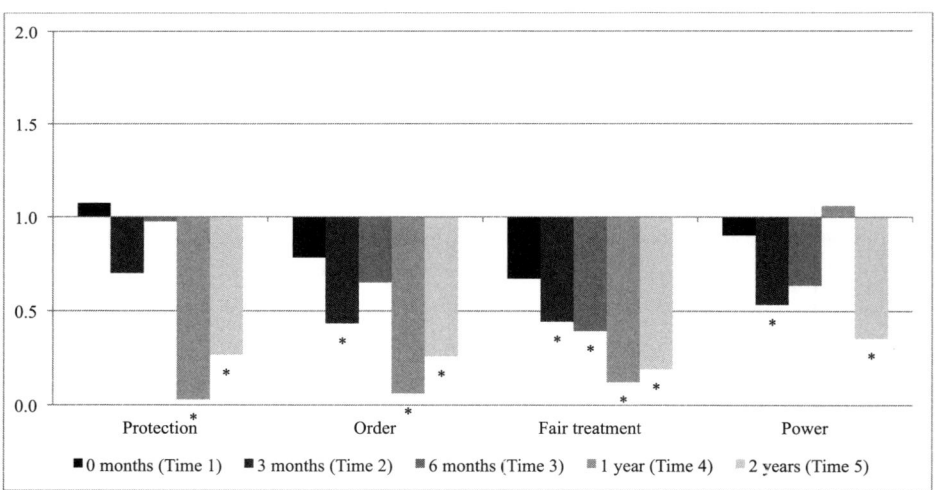

Note: This chart present odds ratios calculated from multivariate ordered probit estimates. These ratios can be interpreted such that an increase of one unit of an independent variable—in this case moving from minority, which is coded as 0, to white, which is coded as 1—increases or decreases the chances of the dependent variable (motivation) by a certain amount, controlling for all other model variables (see the note to Figure 5.4 for a list of each model's variables and for further information about interpretation of odds ratios). An asterisk indicates that the underlying coefficient is statistically significant at the $p < .05$ level. $N = 68$–69, Time 1; $N = 59$–62, Time 2; $N = 59$–60, Time 3; $N = 34$–35, Time 4; $N = 39$–41, Time 5.

Figure 5.5. Predicting Police Motivation: Race

0.75 times more likely to be motivated by these altruistic motives. In addition, the figure reveals that, except for at Time 4, racial minorities were more likely to be motivated by the job's power. Although the trend is nonlinear, the probability of this difference appears to grow over time. These findings support the dispositional expectation that entrants' bureaucratic personalities will, to some extent at least, remain connected to their extraorganizational identities.

The third major point that emerges from this analysis is that the association between organizational influences and motivation was slow to emerge. In the policing literature, some accounts suggest that socialization occurs quickly after cadets enter the academy. For instance, recall the chief of police, quoted in Chapter 2, who said, "The day a new recruit walks through the doors of the police academy he leaves society behind to enter a profession that . . . defines who he is" (Van Maanen 1974, 84). However, this project's analysis shows that after three months inside the police academy there were few strong associations between organizational influences and cadets' motivations (the odds ratios of these organizational variables were small and not statistically significant). In other words, cadets who were influenced by training instructors, who learned from fellow cadets, and who were influenced by the academy's environment were approximately as likely to be motivated by each outcome as cadets who were not.

However, as seen in Figure 5.6, six months after entry (Time 3), training instructors emerged as a consistent predictor of cadets' motivations. In particular, at this time we see that cadets influenced by training instructors were approximately 0.20 times more likely to be motivated by protecting people and keeping order in the streets and 0.30 times more likely to be motivated by treating people fairly. Although these relationships are statistically significant, readers should note the difference in the scales used in Figures 5.4 and 5.6. Comparing these figures, we see that entering motivations are considerably more powerful predictors than training.

The fourth point that emerges from the analysis of entering police officers' motivations is that, from an organizational standpoint, there appeared to be a stronger role for formal influences (training, supervision, monitoring) early in the entry process and a stronger role for informal influences (peers, veterans, culture) later in entry. For example, Figure 5.6 showed some statistically significant relationships between motivation and training at the end of the academy period. However, at that time there were fewer statistically significant relationships between informal influences and motivation.[10] Nonetheless, at the end of their first year in the department (Time 4), there were a roughly equal number of statistically significant relationships (between informal and formal influences and motivation). In

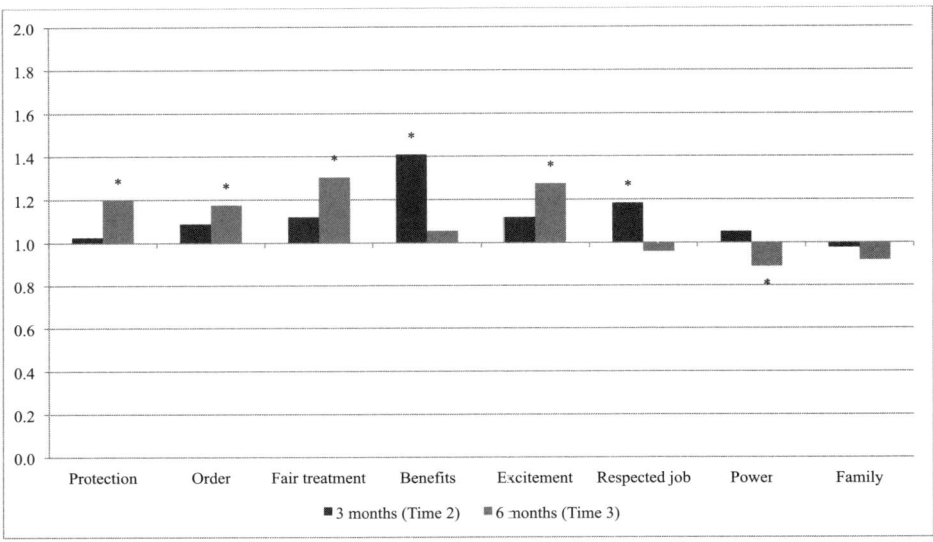

Note: This chart presents odds ratios calculated from multivariate ordered probit estimates. These ratios can be interpreted such that an increase of one unit of an independent variable (training instructors) increases or decreases the chances of the dependent variable (motivation) by a certain amount, controlling for all other model variables (see the note to Figure 5.4 for a list of each model's variables and for further information about interpretation of odds ratios). An asterisk indicates that the underlying coefficient is statistically significant at the $p < .05$ level. $N = 59-62$, Time 2; $N = 59-60$, Time 3.

Figure 5.6. Predicting Police Motivation: Training Instructors

particular, there were associations between veterans and peers and entrants' motivation. Interestingly, there were no consistent patterns in terms of the substance of the relationships—some informal influences, like culture, were negatively associated with altruistic motives, and others, like peers, were positively associated with altruistic motives.

By the end of the study, there were considerably more relationships between informal influences and motivation. Unlike at Time 4, most of these relationships followed a simple pattern: informal influences were negatively associated with altruistic motives. For instance, police influenced by the department's culture were half as likely to be motivated by treating people fairly and 0.65 times less likely to be motivated by keeping order.

Finally, this section reports findings from the individual-level change analysis. This analysis explored if any dispositional or institutional variables explained the likelihood that police entrants would adopt new motivations. The analysis showed that no one variable or set of variables dominated in explaining change. Rather, throughout the study a number of dispositional and institutional variables were inconsistently associated with change. Nonetheless, some influences appeared to be more important than others. Early in training (Time 2), there were few significant institutional predictors of change; however, by graduation (Time 3), variables measuring the influence of culture and training instructors were significant predictors of change. Substantively, these influences appeared to have different effects. Cadets influenced by training were more likely to become motivated by altruistic motives like protecting the public and treating people fairly; cadets influenced by the academy's culture were less likely to become motivated by treating people fairly.

After graduation, two informal influences, culture and veterans, were strongly associated with cadets' likelihood of adopting new motives. For the most part, the substantive effect was the same: officers influenced by the department's culture and veterans were likely to move away from altruistic motivations. For example, officers influenced by the department culture at Time 5 were likely to have shifted away from being motivated by protecting the public, keeping order, and treating people fairly.

Among dispositional influences, age was initially (Time 2) a strong predictor of motivation change. Oddly, older cadets were more likely to adopt new motivations (in the areas of excitement and job respect) than were younger cadets. However, age was not a significant, consistent predictor of cadets' likelihood of changing their motives at other times in the study. In contrast, initially race was not a strong predictor of changed motivations, but after graduation it emerged as important. By the end of the study (Time 5), entrants' racial identities predicted their likelihood of altering their motivations in four areas: protection, fair treatment, benefits, and the job's power. Reflecting the analysis above, whites were likely to become less motivated by protecting the public and treating people fairly; minorities were likely to become motivated by the job's benefits and power.

With this account complete, we now turn to the entering welfare caseworkers to explore what motivated them as they entered the department and how their motives changed or remained static during their first two years on the job.

Welfare Caseworkers' Motivations

Interviews

At the outset of their careers in the welfare office, caseworkers were motivated by the stability and benefits offered by the job. For example, prior to getting a state job, Ralph was not earning enough to make ends meet. In our first interview he commented that the welfare job "had good benefits and paid a lot more than I was making . . . so that was it. There wasn't very much thought about the welfare system, it was more of a survival thing. I needed more money and I qualified for this, which was amazing because I'd been turned away from like hundreds of jobs since I graduated college." Evelyn indicated a similar motivation: she had retired from her first career but found that she could not cover her expenses. At Time 1 she said, "At this point in my life the only reason I am here is because I'm a retiree from [large company] and I needed to go back to work and it just so happened that this was available. . . . This was what was available [laughter] and it's not anything really deep at that point, it's just that this became available . . . it was a source of, I hate to say it this way, but I have to be honest . . . it was a source of money. . . . It was strictly for employment."

Although some newcomers were underemployed prior to welfare, others were unemployed. In fact, some entrants indicated going directly from receiving welfare benefits to working as a welfare caseworker. In the typical telling, an entrant would go down to her local office to apply for benefits. Once there, a caseworker would look at her skeptically but sympathetically and ask, "What are you doing here?" The implication of the question was that the applicant was too "qualified" or "together" to be receiving welfare; rather, she should be on the other side of the desk administering the various programs. The caseworker would then encourage her to take the state civil service exam and try to become a caseworker. Consider the experience of Jasmine, a black caseworker entrant in her mid-thirties: "I ended up having to leave my job. . . . With the four kids I needed medical coverage so when I came in [to apply for benefits] [my caseworker] said, 'You should work here.' So I went down and took the test and that very next day they called me."

After I heard this theme a few times, and calculated that 79 percent of caseworker entrants had received welfare at some point in their lives, it occurred to me that, in addition to determining eligibility, welfare caseworkers may serve as informal job recruiters for the organization. From this perspective, the pool of welfare applicants, in addition to being the organization's "clients," may serve as an important source of human capital.

Though almost all workers were motivated primarily by the job's pay and benefits, some mentioned altruistic goals. For example, Deborah, a mother of young children, was out of work and receiving benefits. She indicated that she needed to find work, but that she was also drawn to the job to make welfare applicants' experiences better.

I wanted [welfare applicants] to have someone who knew what they were going through. And not act like it's their money that they're giving away. 'Cause I come in to get the Food Stamps and some caseworkers are like, "I'll see." And I'm like if I'm eligible for benefits, I'm eligible for benefits. But it's not like I was just living off the system. I had a job and I was in school and I just wanted the benefits. And I'm not just collecting the benefits. I'm doing it so that I can get to a job where I don't get benefits. I was so happy that I was able to close my case. . . . They were rude coming in there to apply for benefits. I didn't want to be totally dependent on them. I just wanted some help with food and medical. And I said if I ever get this job I want to just be nice to the clients, you know?

This feeling was shared by Jessica, who felt that when she was receiving benefits, her caseworker had always made the process of getting benefits seem like a big deal or impossible. She wanted to see if she could do the job in a way that was less onerous for everyone involved. Other caseworker trainees also indicated altruistic reasons for taking the job. For instance, one caseworker wanted to help single mothers with housing problems, while another was drawn to helping immigrants or other "underdogs." However, in nearly all cases, altruistic caseworker entrants also indicated that they were coming from a precarious financial situation and needed a steady job.

Above we saw that some racial minorities entering the police department were motivated by a desire to make sure that police treated minorities equally. Since there has been some tension between welfare departments and minority communities in the past (Kornbluh 2007; Piven and Cloward 1979), it is notable that in my interviews with entering minority welfare caseworkers I did not detect a similar motivation. It is not clear why this was the case. However, it is useful to note that the employees in the city's police department were mostly white and the employees in the city's welfare department were mostly minority. Also, most welfare caseworker entrants, by dint of having received welfare benefits at some point in their lives, had experience with the welfare system and viewed it as a system operated by minorities. As a result, welfare caseworker entrants with altruistic impulses appear to have been focused on making the system generally accessible. Though they did not voice a concern for protecting the interests of minority applicants, by improving the system they may have implicitly highlighted this goal.

When I returned to the question of their motivation later in the study, there was a decidedly simpler response from nearly all interviewees, the job's benefits and pay. For instance, Deborah, who at entry had indicated an interest in making the process smoother for applicants, indicated after two years that she was motivated by "a steady paycheck and benefits. . . . That's it." As they entered the organization and began interacting with recipients, most entrants appeared to move away from the secondary motives that they had articulated previously about helping out the disadvantaged. Due to their understanding that the system was not helping people and that claimants were often trying to "get over," they indicated that they were primarily there to get a paycheck and the job's accompanying benefits.

For example, Tracy initially sought out work in welfare for altruistic reasons. "I like to help people I mean that's sort of my M.O. . . . I was a single mom and so one of my main goals was to provide housing or housing and assistance for other single moms. So I thought this would be good to kind of learn the mentality of people that were out there. Helping people with housing is my ten-year goal." Two years later she had a much simpler motivation: "My paycheck! [laughter] . . . I have a daughter in college." After our conversation she sent me a note that read, "One last comment: I notice that though I came in wanting to help and do all I can for the client, that the system is not really designed to help you help the client. On one hand they want you to be nice and friendly, but because of all the time restraints on you it really is hard."

Surveys

To develop a more rigorous portrait of caseworkers' motivations, on surveys I asked them how much they were driven by six motives: getting a job with good benefits, helping teach clients basic skills, making sure that clients aren't taking advantage of the system, helping clients find work, doing something about poverty, and making sure that clients are treated fairly and equitably.[11] They answered by choosing a single point on a 5-point scale from "not at all" to "a lot." The first motive (benefits) is classified as egoistic, and the other five are classified as altruistic.[12] Figure 5.7 charts entrants' answers to these questions over their first two years inside their organization.[13] As the figure indicates, at each time over 80 percent of caseworkers were motivated by the job's benefits. Over the course of the study, this motivation grew somewhat across the group. Though the number of survey respondents was quite small, this finding by and large aligns with comments that entrants made in interviews.

However, the survey results are also somewhat at odds with the interview data discussed above. Throughout the study, 50 percent or more of entrants indicated being motivated by altruistic outcomes like finding work for clients, doing

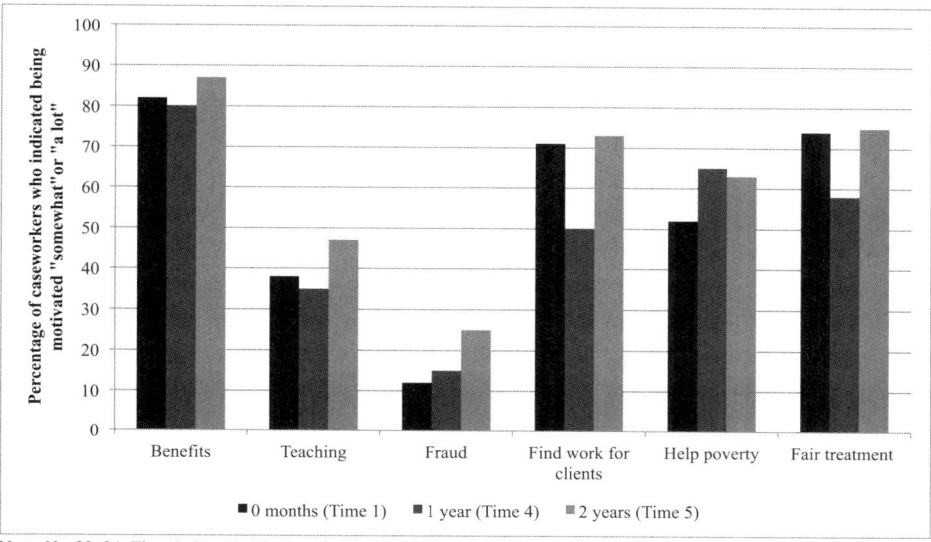

Note: $N = 33-34$, Time 1; $N = 18-20$, Time 4; $N = 15-16$, Time 5.

Figure 5.7. Caseworker Motivation

something about poverty, and treating people fairly. In fact, at the end of two years in the department, over 70 percent of entrants indicated being motivated by helping clients find work and treating people fairly. This trend is surprising since most entrants indicated that they had a single, all-encompassing motive after entry: the job's pay and benefits.

To understand the relative importance of these motives, I also asked entrants to indicate their top motivation from this list. Figure 5.8 charts entrants' primary motivations over their first two years. Clearly, the job's benefits were the largest and most consistent primary motivation for welfare caseworker entrants. Approximately 70 percent of the caseworkers ranked benefits first. No other motive was mentioned by more than 20 percent of this group. However, it is notable that the percentage of entrants primarily motivated by fair treatment rose at each time. By the end of the second year, nearly one-fifth of entrants were primarily motivated by fair treatment.

We also need to consider the spread of caseworkers' motivations throughout the study to determine whether, collectively, their motives moved closer together, as the institutional perspective would expect, or diverged/remained static, as the dispositional perspective would expect. To do this, I examined the standard

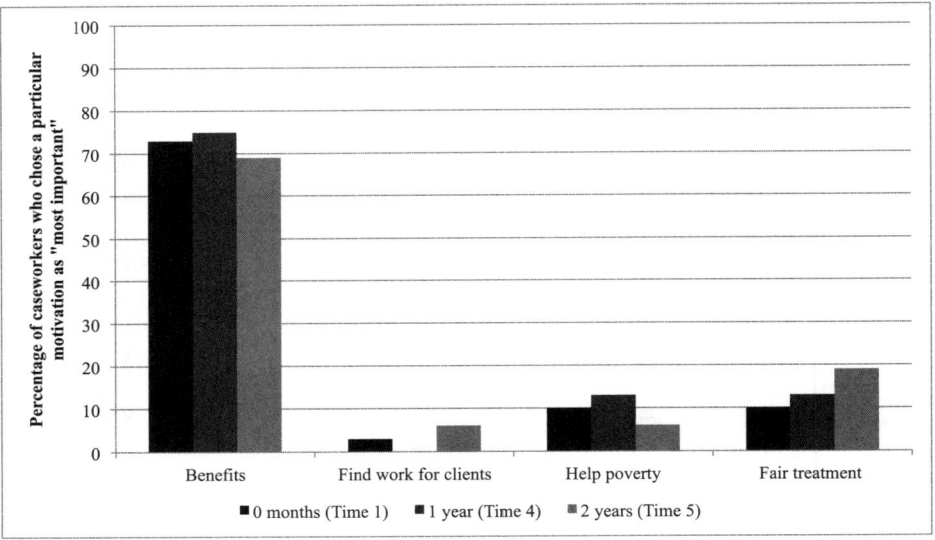

Note: $N = 30$, Time 1; $N = 8$, Time 4; $N = 16$, Time 5. "Teaching" and "fraud" are not included in this figure because they never represented more than 5 percent of respondents' top motivations.

Figure 5.8. Caseworker Motivation: Primary

deviations of the population's responses to each motivation question over time. This analysis revealed that in five of the six motives, there was a decrease in the standard deviation from Time 1 to Time 5. The only motivation question in which caseworkers' views appeared to diverge over time was fraud detection. The narrowing of the spread of caseworkers' motivations is in direct contrast to the situation for police and supports the institutional perspective on entrant development.

Thus far, the survey data have been used to make comments about change and continuity across the general population of entrants. As discussed in the police section, it is also important to understand the extent to which individuals changed or remained static. Therefore, I conducted a cross tabulation of entrants' top motivations after dividing their motives into altruistic and egoistic. These calculations showed that, as with police entrants, over two-thirds of caseworker entrants (67 percent) had the same type of motivation at Times 4 and 5 that they reported at Time 1. Thus, though the number of respondents is quite small, we see strong hints of motivational continuity. Furthermore, I sought to understand the extent to which entering caseworkers altered their motivations over the course of the project by calculating the absolute value of the difference between each caseworker's entering and subsequent motivations. Figure 5.9 charts the mean change of caseworkers' motivations in scalar points; since the figure shows absolute values, each bar indicates total change, not change toward a particular position.[14]

This figure shows that, in broad terms, there was consistency in caseworker entrants' motives: by the end of the study, the largest mean change, fair treatment, was still below 25 percent (one scalar point). It also shows some ambiguity about the direction of change: the amount of change appears to be increasing for three outcomes (benefits, fraud, and poverty) and decreasing for three outcomes (teaching, helping, and fair treatment). Nonetheless, this figure generally supports the dispositional perspective of bureaucratic socialization.

Statistical Analysis

This section continues the inquiry by discussing the findings from a bivariate statistical analysis of caseworkers' responses to motivation survey questions.[15] Since responses to questions are ordered, ordered probit was used to analyze the relationship between dependent and independent variables. As discussed above, probit coefficients are difficult to interpret on their own; therefore, the chapter presents

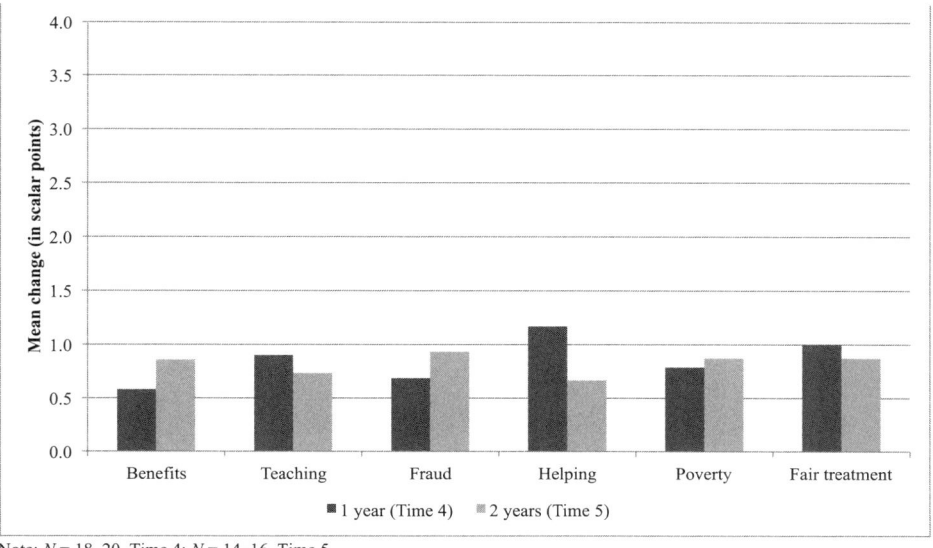

Note: $N = 18–20$, Time 4; $N = 14–16$, Time 5.

Figure 5.9. Caseworker Motivation: Mean Individual Change

the findings from odds ratio calculations that detail the probability of a certain outcome based on variation in an independent variable. Also, like the police analysis, this section discusses results from "real-time" and change analyses.

To begin, the analysis showed that there was a strong and consistent relationship between caseworkers' entering and subsequent motivations at the one-year point. Even though caseworkers had undergone six months of training and six months of work in their offices, they remained strongly tied to their entering motivations. Figure 5.10 shows the relationships between entering and subsequent motivations over the two years of the study. A caseworker motivated by benefits at entry was approximately 1 time more likely to be motivated by benefits at Time 4. An entrant motivated by detecting welfare fraud at entry was 1.70 times more likely to be thus motivated at the one-year point. Perhaps because entrants remained connected to their entering motives, there was a dearth of associations between organizational influences and entrants' motivations at the one-year point. In particular, it is striking that training and supervision, noted as important aspects of entry in Chapter 4, were not strongly associated with entrants' motives.

Despite continuity at Time 4, the analysis shows a general decline (four of six

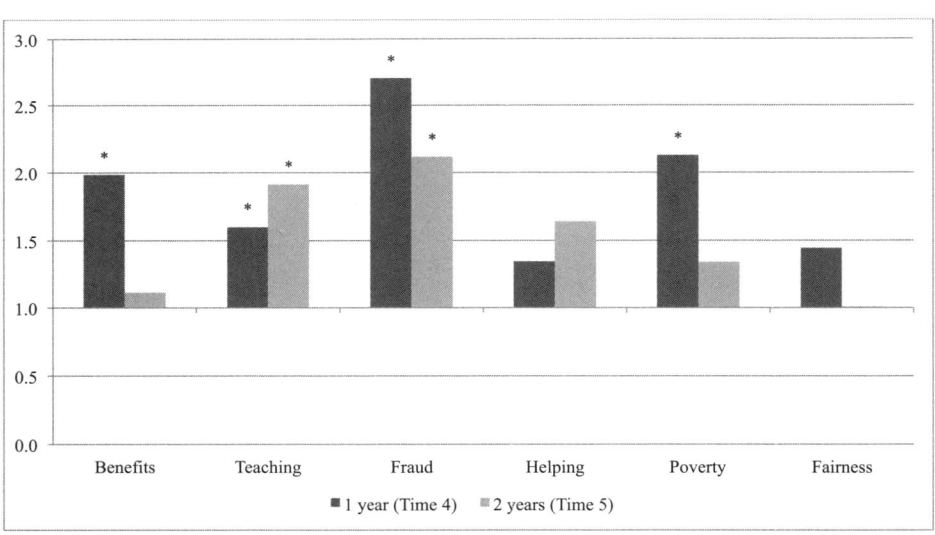

Note: This chart presents odds ratios calculated from bivariate ordered probit estimates. These ratios can be interpreted such that an increase of one unit of an independent variable (entering motivation) increases or decreases the chances of the dependent variable (subsequent motivation) by a certain amount (see the note to Figure 5.4 for further information about odds ratio interpretation). An asterisk indicates that the underlying coefficient is statistically significant at the $p < .05$ level. $N = 14$–20, Time 4; $N = 12$–16, Time 5.

Figure 5.10. Predicting Caseworker Motivation: Entering Motivation

motives) in the consistency and strength of the relationships between entering and subsequent motivations at Time 5. In fact, only two entering motivations (teaching and fraud) were strongly associated with subsequent motivations at this time. This is impressive when compared with the police, who, even at Time 5, remained strongly tied to their entering motives.

In conjunction with the diminishing connection between entering and subsequent motives, analysis of entrants' views at that time shows a modest emergence of organizational influences. No one organizational influence or class of influence had a patterned relationship with caseworkers' motives. However, the most consistent influence at Time 5 was training. Figure 5.11 shows the relationship between training and caseworkers' Time 4 and Time 5 motives. As the figure shows, caseworkers who continued to draw from their training at Time 5 were 0.75 times more likely to be motivated by rooting out fraud, 1.20 times more likely to be motivated by helping clients find work, and 0.70 times more likely to be motivated by doing something about poverty. Although this finding may seem contradictory at first, both messages are consonant with the post–welfare reform "work first" philosophy that sees work and fair use of welfare as paths out of poverty. Taken

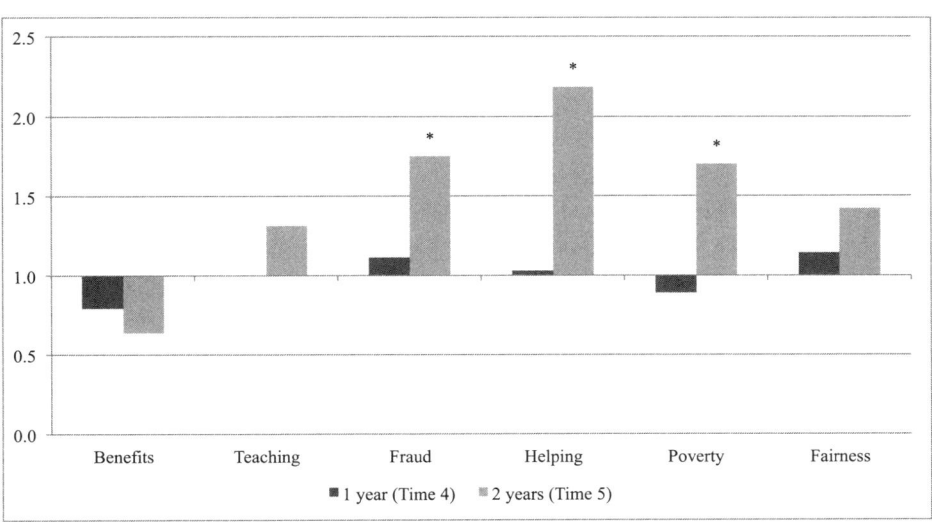

Note: This chart presents odds ratios calculated from bivariate ordered probit estimates. These ratios can be interpreted such that an increase of one unit of an independent variable (training) increases or decreases the chances of the dependent variable (motivation) by a certain amount (see the note to Figure 5.4 for further information about interpretation of odds ratios). An asterisk indicates that the underlying coefficient is statistically significant at the $p < .05$ level. $N = 14$–20, Time 4; $N = 12$–16, Time 5.

Figure 5.11. Predicting Caseworker Motivation: Training

in sum, this figure appears to corroborate the comments of welfare entrants about the importance of their training supervisors.

Third, there were few extraorganizational predictors of entrants' motivations. In other words, when entrants began their careers in the welfare office, characteristics like race, gender, and age were not strongly associated with entrants' motives. As they underwent training and began work, these dispositional variables remained inconsistent, weak predictors of their motivations. Thus, even as entrants remained relatively connected to their entering motivations, demographic characteristics did not explain much of the variation in their motives at each time that survey data were collected.

Finally, there were few strong, consistent predictors of the likelihood that caseworker entrants would adopt new motivations or maintain their current motives. This was true for extraorganizational demographic characteristics, like age, race, and gender, that were generally expected to have a stabilizing effect on entrants' motives. For example, throughout the study younger caseworker entrants were just as likely to maintain their motivations as older entrants. The inconsistency was also true for institutional variables. However, entrants influenced by the department's culture appeared to be more likely to shift their motivations in some areas. For example, entrants influenced by the department's culture were less likely to become motivated at Time 4 by preventing fraud; at Time 5, caseworkers influenced by their department's culture were more likely to become motivated by helping clients find work and doing something about poverty. These relationships are surprising because they indicate that the department culture pushed entrants to embrace client-friendly motivations. Though this finding is interesting, it is important to note that such relationships were rare and there were no consistent dispositional or institutional predictors of caseworkers' likelihood of adopting new motivations.

Conclusion

This chapter has begun the task of exploring entrants' bureaucratic personalities during the first two years of their careers by focusing on their motivations. In general, we see that most welfare caseworkers were primarily motivated by the job's benefits throughout the two years of the study. Although many police were motivated by benefits and other egoistic motives, a greater percentage were also primarily motivated by altruistic motives. In part this may result from entrants' pre-entry financial situations: in interviews, many caseworkers indicated that they came directly to administering welfare from claiming welfare or being in jobs in which the pay was insufficient. Thus, for many caseworkers the draw of the job may have been stability and a paycheck, not necessarily the opportunity to "give back" or serve others. In contrast, police officers indicated that they came from steady jobs with relatively equal pay and that, should they give up policing, they could find comparable work elsewhere. Although initially most police (60 percent) were primarily motivated by an altruistic motive, the chapter shows that as they began interacting with the public, and doing their work, the number of police officers driven primarily by an altruistic motive decreased (to 46 percent).

In addition to description, the chapter explored and analyzed entrants' motivations. This analysis reveals a few broad conclusions. To begin, both groups remained at least somewhat tied to their entering motivations. Cross tabulation showed that about two-thirds of entrants from each group maintained their primary general motives (altruistic or egoistic) throughout the two years of the study. In other words, a caseworker or police officer primarily motivated by altruism at Time 1 was very likely to report being so motivated at Time 5. This analysis also showed that during training, and after beginning their work, newcomers' entering motivations remained a strong, positive predictor of their subsequent motivations. This was especially true for police. In addition, racial identity remained a strong predictor of motivation for police even after entry. These findings are surprising because police socialization is typically depicted as strong. Also, police were, as a group, younger than entering caseworkers. Based on an understanding that personality stabilizes with age (see Chapter 2), and police socialization is strong, caseworkers would have seemed more likely to remain tied to their entering views.

The finding about race and the police is also important because many works have sought to understand how minority officers think and act once they become police officers (Wilkins and Williams 2008). At the outset of their careers, many black officers indicated an interest in providing better services to black communities or improving relations between their communities and the police. For instance, Reggie, a black entrant, commented, "I took [this job] because I like helping people and because I want to make a difference in my community." The findings here suggest that this motivation remained intact for many minority officers through the end of their second year inside the department. Interestingly, race was not a strong predictor of entering caseworkers' motivations.

On the organizational side, we see that training appeared to have an influence on both groups. Although it is difficult to tell for sure, the influence in both cases seemed to push entrants toward goals that the organization favored. Caseworkers influenced by training were more likely to be motivated by two of the goals of welfare reform, detecting fraud and helping clients find work; police influenced by training were more likely to be motivated by keeping order and treating people fairly. Thus, it appears that the resources spent by organizations to get entrants to think in particular ways had some effect. However, for the police, informal influences like peers and veterans also played an important developmental role. Although the effect of informal influences was initially ambiguous, by the end of the study police influenced by informal influences were less likely to report being motivated by altruistic motives.

In sum, we have the beginning of a portrait of how these two groups developed as they entered their organizations. We also have some idea of which factors shaped their thinking at different times. Now we turn to the second component of bureaucratic personality: bureaucratic identity.

CHAPTER 6

Bureaucratic Identity:
Rules and Loyalty

After two years on the force, Phillip, a white police officer who had previously served in the armed forces, described his approach to policing: "You gotta have a dual personality like you'll know when the good, honest, hardworking people you're dealing with, and I treat them like a good, honest person should be treated. But when I'm dealing with a crackhead, or if I'm dealing with somebody that I just locked up for something else, they're usually a bunch of assholes and so you tend to be an asshole to them too." Phillip's comments align nicely with the logic of appropriateness theory put forward by March and Olsen and suggest that understanding the actions of government officials requires grappling with their bureaucratic identities—the internal self-conceptions that they have about themselves as organization members. One of the goals of this book is to understand how such identities are formed. Some studies imply that workers bring their identities with them into their organizations (DeHart-Davis 2007; Kaufman 1960; O'Leary 2010; Portillo and DeHart-Davis 2009; Selden, Brudney, and Kellough 1998), while others suggest that they are built inside organizations (Maynard-Moody and Musheno 2003; Van Maanen 1975; Wilkins and Williams 2008).

This chapter brings evidence to bear on these competing expectations by studying how police officers and welfare caseworkers developed their bureaucratic identities during their first two years on the job. It analyzes entrants' general bureaucratic identities as well as their rule-following identities—their understanding of themselves vis-à-vis their organization's rules. In addition, the chapter asks about loyalty, the level of allegiance that entrants felt toward their organizations.

In short, the chapter shows evidence of change and continuity. Both sets of entrants shifted toward greater acceptance of discretion use and maintained their entering levels of loyalty to their departments. The main finding from the chapter's statistical analysis is that police and caseworker entrants remained strongly connected to the identities that they articulated at entry.

Police Officers' Bureaucratic Identities

Interviews

In my initial interviews, police discussed how they expected to act when they graduated from the academy and started work on the streets. The main theme from these conversations was that they envisioned themselves as authoritative professionals who would command respect. Commanding respect required having a good sense of right and wrong and being confident in your decisions. Essentially, cadets expected that they would enter difficult situations and would need to assert themselves. However, they recognized the limits of their authority: even though they would have power, and needed to show themselves as powerful, they also expected to act properly and show the public that they did not misuse their authority. Indeed, some indicated seeing themselves as merely the first step in the criminal justice system. For instance, David commented, "It's really not up to me to determine if a criminal goes to jail for ten years. That's up to the court system. It's up to me, though, to take that person into custody." As these comments suggest, entrants were conscious of their power and intended to use it. However, they did not see themselves as all-powerful.

The initial interviews also revealed that there were some differences across the group. Some entrants expected to be open and collaborative. To them, the goal was not to be a "bad ass," Rambo-type officer who was rough and brusque with people. Rather, they wanted to be "public servants" whom someone could approach with a problem; by not being a robot, they could show people that they cared. Other officers envisioned themselves as imperious figures whose authority would not be challenged. To these officers, interactions with the public were not an opportunity for dialogue but moments when police should impose their will. Those who were honest and cooperative may get a break, but the dishonest, argumentative, and disrespectful would not.

Another theme in these first interviews was that being a police officer meant walking a fine line between passivity and aggression. An officer who was too passive would get disrespected on the street, but an officer who was too aggressive would provoke fights and inflame already difficult situations. For instance, Reggie commented,

You can't go out there and be overly aggressive. But at the same time you can't be passive. If the situation warrants for you to go all hell, so be it. But, every situation is different and you've got to keep that in mind. . . . Even if you have to put your hand on someone, you do it in a respectful manner. It sounds funny, but it makes a lot of sense if you really think about it. And what I'm saying is if the situation calls for you to become physical, when I say you be respectful, I'm not saying you respect the person that you know, while you're being physical with them, you're nice, what I'm saying is that you don't do anything to disrespect yourself, you don't do anything to disrespect the organization that you represent, you don't do anything to disrespect your family. So you use the force that's necessary, but you don't go overboard. And then you stop when you have to stop, just enough. That's what I mean by being respectful even if you're physical.

Many cadets also indicated that they would take the high road when they interacted with the public. They knew that as police they would encounter abuse and that they might be tempted to retaliate. However, most indicated that they would be the type of officer who would not respond to negativity. Phillip said, "People can [curse] us and whatever they want as long as they're not breaking the law. Technically under the First Amendment they have that right. . . . So if someone's mother f-ing me and all that I'll say, 'Yes sir' and 'calm down.' I'm not gonna fall into being the same way they do because when you do that's when things get heated up, and that's when problems arise." This desire came, it seemed, from his loyalty to the department and his wish to protect its reputation.

Cadets also talked about how they saw themselves vis-à-vis the rules. The major rules-oriented theme at the outset was that they expected to be neutral agents who approached each situation the same and enforced the law equally. In this sense, cadets were articulating the Weberian ideal that like cases should be treated alike. Accordingly, deviations from neutrality were "unjust" or "profiling" and were therefore inappropriate. For example, one officer commented, "The main thing is just to be fair and impartial. You can't have any biases or prejudices against anything."

However, their entering sense of themselves and the rules also differed from Weber's "formalistic impersonality." Although they expected to enter situations neutrally, they were comfortable with the idea that they would then respond and treat each situation or case as appropriate. In other words, for entering police, appropriate behavior meant going into situations without any preconceptions and then making decisions based on interactions with individuals. In this way, they were able to balance the potentially competing notions of themselves as rule followers and discretion users. According to Reggie, "Well, you know, justice is supposed to be blind. So objectivity, it's pretty much what it is.... But, every situation is different and you've got to keep that in mind. You know, you can't talk to everyone the same way, but what you do is you always approach a situation or individual with the intent of being respectful." As this quotation shows, mirroring the comments of veterans in Chapter 3, a key part of police cadets' expectations of how they would act was tied to the situation. If the person whom they were dealing with was respectful and calm, they would be too. In this way they were able to see themselves as neutral but also responsive.

I again interviewed police entrants after they had spent a year in the department and had worked on the streets for six months. My goal at that time was to understand how they saw themselves acting on the job. Many new officers characterized themselves as powerful actors comfortable with exercising authority in difficult situations. Most also seemed generally positive about the department, even if some voiced the concern that the academy had not prepared them enough. However, I also discovered a few themes that I had not heard at the outset. Whereas police at Time 1 saw themselves as an important part of the criminal justice system, at Time 4 I detected that some saw their power and authority as more final. For example, one officer noted, "Being a police officer . . . you have to resolve and take control of all the different scenarios that go on in communities. That's what you got to do. Because there's . . . nobody else to call . . . there's nobody higher than the police. We come in and there's nobody higher to resolve the problem."

Another new theme that emerged after one year (Time 4) was the view that the police were "parents" to the "children" in the public. They understood their role as teaching the public about how to act and being the adult when people were behaving badly. For instance, in our second interview, Henry said, "The place where I work at, the place is reliant on the police. They're dependent on us and they don't know how to act unless we tell them how to act." This view of interactions with citizens was strikingly different from the collaborative image envisioned by some cadets at Time 1.

Echoing a theme from Chapter 3, at Time 4 some officers indicated that they felt disconnected from the messy, stressful situations that they encountered on the job. By disconnecting themselves in this way, officers indicated they could maintain emotional stability. For instance, Steven, a white officer in his mid-thirties, commented that he had learned to depersonalize. When I asked him what that meant, he said,

It means don't become emotionally involved like, "Oh my god this poor kid he's got it rough" or this [or] that occurred or . . . you can empathize and say, "I know what you're going through" and "I went through a similar instance" . . . but you can't get emotionally attached . . . to the citizens because you could be going through like sixteen to twenty extremely emotional instances within eight hours. You handle sixteen to eighteen jobs in eight hours and if you go through all that and get, not attached but, you get affected emotionally by all those, you'll get home at the end of the night feeling like you just went through a war. And that's how I felt when I first started. I'd come home and said man I don't feel like doing anything, I'm beat. And I realized I'm getting too emotionally affected by the situations. And now I go in and the person's all affected emotionally and they're talking in your face and you're supposed to get into that mode with them, but I'm not and I'm just like ok this person's going through this, that person's going through that. I can see their expression and I want to give them a sincere look and handle this in a respectful manner, but in the back of my head I really don't care. I don't care because I hear this all day. So that's how you become after being on the job, handling the jobs over time. And there's people that, there's nothing wrong with it, you know you're an emotional person or you see things emotionally or are affected emotionally, nothing wrong with that, but it'll have a greater toll on you stresswise being in those stressful situations all the time, so that's why I was saying stress management is very important.

For some police, then, emotional management was an important aspect of their development. Disconnecting emotionally was appropriate because getting involved in the details of every citizen's life would make the work too punishing.

In terms of the rules, most police at Time 4 reported acting as they had expected: they indicated being unbiased and neutral at the outset of encounters and then adjusting their actions and selves as appropriate. For example, Allen commented, "Each situation is different but you treat everyone with respect, I mean the same way you would with the next person. You just handle the situation differently. But at the same time it also depends on the type of attitude that they give you. But even if it is you get attitude from them, you want to keep it positive or as neutral as possible."

Though the police aimed for neutrality, I also detected a growing comfort that they, as authority figures, could reward the deserving and punish the undeserving. One officer noted that he dealt with "average" people differently from "criminals," and others noted that recidivists or the disrespectful would be loaded up with extra tickets or fines. As Phillip's quotation at the start of the chapter showed, he indicated being an "asshole" to "crackheads" and the like. In this way, some officers appeared to embrace the "low road" approach to policing that they wanted to avoid at the outset.

By Time 5, officers had spent two years in the department and had worked on the streets for a year and a half. At this time many felt connected to their partners and peers. However, as discussed in Chapter 4, some officers had soured on key aspects of the department like the academy, superiors, and veterans. When I asked entrants about how they saw themselves interacting with the public, many sounded like Steven—they depicted themselves as professional and calm but emotionally removed. Since their jobs required encountering difficult, volatile situations, these officers believed that their best approach was a cool, phlegmatic demeanor. For example, one officer indicated that he had developed a "thick skin," which was necessary when interacting with the public. Similarly, officers indicated that they were generally civil with the public, but that they could not be "Mr. Nice Guy" or "Officer Friendly" or else people would take advantage of them. In this approach to policing, officers believed that they could not be too willing to listen to people—in terms of both complaints and excuses—because "everyone has a story" and they would not be efficient or effective. As at Time 4, some officers also saw themselves as parents/teachers responsible for the tutelage and control of children/students.

In regard to themselves and the rules, police maintained the view that they articulated at Time 1: most saw themselves as neutral and using discretion. They understood themselves as entering situations neutrally, without bias or preconception, and adjusting or responding as they saw fit. In this way there was strong continuity throughout the study. For example, at Time 1 Reggie indicated an interest in being objective, responsive, and fair. Two years later he described himself as follows:

> Just fair. I take the same approach at all jobs and um I don't go into a job with a certain attitude. My attitude is developed once I get there. I'm not a passive individual, so if you come off at me a certain way I do kinda come back. Which I guess some people wouldn't call professional, but like I said it is what it is. . . . If I go into a hostile environment, I mean you go into any situation alert but if I go into a situation and I perceive it as hostile, I myself become hostile. You know what I'm saying, that way I'm better prepared to react if I have to react.

As Reggie shows, police articulated rule-following identities that enabled them to see themselves as neutral but responsive. Although an outsider might see this as bias, to police entrants this was the appropriate way of balancing potentially conflicting approaches to policing.

Surveys

To develop a more detailed portrait of police entrants' bureaucratic identities, I asked them to respond to the following statements and questions each time I surveyed them: "I am someone who follows the rules even if I don't agree with them"; "People and situations are unique and should be treated on a case-by-case basis"; "As a police officer it is important that things be done 'by the book' no matter what"; "Sometimes it's okay to bend the rules to help out a person who deserves it"; "When you think about being a police officer and enforcing the law, do you think you'll generally be lenient or strict?" (at Times 4 and 5: "As a police officer and enforcer of the law, do you think you're generally lenient or strict?"); "I would be harder on a criminal who had lots of opportunities in his life than one who didn't"; and "I feel a sense of loyalty to the [department]." These statements and questions were meant to explore entrants' views of themselves in relation to the department, its rules, and particular types of interactions with the public.

Figure 6.1 charts police entrants' answers to the statements and questions listed above. Focusing on the first five statements from the left, the general theme of this figure is that most police entrants initially saw their role as one of strict law enforcement: they would follow all rules, do things "by the book," and generally act objectively. As cadets entered the academy, interacted with instructors and peers, graduated, and began working on the streets, their views shifted. No longer did they see themselves as strict rule followers devoted to the administrative ideal of neutrality. Rather, they depicted themselves as less constrained, more lenient, and more willing to reward the deserving and punish the undeserving. It is notable that at Time 5, fewer than a third of entrants believed that things should be done "by the book," and over half indicated that they would bend the rules for a person who deserved it.

Interestingly, only one statement deviated from this general trend: throughout the project, at least 80 percent of police indicated that they agreed that people and situations were "unique" and should be treated on a "case-by-case" basis. The extended interviews, discussed above, provide some useful guidance in interpreting these findings: officers saw themselves as beginning interactions neutrally, but

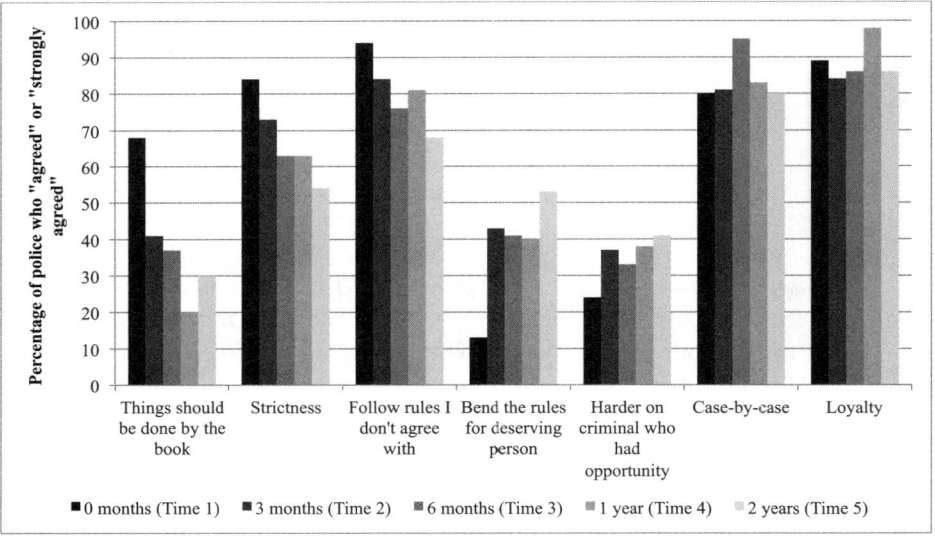

Figure 6.1. Police Bureaucratic Identity

then deviating as required by the situation. Although this may seem like a contradiction, it shows that most workers at the outset shared this logic. Over time, their devotion to the rules waned, but they retained their view that people should be treated on a case-by-case basis.

Another area where we see continuity as opposed to change is officer loyalty: there were high levels of loyalty over the course of their entry. At the outset, almost all cadets indicated feeling loyal to the department. Although Chapter 4 showed that some entrants had mixed views about training, and other elements of the department, the survey results suggest that they generally retained their feeling of loyalty to the department.

In addition, it is important to consider the spread of officers' responses to identity questions throughout the study to determine whether, as a group, officers' identities moved closer together (as the institutional perspective would expect) or diverged/remained static (as the dispositional perspective would expect). To do this, I examined the standard deviations of the population's responses to each identity question over time. This analysis revealed that for six of the seven questions, there was an increase in the standard deviation from Time 1 to Time 5.[1]

At Times 4 and 5, I presented entrants with a list of officer attributes: efficient, friendly, authoritative, investigative, respectful, sympathetic, skeptical, and responsive. I asked police to indicate the extent to which each attribute described them as they interacted with civilians on a 5-point scale from "none" to "a lot." In another section of the survey, I gave police entrants the same list of attributes and asked them to indicate the extent to which the department wanted them to act in these particular ways. This design facilitates comparison of entrants' self-descriptions with their views of how the department wanted them to act.

At Times 4 and 5, approximately two-thirds of officers saw themselves as efficient, authoritative, investigative, respectful, skeptical, and responsive. Over half of officers saw themselves as friendly, but fewer than half described themselves as sympathetic. In terms of the department, at both times approximately two-thirds of officers believed that the department wanted them to be efficient, friendly, authoritative, investigative, respectful, and responsive. Fewer than half believed that the department wanted them to be sympathetic or skeptical. Taken together, the identities officers articulated were aligned with the identities that they believed the department wanted them to have. The only area in which there was a major difference between how officers acted and how they perceived the department as wanting them to act was skepticism: most officers described themselves as skeptical, but relatively few believed that the department wanted them to act that way.

Thus far the survey data have been used to examine entrants' identity responses and note changes and continuities. Though useful for understanding population-wide trends, this approach isn't helpful for explaining individual-level change—due to nonresponse or attrition, the group of respondents was somewhat different at each time.[2] Consequently, I sought to understand the extent to which individual newcomers changed over the course of the project. To do this, I calculated the absolute value of the difference between each officer's entering and subsequent answers to the questions listed above. Figure 6.2 charts the mean change of officers' answers in scalar points; since the figure shows absolute values, each bar indicates total change, not change toward a particular position.[3]

This figure shows consistency and change over two years. On the consistency side, we see few radical changes across the questions. However, across almost every outcome we see gradual, increasing change. By the end of their second year, the mean change for two questions ("by the book" and "bend the rules") was 25 percent or greater. For example, at Time 1 the average score to the "by the book" question was 3.9 on a 5-point scale (agree); at Time 5 the average score was 3.0 (neutral). Recall from Chapter 5 that by the end of the second year, no motivation

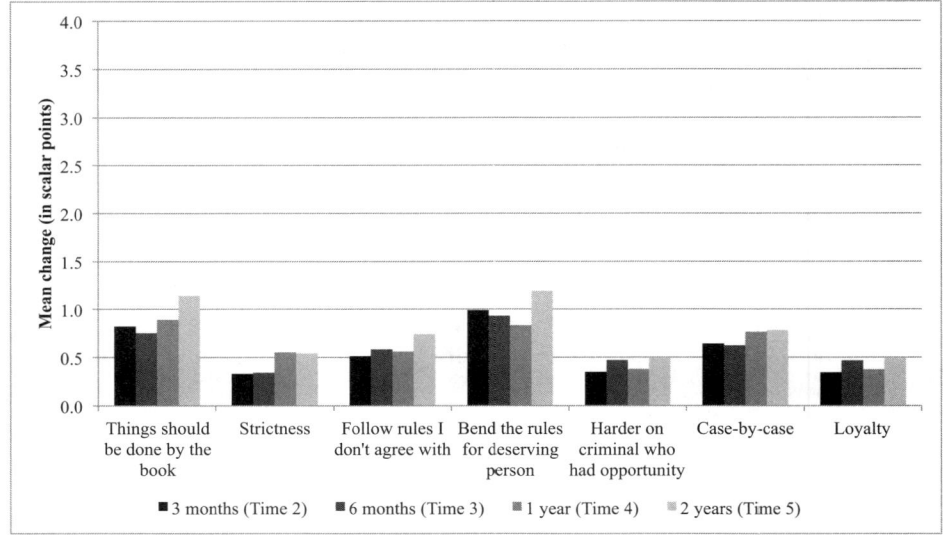

Note: $N = 64$–75, Time 2; $N = 61$–73, Time 3; $N = 37$–41, Time 4; $N = 44$–50, Time 5.

Figure 6.2. Police Bureaucratic Identity: Mean Individual Change

questions reached this average amount of change. Thus, there is evidence that police officers shifted their identities more than their motivations, but across all identity questions, the scope of change was modest.

Statistical Analysis

This section continues the inquiry by discussing the findings from a multivariate statistical analysis of officers' responses to identity survey questions.[4] As in Chapter 5, the statistical analysis was performed utilizing ordered probit and the figures present odds ratios (for interpretation information see the notes under Figure 6.3). Initially, the analysis examined the "real-time" relationship between independent and dependent variables. For example, it analyzed whether cadets influenced by training before graduation (Time 3) had different bureaucratic identities than those who were not. Such an analysis is useful for discussing the relationship between variables as they occurred. Second, the analysis examined the likelihood that police entrants would report different bureaucratic identities after entry. This part of the analysis used individual-level change data (calculated by taking the difference between newcomers' entering and subsequent responses) as dependent variables. Several points emerged from this analysis.

First, the strongest and most consistent predictors of police officers' identities were their entering identities. This strong continuity reveals a basic consonance with the analysis of police motivations in Chapter 5 and generally supports the expectations drawn from the dispositional perspective. For instance, consider Figure 6.3. Controlling for extraorganizational, informal organizational, and formal organizational influences (see the note to Figure 6.3 for a list of all model variables), an officer who indicated an interest in going "by the book" at entry was nearly four times more likely to indicate going "by the book" after two years inside the department. Similarly, entrants who indicated that they felt loyal to the department at entry were one time more likely to be loyal after two years. Although entering responses were significantly associated with subsequent responses in five of the seven questions, the figure also shows that this relationship may have receded. In five of the seven questions, the likelihood is lower at Time 5 than it was at Time 2.

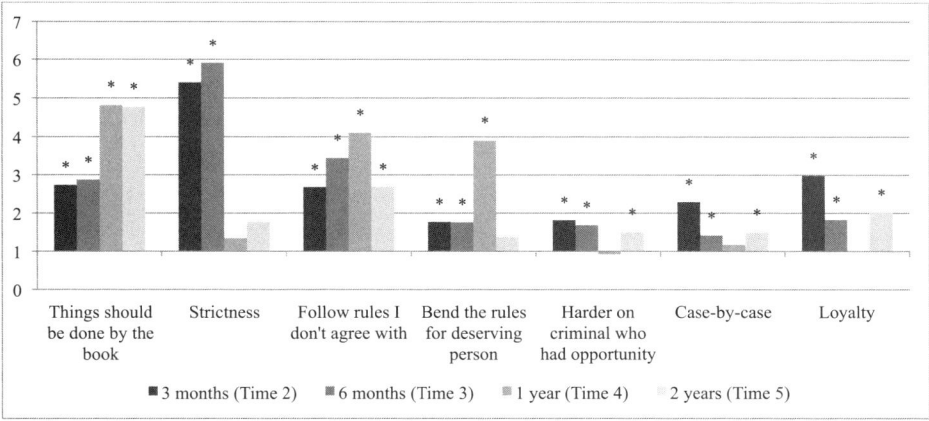

Note: This chart presents odds ratios calculated from multivariate ordered probit estimates. These ratios can be interpreted such that an increase of one unit of the independent variable (entering identity response) increases or decreases the chances of the dependent variable (subsequent identity response) by a certain amount, controlling for all other model variables (at Times 2 and 3 the model included education, age, pre-entry family income, welfare receipt, race, service in the armed forces, political ideology, academy instructors, culture, and academy peers; at Times 4 and 5 the model included education, age, pre-entry family income, welfare receipt, race, service in the armed forces, political ideology, academy training, department culture, supervisor, peers, veterans, amount of work, and monitoring). An odds ratio of 1 implies that the outcome is equally likely; an odds ratio of 1.25 indicates that the outcome is 0.25 times more likely due to an increase in the independent variable; an odds ratio of 0.75 indicates that the outcome is 0.25 times less likely due to an increase in the independent variable. An asterisk indicates that the underlying coefficient is statistically significant at the $p < .05$ level. $N = 56–62$, Time 2; $N = 55–60$, Time 3; $N = 32–35$, Time 4; $N = 38–41$, Time 5.

Figure 6.3. Predicting Police Bureaucratic Identity: Entering Bureaucratic Identity

The second major theme to emerge from the analysis is, like in Chapter 5, the relative unimportance of extraorganizational, demographic influences. Throughout the period of entry, including Time 1, entrants of different ages, education levels, and class experiences, for example, did not have statistically different bureaucratic identities. In particular, it was surprising to note that military veterans did not have significantly distinct rule-following identities. Due to their experiences in organizations that emphasize obedience, I expected veteran entrants to be more likely to identify as strict rule followers. Although there were particular times in which veterans saw themselves as more "by the book" than others, in general there were few strong patterns throughout the study.

As in Chapter 5, the influence of the organization was slow to emerge. Based on the police socialization literature, it was expected that entry would be a time in which cadets quickly adopted new identities and that influences from the organization would be strongly associated with their new identities. As seen in Figures 6.1 and 6.2, there was some modest change in this area during the first three months of

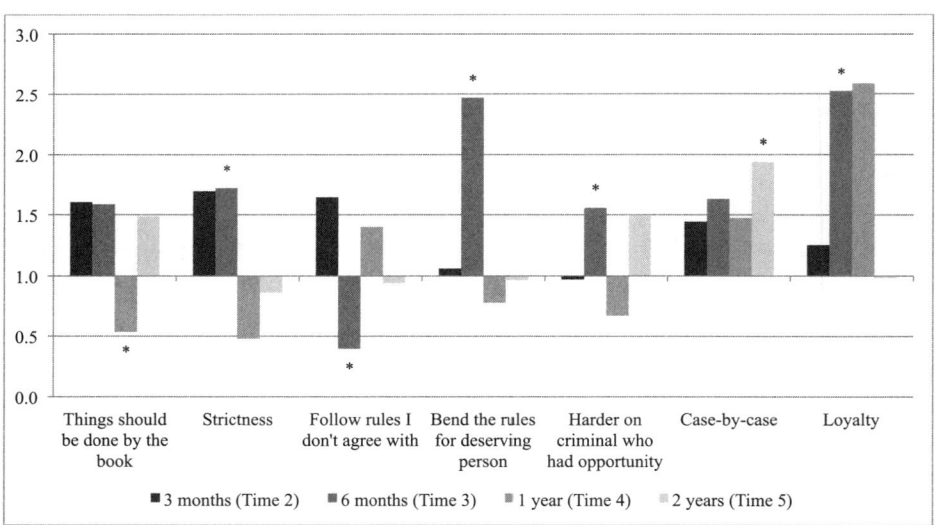

Note: This chart presents odds ratios calculated from multivariate ordered probit estimates. These ratios can be interpreted such that an increase of one unit of the independent variable (culture) increases or decreases the chances of the dependent variable (identity response) by a certain amount, controlling for all other model variables (see the note to Figure 6.3 for a list of each model's variables and for further information about interpretation of odds ratios). An asterisk indicates that the underlying coefficient is statistically significant at the $p < .05$ level. $N = 56–62$, Time 2; $N = 55–60$, Time 3; $N = 32–35$, Time 4; $N = 38–41$, Time 5.

Figure 6.4. Predicting Police Bureaucratic Identity: Culture

the academy (Time 2). However, the statistical analysis revealed few strong associations between organizational influences and cadets' responses to bureaucratic identity questions at that time. Nonetheless, toward the end of the academy (Time 3), the analysis showed that an informal influence, culture, was a consistent predictor of cadets' responses. Substantively, culture appears to push cadets in ambiguous ways. For instance, as seen in Figure 6.4, cadets who indicated being affected by the academy's culture at Time 3 were 0.70 times more likely to indicate that they would be strict enforcers, but 0.60 times less likely to indicate that they follow rules with which they didn't agree. Although culture appeared to be a strong influence at Time 3, the figure also shows that after graduating from the academy the department culture was not a strong predictor of officers' responses.

After graduation from the academy, cadets were assigned to districts around the city and partnered with veterans who were expected to teach them more about the job. In Chapter 4, and the broader policing literature, there is evidence that police veterans play an important role in shaping graduates' views about how to

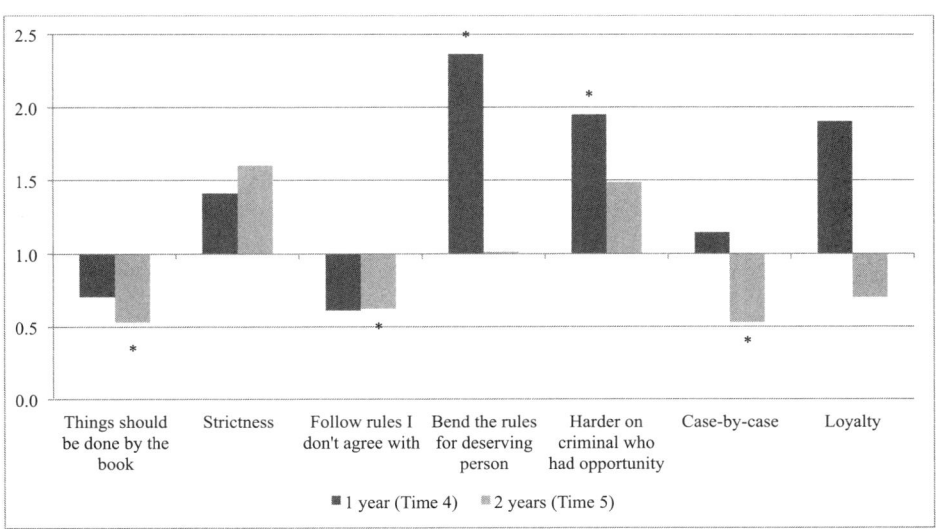

Note: This chart presents odds ratios calculated from multivariate ordered probit estimates. These ratios can be interpreted such that an increase of one unit of the independent variable (veterans) increases or decreases the chances of the dependent variable (identity response) by a certain amount, controlling for all other model variables (see the note to Figure 6.3 for a list of each model's variables and for further information about interpretation of odds ratios). An asterisk indicates that the underlying coefficient is statistically significant at the $p < .05$ level. $N = 56$–62, Time 2; $N = 55$–60, Time 3; $N = 32$–35, Time 4; $N = 38$–41, Time 5.

Figure 6.5. Predicting Police Bureaucratic Identity: Police Veterans

be a police officer. The analysis shown in Figure 6.5 reveals some support for this perspective. For example, after six months in their districts (Time 4), officers who were influenced by veterans were 1.4 times more likely to agree that bending the rules for a deserving person is acceptable and 0.95 times more likely to agree that they would be harder on a criminal who had lots of opportunity in life. Substantively, this same trend continued at the two-year mark (Time 5): police influenced by veterans were 0.45 less likely to agree that things should be done "by the book" and 0.38 less likely to agree that they follow rules with which they disagree. Although this evidence suggests that veterans may have played an important role in shaping the identities of incoming officers, it is important to note that compared with entering responses (Figure 6.3), experienced workers were a less consistent and less strong influence.

One of the key ways that police departments maintain accountability is via monitoring—finding ways to chart the actions that officers take as they complete their official duties. Monitoring the police has always been a difficult task since they operate outside of the gaze of superiors. Though modern police statistics systems have tried to create more accountability, police are often asked to produce the materials (paperwork) that will be used to assess their performance.[5] Thus, it was interesting to see that when controlling for many other extraorganizational and organizational factors, monitoring had a small and inconsistent relationship with officers' responses to identity questions. For example, at Times 4 and 5, there was one statistically significant relationship between monitoring and the questions listed above (loyalty). As such, there is little evidence here to support the view that variation in monitoring is associated with the bureaucratic identities that police articulated.

Finally, the analysis also examined which variables, if any, helped explain entrants' likelihood of altering their responses. In these tests, the dependent variable was the difference between newcomers' entering and subsequent responses to bureaucratic identity questions. The analysis showed that there was no single dominant explanation for change or stability. Rather, the likelihood of changing one's identity responses was inconsistently associated with an array of variables. After three months inside the academy, there were few strong institutional predictors of changed response. However, as cadets neared graduation, culture emerged as a significant influence. In these cases, cadets who indicated that they had been influenced by the academy's culture were more likely to indicate that they were comfortable exercising discretion. After graduation, there were no strong institutional predictors of officers' likelihood of providing new responses to bureaucratic identity survey questions.

Of the dispositional variables, again there was no single dominant predictor of change. However, some variables were more strongly associated with change than others. During their first year on the force, those who had served in the armed forces altered their responses at somewhat different rates than those who hadn't. In general, as the group shifted toward embracing discretion, former members of the armed services were more likely to retain a by-the-book approach to policing. However, at the end of the second year, there were no differences between veterans of the armed services and nonveterans. Education was also related to the likelihood of change. Oddly, its effect was variable: for some questions higher-educated entrants were more likely to adopt new views, and in some cases they were less likely to do so. In terms of the rules, education didn't have a uniform relationship in predicting changes.

With this account complete, we turn to welfare caseworker entrants and their identities during their first two years on the job.

Welfare Caseworkers' Bureaucratic Identities

Interviews

As shown in Chapter 5, most caseworkers were initially drawn to work in welfare because of the benefits and stability offered by the job. However, some had secondary altruistic motivations. For instance, some caseworker entrants who had previously received welfare hoped to become "good" caseworkers who were pleasant and did not act like it was their money they were giving away. Did they meet this goal and become this type of worker? This section addresses this question and others like it by describing caseworkers' identities and expectations at the outset of their careers and then tracing them over two years of the study.

At the outset of their careers, many entrants expected to be good, positive caseworkers. For example, one caseworker envisioned herself as polite and respectful and expected to treat welfare recipients like the customers whom she had served when she worked at a retail store. Others, who came directly from receiving assistance, vowed to be better caseworkers than the ones whom they had interacted with in the past. In essence, they wanted to be approachable, sensitive, and connected to the people whom they served.

Like police academy cadets, entering welfare caseworkers had a complicated view of what was appropriate conduct vis-à-vis the rules. Initially, nearly all caseworkers indicated allegiance to the idea of themselves as neutral, rule-following agents. In this version, welfare applicants were expected to provide the necessary paperwork and verification, and the caseworkers would give them benefits if they were eligible. For example, Mary indicated that she saw herself as a "by-the-book . . . compliance person" who would be nonjudgmental as long as welfare recipients complied with the rules. Abigail drew on her prior work as a nurse in describing her allegiance to neutrality: "Well, having been a nurse you're not allowed to be prejudicial, you have to treat everyone equally. So that's kind of engrained in the back of my skull. Everyone gets treated the same, they're all entitled to the same programs if they qualify, if they meet the eligibility."

Despite allegiance to the rules, many also indicated a strong desire to help people and an interest in finding ways to reward those who deserved it. Ralph indicated that he would treat people the same until he learned how to work the system more effectively so he could carve out exceptions for people in need. Others noted that they hoped that they would treat people neutrally but suspected that they might not. Some workers indicated wanting to help those who needed it even if it meant risking trouble. As this impulse hints, entrants expected to have some power in their work—giving advice or guidance, extra information, or special treatment.

Though they reported seeing themselves and their future selves positively at the outset, few entrants indicated feeling loyal to the organization. This is not to say that at the outset no workers felt connected to the agency. Maurice noted that it was not part of his identity, but he felt connected because he drew his salary from them. Heather felt connected because she realized she would now be seen as a lazy government employee. Nonetheless, especially when compared with the police, there was fairly limited loyalty to the welfare department at the outset of their careers.

After training, welfare caseworker entrants left the training facility and began their work. In a variety of ways, my interviews suggested that the identities that they developed differed from the ones that they expected to develop. At the most general level, the identities that caseworkers reported at Times 4 and 5 were less oriented around helping than the identities that they imagined when they started. Although no workers described themselves as "bad" or "mean," many described themselves as tough, investigative, and judgmental after a year or two on the job. The goal for many workers was to convey to applicants that they were not "playing games" so that when they gave applicants directions, they would do as they were told. Caseworkers indicated that they needed to project a tough side and be willing to close clients' cases for failure to provide verification. If they did not act that way, clients would lie or procrastinate and prevent them from processing their cases.

This fear of being deceived played an important role in caseworker development. In essence, workers found that they needed to develop strategies or selves to defend themselves against the clients' tricks and scams. Evelyn indicated that she initially was giving welfare applicants the benefit of the doubt, but had to shift her approach after being burned many times. "Now, now I tend to say, my attitude is prove to me that you need it. I used to say get me this or that. Now I say you prove to me that you deserve it. . . . The burden of proof is on you and I don't feel bad by saying: 'I'm not buying that story. It doesn't sound right. It don't make good sense. So call me up when you get your stuff.'" Terrell indicated that he would play the "nice guy" in interacting with clients because he was wary that they were lying to him. Once they felt comfortable with him, he would try to discover information that would disqualify them for benefits.

Although many expected to be able to have some impact on individuals, few reported feeling powerful after becoming caseworkers. Rather, echoing veteran caseworkers in Chapter 3, entrant caseworkers tended to feel like they were not able to reach individuals or provide many services. Interestingly, for some workers this powerlessness related to their inability to punish clients who did not do as they were instructed. This feeling of impotence was driven in part by the recognition that if the client challenged a caseworker's decisions, or made an appeal, the caseworker would not be supported by administrators.

Though many caseworker entrants felt impotent, in our conversations I would occasionally get glimpses of a different reality in which they had real power to affect individual welfare claimants. For instance, Mary described her supervisor as "generous" and "client-oriented" but also rigid when it comes to ensuring compliance with rules and regulations. In some cases, Mary would challenge her supervisor's instructions and defend the interests of the claimant:

> There are days when [my supervisor says], "No . . . just go ahead and close them [end their benefits]." But I know the client better than her because I work with the client directly so because I work with the client I have to use my judgment in that area. Because [my supervisor is] just looking at information on a piece of paper she doesn't deal with the person so I can't do that to the person . . . [so] I get right in there and say what I have to say. And what I've found out is that with [my supervisor], her decisions are solely based on what she sees on paper and so if you don't remind her that, "No, she really did this," or "No, we really talked about this," she's only going to go by what she sees on paper. So you have to go in and fight for what you know because sometimes she's wrong.

Aside from their relative potency, the ambiguous feeling that entrants reported at Time 1—wanting to be neutral and wanting to treat people individually—continued at Times 4 and 5. For example, one caseworker indicated that he was strict, but not with everyone; another indicated being strict, but only with those who had been on welfare a long time. Jessica, repeating the words of training instructors, indicated seeing herself as policy incarnate—"I'm always policy, whatever policy is." However, she also indicated that she was willing to diverge from the norm when appropriate. Although some workers indicated that they saw themselves as by the book or treating all of their clients the same, they also provided stories indicating special attention or bending of the rules for some clients. For example, Mary, who above indicated fighting for particular clients, also said, "I actually just follow policy. I'm not going to lie." Like the police then, caseworkers appeared to be comfortable with treating people the same but also making exceptions. In this way they saw themselves as responding to individuals and the rules.

Another important development during their first two years on the job was an emotional detachment that caseworkers reported in their interactions with claimants. For example, Evelyn said, "I think this job, more than any I've ever had, I'm not able to show who I am. I believe that the job itself dictates that more than any other job I've ever had. In other words I can't really be a person. I have to be a case manager. I got to be policy. In other words I should be walking policy." There were a variety of ways in which caseworkers described this general approach—professional, pleasant but not nice, and impersonal—but the sentiment was the same. In order to do their jobs effectively, many workers indicated that they had to disconnect themselves emotionally from clients. For those workers who were not drawn to the work to help others, this was fairly easy. But since some workers were drawn to welfare, at least partly out of a desire to help, this was difficult.

To highlight this development, it is useful to consider one worker who was unable to emotionally disconnect from the job. Karen was an African American female who grew up in a poor working-class family with many siblings.[6] She began her career in welfare at an older age than most because she needed extra income. She also wanted to help. By her own admission, she quickly became overwhelmed upon leaving training and encountering the public. She felt that she never got a handle on her caseload or developed an efficient way of interacting with clients because she was unable to stop caring. Karen was surprised by the actions and attitudes of other workers in the office: "They'd have stacks and stacks of papers on their desks and they'd be like . . . 'I ain't worried about that. I get to it when I get to it. If their benefits get suspended I will reinstate.' There was no human conscientiousness about the caseworkers and no feelings. And they'd tell me you have to disconnect your feelings from the job." In response, I asked her if she was able to do that.

> In most cases no. [Other caseworkers] would tell me . . . "you got to separate yourself from the job." . . . They knew that job wasn't for me. After a while they could tell and they knew I couldn't disconnect myself from it. But then again they didn't know [that I grew up poor]. . . . [So] I was under a lot of stress. My hair fell out, I was getting rashes on my skin, on my face, on my nose and I didn't realize what it was until the doctor told me it was stress. I was losing sleep and I just couldn't even concentrate I was forgetting stuff so bad. The job became my, the job became my albatross. I'm serious. I'd take it home. I'd dread walking into work that day. I really did.

Near the end of her first year, Karen gave the job one last chance by trying to disconnect from the clients. She also began working unpaid and unreported overtime and taking work home with her at night and on weekends. On many days she skipped lunch to keep working. When I asked how she saw herself at this point, she responded, "While I was working I changed. I became a different person. I started disliking the clients. I started disliking my supervisor. I dreaded coming to work. I was to the point where I hated the job. I liked the money but I hated the job. . . . I actually disconnected myself from the whole welfare system: the money, the clients, everything. I became a robot just going in and doing what you have to do and get out." Eventually, after nearly having a nervous breakdown on the job, she quit.

Although Karen's case is extreme, it highlights the importance of emotional detachment. It also may suggest that the caseworkers who were able to continue on in the job were better able to emotionally compartmentalize than those who could not. Whatever the reason, after a year or two many caseworker trainees indicated a detachment from the people whom they served. To them, the job was just a job which, after 5 P.M., they left.

Surveys

To develop a more detailed portrait of caseworker entrants' bureaucratic identities, I asked them to respond to the following statements and questions at each time: "It is important that things be done 'by the book' no matter what"; "When you think about being a caseworker, do you think you'll generally be lenient or strict?" (at Times 4 and 5 the question was "In managing your caseload, do you think you're generally lenient or strict?"); "I intend to go out of my way to help certain clients that really need help" (at Times 4 and 5 the statement was "I go out of my way to help certain clients that really need help"); "I am someone who follows the rules even if I don't agree with them"; "Sometimes it's okay to bend the rules to help out a person who deserves it"; "People and situations are unique and should be treated on a case-by-case basis"; "One of my job duties is to punish clients who are scamming the system"; "I feel a sense of loyalty to the [welfare department]"; and "My job with [the welfare department] is an important part of who I am." These statements were meant to explore entrants' views of themselves in relation to the department, its rules, and particular types of interactions with the public. Figure 6.6 charts caseworker entrants' answers to identity statements.[7]

This figure shows evidence of change and continuity. From the first days of their careers until the end of their second year, most caseworkers agreed that people and situations should be treated case by case. However, they also consistently believed that in interacting with clients, they followed rules with which they

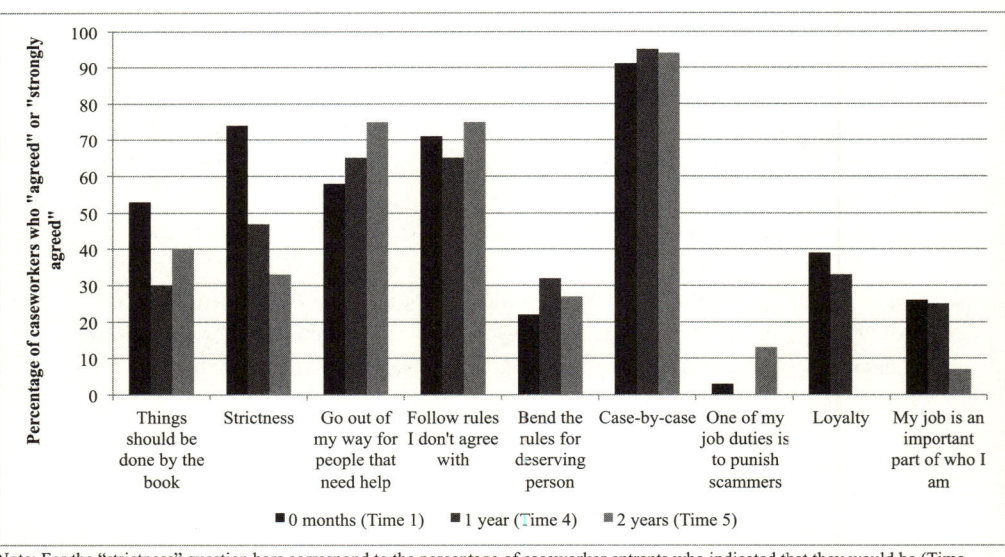

Note: For the "strictness" question bars correspond to the percentage of caseworker entrants who indicated that they would be (Time 1) or were (Times 4–5) more strict than lenient (choices 4–5) on a 5-point scale. $N = 28$–34, Time 1; $N = 17$–20, Time 4; $N = 15$–16, Time 5.

Figure 6.6. Caseworker Bureaucratic Identity

disagreed and would not bend the rules even for a deserving client. At each time few caseworkers saw punishing scammers as one of their job responsibilities

Nonetheless, we do see some changes. On the left side of the figure we see that, after entry, fewer caseworkers agreed that things had to be done "by the book" or that they were strict. Also, at each time there was an increase in the percentage of caseworkers who said that they go out of their way for a client who deserves help. At first blush, this desire would seem to contradict earlier findings about emotional disengagement. However, it is important to recall that workers indicated retaining an interest in helping the deserving. Putting these two trends together, we get a sense of how caseworkers saw themselves at the outset and how their views changed. Initially they saw themselves as bound by the rules and law but wanting to treat people individually. They continued to see the rules as serious but also saw themselves as able to treat people individually by not going "by the book" or acting strictly.

On the right side of the figure we see how caseworkers saw themselves vis-à-vis the job and how loyal they felt toward their organization. Whereas at least 80 percent of the police felt loyal to the department throughout their first two years, the percentage of caseworkers feeling loyal began under 40 percent. From there, at each subsequent time, the percentage dropped until Time 5, when no caseworkers indicated a sense of loyalty to the department. Similarly, approximately a quarter of entering caseworkers initially saw the job as an important part of who they were, but this figure dropped to less than 10 percent by Time 5.

In addition, it is important to consider the spread of caseworkers' responses to identity questions throughout the study to determine whether their identities moved closer together or diverged/remained static. To do this, I examined the standard deviations of the population's responses to each identity question over time. This analysis revealed that in five of the nine questions, there was an increase or no change in the standard deviation from Time 1 to Time 5.

At Times 4 and 5, I presented entrants with a list of caseworker attributes: efficient, friendly, skeptical, investigative, and respectful. For each, I asked entrants to indicate the extent to which each described them as they interacted with clients. In another section of the survey I gave entrants the same list of attributes and asked them to indicate the extent to which the department wanted them to act in each particular way. This enables a comparison of entrants' self-descriptions with their views of how the department wanted them to act.

Approximately two-thirds of these caseworkers viewed themselves as efficient, friendly, and respectful at Times 4 and 5. Few saw themselves as skeptical as they interacted with clients. These data seem somewhat at odds with the interview data discussed above. In particular, it was surprising to see that so many caseworkers saw themselves as friendly when one of the themes of the interviews was that caseworkers were emotionally removed from clients. The explanation for this may be in how caseworkers understood the term "friendly"; in their version, friendly may mean pleasant but not emotionally connected. In terms of the department, approximately two-thirds of entrants believed that the department wanted to them to be efficient, investigative, and respectful. The major differences between how they saw themselves and how they believed the department wanted them to act were in regard to skepticism and friendliness. Most caseworkers described themselves as friendly, even though they did not think the department wanted them to be, and few described themselves as skeptical, although approximately a third believed that the department wanted them to be. This analysis suggests that there was less bureaucratic identity congruence in the welfare department in comparison to the police department.

Though useful for understanding population-wide trends, the above analysis is limited in explaining individual-level change because, due to nonresponse or attrition, the group of respondents was somewhat different in each wave.[8] As such, I sought to understand the extent to which individual newcomers altered their

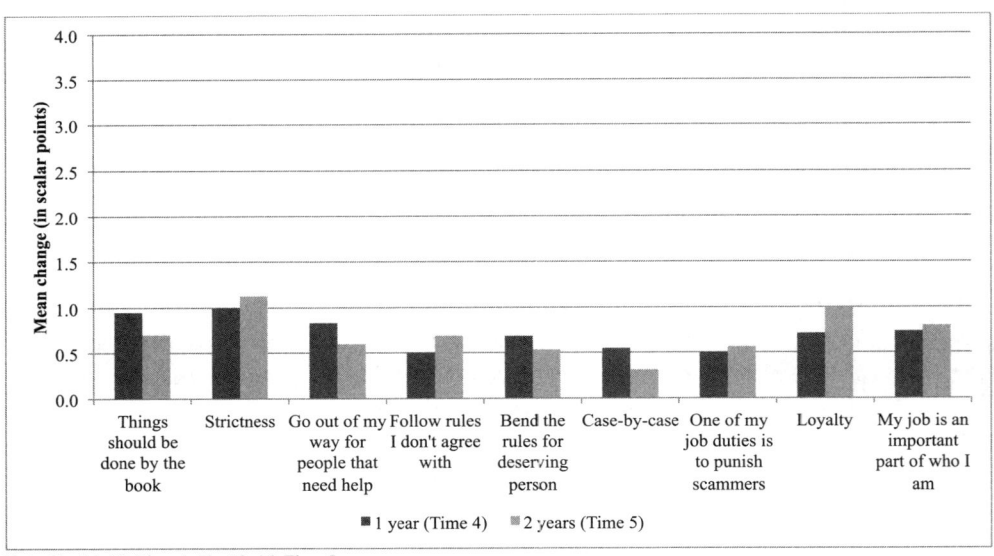

Note: N = 14–20, Time 4; N = 12–16, Time 5.

Figure 6.7. Caseworker Bureaucratic Identity: Mean Individual Change

answers over the course of the project. To do this, I calculated the absolute value of the difference between each caseworkers' entering and subsequent responses. Figure 6.7 charts the mean change of caseworkers' responses in scalar points. Since the figure shows absolute values, each bar indicates total change, not change toward a particular position.[9]

This figure shows some consistency and some change. In eight of the nine questions there was relative stability (25 percent change or less) from entry to the end of the second year; also, in four of the nine questions there was a decrease in change by the end of the second year. Illustrating this, we see that the mean response to the "case-by-case" question at Time 1 was 4.6 and at Time 5 was 4.3. Both responses are between agree and strongly agree on the 5-point scale.[10] Also, compared with the police, there appeared to be less movement in caseworkers' responses to bureaucratic identity questions over the course of the study. Consequently, the descriptive data about caseworkers' identities suggest support for the dispositional approach.

Statistical Analysis

To continue the inquiry, this section discusses the findings from a bivariate statistical analysis of caseworkers' responses to bureaucratic identity survey questions.[11] The statistical analysis utilized ordered probit as an estimation tool and presents the findings from odds ratio calculations (for interpretation information see the notes to Figure 6.3). As with the police, it examined the "real-time" relationship between independent and dependent variables and the likelihood that caseworker entrants would give different responses to bureaucratic identity survey questions after entry. There are a variety of points that emerged from this analysis.

As with the police, there was evidence of considerable continuity: at the one- and two-year points of the study, caseworker entrants remained strongly connected to their entering identities. Figure 6.8 summarizes the relationships between caseworkers' entering and subsequent responses to identity questions. In six of nine questions, after a year inside the department (Time 4), entrants' early responses were strong, positive predictors of their subsequent answers. For instance, entrants who indicated that they would follow rules with which they didn't agree at entry were 1.4 times more likely to follow rules at Time 4. On the other side of the discretion coin, entrants who indicated that they would bend the rules for deserving clients were, at Time 4, approximately 1.0 time more likely to indicate that they do so as caseworkers.

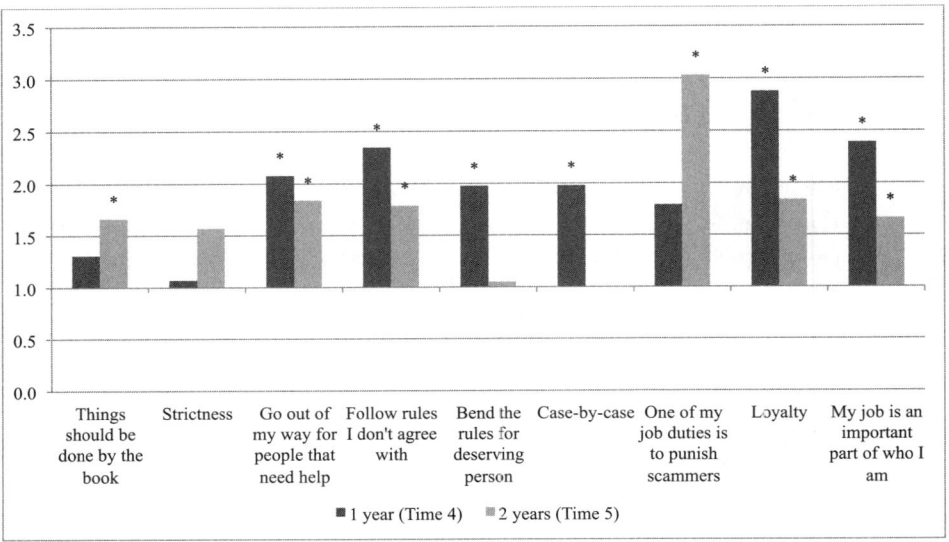

Note: This chart presents odds ratios calculated from bivariate ordered probit estimates. These ratios can be interpreted such that an increase of one unit of the independent variable (entering identity response) increases or decreases the chances of the dependent variable (subsequent identity response) by a certain amount (see the note to Figure 6.3 for further information about interpretation of odds ratios). An asterisk indicates that the underlying coefficient is statistically significant at the $p < .05$ level. $N = 14–20$, Time 4; $N = 12–16$, Time 5.

Figure 6.8. Predicting Caseworker Bureaucratic Identity: Entering Bureaucratic Identity

After two years, the strength of the relationship between newcomers' entering and subsequent bureaucratic identity answers receded (compared to Time 4) in six of nine questions. In other words, entrants' initial expectations about how they would act were weaker predictors of their stated ways of being at Time 5. However, given the small number of respondents by this time, and the difficulty of achieving statistical significance, it is impressive that their entering responses were positive, statistically significant predictors of subsequent identity answers in six of nine questions.

In addition, the analysis revealed some connections between extraorganizational influences and caseworkers' bureaucratic identity responses. For example, after a year inside the department, female caseworkers saw themselves somewhat differently than male caseworkers: women were approximately four times more likely to see themselves as efficient and respectful while interacting with recipients. Similarly, even after entry, white caseworkers were less likely to see themselves as strict or investigative. These findings complement the comments reported in Chapter 4 about the importance of race and gender in welfare casework. Specifically, interview respondents said that only black women could be effective caseworkers because others were "naïve" toward client "shenanigans." Although not all extraorganizational influences were strong predictors—age in particular was not—taken in sum, the analysis showed some support for the expectations set forth in the dispositional perspective.

Another theme that emerged in the analysis was the inconsistent and insignificant relationships between organizational factors and caseworkers' views of themselves vis-à-vis the organization. For instance, at the one-year point (Time 4), caseworker entrants had completed six months of classroom training and approximately six months of probationary training under the careful tutelage of a training supervisor. By entrants' own words (Chapter 4), their training supervisors had a big influence on how they operated as caseworkers. Despite this, caseworkers indicating that training or supervisors shaped their actions were just as likely to be rule followers or discretion users as those who indicated that these influences did not affect them. Although there were some instances in which an organizational influence was associated with caseworkers' identities, these relationships were inconsistent and, in comparison to the strength of the association between entering and subsequent responses, weak.

Finally, there were few strong, consistent predictors of caseworkers' likelihood of altering their responses to bureaucratic identity questions. This was true for demographic characteristics like age, race, and gender that are commonly thought to have a stabilizing effect on entrants' bureaucratic identities. For example, throughout the study female caseworker entrants were just as likely to maintain their identity responses as male entrants. Some institutional variables were more associated with the likelihood of change than others; in particular, variables capturing the effects of supervisors and the culture were associated with adopting new bureaucratic identities. However, the strength and consistency of these relationships varied, and no coherent trends emerged from the analysis.

Conclusion

In this book's bureaucratic personality concept, and March and Olsen's logic of appropriateness theory, identity plays a central role. As organization members confront a situation they must assess the situation and people they are interacting with and choose an appropriate self. This chapter contributes by describing and explaining a variety of possible selves that entrants developed over their first two years on the job. Comparing the two groups, we see some similarities and some differences. At least some members of both groups developed detached, professional identities that deemphasized personal connections with civilian-clients. This shift may have been an effort in stress reduction or emotional protection for workers entering jobs where they encountered endless reservoirs of need. By removing themselves from the human dramas unfolding before them they may have been able to better process large numbers of people each day. In addition, both groups began their work with nuanced views about themselves and the rules: they expected to be neutral at the outset of encounters and then respond based on the nature of the interaction. Although both groups shifted away from seeing themselves as "by the book," by and large they maintained these approaches to administration. In this way, they saw themselves as "unbiased" and "responsive."

Moreover, the analyses in the latter half of each section showed that both groups remained strongly connected to their entering bureaucratic identities. Although this connection appeared to wane in some areas, it was the strongest and most consistent predictor of entrants' bureaucratic identity responses at each time I surveyed them. This is an impressive development for organizational newcomers who entered situations in which they were bombarded with messages by organizations that were consciously trying to shape their thinking and ways of acting. Coupled with the findings from Chapter 5, which suggested that entrants' Time 1 motivations remained strong predictors of their subsequent motivations, we see a pattern of continuity across two aspects of bureaucratic personality.

In terms of the institutional perspective, the chapter shows some instances in which organizational influences were associated with entrants' views. This was especially true for the police. As in Chapter 5, informal influences played an important role in shaping police entrants. Substantively, the police culture appeared to send ambiguous messages about rule following. Veterans, in contrast, had a clearer effect on entrants' identity responses: pushing rookies away from the rules and toward discretion. On the welfare side, there were few strong, consistent organizational influences on entrants' identity responses.

It is also important to consider what this chapter's findings imply for the traditional understanding of the term "bureaucratic personality." Recall from Chapter 1 that midcentury accounts expected that organization entrants would become process-loving rule followers after encountering their organization's social forces. In this chapter, there was little support for this expectation. In fact, we see that entrants' devotion to the rules waned over time. Rather than becoming rule followers they moved, in many cases, toward identities that emphasized discretion. This does not mean they saw the rules or laws as unimportant. However, in both cases we saw a shift away from the by-the-book neutrality that the traditional bureaucratic personality thesis expects will develop inside bureaucracies.

Based on this chapter and Chapter 5, we now have a good sense about how these two groups developed by the end of their second year. However, the logic of appropriateness, as described in Chapter 1, suggests that who organization members choose to be depends considerably on how they read the people and situations that they encounter on a daily basis. Since this chapter showed workers moving toward using discretion, it reemphasized the importance of understanding entrants' attitudes about the world and the people whom they serve. It is to this topic that we turn in the next chapter.

CHAPTER 7

Attitudes:
Social Problems, Race, and Deservingness

The first time that we spoke, Mary talked at length about other caseworkers whom she had observed.

> What I have seen is some of the [caseworkers] are very biased in their thinking. . . . And because of their way of thinking they treat people kind of bad. But you have other workers who the clients are so many, and the caseload is so high, that they just gotta get it done, get it done, get it done. So they're just disconnecting themselves from the person under the record number because they've just gotta get it done. . . . So we have all these different kinds of people in the office, and you hear all these things that you have to close your ears and not let the biases scare you and not let the high caseload scare you. And just come in here with my mind made up that I'm here to help and I'll do it for as long as I can. Because I've heard some negative things. I've heard them say . . . all clients are on welfare because their mothers are on welfare, their aunts on welfare. That's not true. I know that's not true. So you have to be careful what you allow to get into your psyche.

By linking caseworkers' attitudes and actions, Mary implicitly invokes March and Olsen's logic of appropriateness theory and highlights the importance of studying bureaucrats' attitudes. As shown in Chapter 4, Mary's sympathetic views match the messages sent by the welfare department trainers during training. However, they are in stark contrast to the views expressed by experienced caseworkers in Chapter 3. Did Mary adopt new views about welfare clients after beginning work and interacting with clients? Did police entrants adopt new views about crime and poverty as a result of their experiences during entry?

This chapter answers questions like these by cataloguing entrants' attitudes at entry and following their evolution over the course of two years. Because street-level bureaucrats play a particularly significant role in the lives of low-income people, this chapter focuses on workers' views about poverty, criminality, and racial inequality. In each of these areas, the chapter conceives of entrants' views as falling somewhere on a continuum from structural to individual. Structural explanations of social problems point to macro forces beyond an individual's control; individual explanations locate responsibility for problems on people's choices and character (Reingold and Liu 2009; W. Wilson 1996). Given that street-level bureaucrats have a significant amount of discretion, and prior research suggests that they use it to reward the deserving and punish the undeserving (Maynard-Moody and Musheno 2003), the chapter also charts entrants' views about deservingness.

Descriptively, the chapter shows that police officers altered their views about the causes of criminality and welfare caseworkers developed skepticism about the role played by racism in limiting minorities in society. In this way, they both moved toward adopting individual-centered views. However, changes for both groups were modest, and the chapter's main finding is that entrants largely remained connected to their entering attitudes throughout the course of the study.

Police Officers' Attitudes

Interviews

At the outset of their careers, police cadets focused on one main theme in determining the deservingness of the civilians with whom they would interact: their demeanor. They expected to go easier on civilians whom they judged to be pleasant; those who were rude or ill-tempered would not receive a break and might even be punished. In particular, they saw civilians who were polite, honest, apologetic, and passive as deserving. In essence, even at the outset of their careers, police had positive views about people who did not question them or their authority. Consider the comments of John, a younger police cadet with military experience, when talking about how he might use his discretion on the job:

> Like when you pull somebody over and they blew through a stop sign and they're very apologetic, they're very polite and everything. You just might let that one go. If you pull somebody over and they're very rude from the get-go and they say, "You're wrong," saying "I didn't run [the stop sign]"

of course you're going to, you know, if you want to be an asshole you're going to get a ticket. If you wanna be apologetic and say, "Look officer, I'm sorry I was in a rush my daughter's in the hospital," then of course you're going to be more lenient.

Another characteristic that cadets saw as deserving was an individual's industriousness. Individuals whom they perceived as "hardworking," or who were employed and contributing to society, were perceived as more deserving than the unemployed or the lazy. Although this is somewhat different from one's attitude or demeanor—conceivably an employed person could be rude—in some cadets' minds these traits were linked. For instance, Phillip presented the following hypothetical in discussing how he might use his discretion:

Let's say I pulled you over. "I know officer I blew that stop sign and I shouldn't have done it." And then just be truthful. "I was in a rush and I shouldn't have blown the stop sign, I was late for work and was going I went right through it, I didn't see it and it's my fault." . . . Hey you gotta get to work and everyone's been late for work and blew a stop sign. I understand that. But don't try and sit there and beat around the bush and lie and say, you sure I didn't come to a complete stop? I thought I came to a complete stop. Don't sit there and try to lie or anything, just be truthful that's all. If people would just realize that they'd realize cops aren't jerkoffs like a lot of people think. We're just out there doing jobs like they are at their workplace.

Carl made a similar comment and indicated that he saw demeanor and industriousness as linked:

But the kinds of things that would make me let someone go if I did pull someone over is if he's a working-class guy who's trying to get home to his family. . . . And he's like, "You know officer I didn't put on my turn signal and I'm sorry." If it's a working guy. If it's some clown or he's rude, obviously you're gonna write him a ticket, you have the discretion. So I feel like any kind of a regular working-class guy or girl who honestly made a mistake and is contrite about it.

As these quotations show, even before becoming police, entrants had views about which citizens deserved their help. These views align with those held by many in the public about the importance of work (Gilens 1999). They also closely match the views held by veteran police (Chapter 3).

In addition, I tried to understand cadets' views about criminality, poverty, and racial inequality. At the outset of their careers, most cadets had balanced views about the causes of these problems: few thought that they were solely a matter of individual behavior or morality, and few thought that they were solely the result of structural trends. For example, they saw criminal behavior as a choice, but also recognized that it was influenced by processes that were bigger than individuals. Consider Mark's words when I asked about the causes of criminality: "Well, you know what they say that there's a lot of different reasons—lack of jobs it's at the same time it's . . . I guess it's lack of jobs, they don't have the money because times are tough but, at the same time there are programs out there to help them to get a job so. To me it's the difference between someone who wants to have a job and can't get it and [people that don't want to work]." Similarly, when I asked about poverty, cadets spoke of broad historical trends like intergenerational cycles of poverty, education, and politics, but also of industriousness and consumer choices.

Although most cadets saw these social problems as caused by a variety of factors, whites tended to see them through the lens of individual choice or character while minorities saw them as more driven by structural factors. In this way, their views mirror general differences between whites and minorities (Thompson and Bobo 2011). For instance, when I asked about the overrepresentation of minorities among the poor, Denise, a black female officer, replied,

> Um, I guess if you look at how the history of even how the country began in the sense that slavery, the whole nine, that's not something that you can remedy in a matter of a one hundred years. Even though let's say that slavery has been abolished approximately one hundred years now, one hundred-plus years, that's not something that I think you can remedy over night. And I know that might sound like you know over one hundred-plus years is a lengthy period of time, but the reality is that you still have obstacles that you're faced with on a daily basis. There's just certain things that I can relate to what a black male goes through. And actually my eyes were opened to that when I was once pulled over in [a neighboring state] by a police officer and I had a baseball cap on; well, I wear my hair very, very close and I go to the barbershop so that tells you how close I wear my hair. I knew the only reason I was pulled over and the reason I was profiled because he perceived me as a black male. And I know that's kind of off the subject. Even though it's been some time, it's not something that can

be remedied over night and just based on the structure of the social structure and how we came together blacks, whites, Native Americans and all other cultures; it's something that even one hundred-plus years can't be remedied over night.

In her answer we see an explanation that links racial inequality with the historical legacy of racial discrimination and current racist practices. However, white officers tended to see social problems, especially minority poverty, as mostly driven by choice and industriousness. For instance, Phillip was loath to "pinpoint a certain thing because there's so many things that can factor in," but indicated racial inequality was mostly about effort:

I don't know if it's maybe because if some people still have a grudge of the past and history and the past. . . . I don't know if it's because people hold that grudge and that causes it. . . . But I don't know if the assistance programs like welfare plays into it. Because people think, "Oh, I'm making all this money by just having a bunch of kids. Why should I have to go to work?" But that's the whole pride factor. If you don't have pride, well, "I don't care what people think of me, I'm gonna do my best I can to make kids to think I'm a great person so they can see I bust my butt and they'll bust their butts to become something better."

When I asked him about other factors like slavery or segregation, he conceded that they played a small part, but mostly racial inequality was driven by welfare and laziness.

Over the subsequent two years, when I returned to interview these police entrants, I heard responses mostly similar to the ones from entry. All police continued to see civilians who were deferential and apologetic as deserving of a second chance or a break. Those who were aggressive or uncooperative were unlikely to be seen as deserving. For example, after one year on the job, Denise commented,

Sometimes [you] come across someone that's, um, not pleasant and their attitude is, you know, poor and maybe they're calling you obscenities or whatever, and when you investigate their situation a little further you find out that certain things like licenses might be suspended or other things might come up as far as registration or insurance. In which case, yes, I will take your vehicle. You're not making my job any easier, so why should I make it easier on you?

Similarly, white and minority officers continued to see problems like poverty and racial inequality as a consequence of structural and individual factors. However, in one area it was noticeable that entrants' views shifted: the causes of criminality. Whereas most entrants had seen the causes of criminality as balanced at entry, over time they came to understand it in individual terms. For example, at entry Reggie talked about the varied reasons people commit crimes:

> You know, everyone that commits a crime is not necessarily a bad person. Different guys have different reasons for doing things. You have murderers that murder because they were actually protecting themselves. . . . You have people that steal because they're trying to feed their families. You have people that sell drugs because they can't get a legal job. And they just got tired of struggling. I [was previously] out of work for four years. And I was out there looking and no one would respond, so it just got hard out there. So I don't stereotype, I don't prejudge.

When I spoke with him two years later, he embraced a much more individual-centered explanation of crime:

> Choice. It's not a circumstance where everybody gotta do what they do. People choose what they do. So when you choose to do what you do you gotta be prepared to deal with the consequences. So you are out there and you deal the drugs, you decide to play the game. So that means you're going to live your life looking over your shoulder, either for us to come get you or for somebody that you made an enemy out of to get you. So that's basically what it boils down to. I would say ignorance; ignorance plays a part of it, but people are happy in your ignorance so if you're blissful in your ignorance it is what is it. Again, it's what I opened up with you know you make a choice and you don't learn from your mistakes and you do it again and again.

In the other areas that I investigated—the causes of poverty and racial inequality—minority and white police also saw these problems in nonstructural terms. However, in most of their answers in those areas, entrants usually acknowledged the importance of choices and environments. Perhaps because crime was their main focus, they came to see it as a decision or an indication of one's character.

Surveys

To provide a more detailed portrait of police entrants' attitudes, this section describes their responses to the following survey statements: "Criminals often commit crimes because they come from disadvantaged backgrounds"; "Most criminals commit crimes because they are bad people"; "Minorities have a tough time succeeding in our society because of racism"; "More minorities are poor because they don't work as hard as others"; "Poor people are poor because they make bad decisions"; "Hardworking poor people deserve a second chance every now and then"; "People are poor because there aren't enough good jobs"; "Poor kids (age sixteen and under) that get into trouble don't deserve any special treatment"; and "Poor pregnant girls that aren't married have no one to blame but themselves." For all statements, entrants indicated how much they agreed with the statement on a five-point scale from "strongly disagree" to "strongly agree."

Figure 7.1, which summarizes police officers' responses to statements about crime and racism, shows that from entry through the end of two years on the job, there was relative continuity in police officers' views about crime and racial inequality. Nonetheless, we do see some shifting in each of these statement clusters.

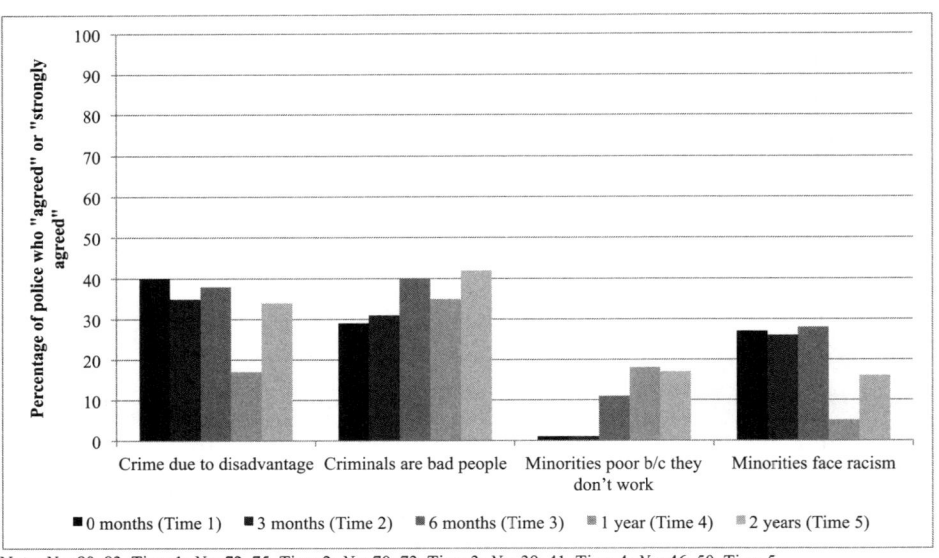

Note: N = 80–83, Time 1; N = 72–75, Time 2; N = 70–73, Time 3; N = 39–41, Time 4; N = 46–50, Time 5.

Figure 7.1. Police Attitudes About Crime and Racism

In regard to the causes of crime, there was a downward trend in the percentage of police who agreed that it results from disadvantage and an increase in the percentage who agreed that criminals commit crimes because they are "bad people." Initially there was relatively scant support for the idea that racial inequality resulted from a poor work ethic; over two years the percentage who agreed with this explanation rose somewhat, but still was less than 20 percent. Similarly, the percentage of police who agreed that minorities have a tough time succeeding because of racism began low and then dropped after police began their work.

Police officers' views about poverty are summarized in Figure 7.2. Initially, relatively few entrants agreed that people were poor because they had made bad decisions; over time there was some volatility, but at Times 4 and 5 the number who agreed with this statement rose. On the other hand, few officers initially agreed that people were poor because there were not enough jobs. Throughout the academy and then working on the streets, this view remained largely stable. The three statements on the right try to ascertain officers' views about the deservingness of three types of people: poor pregnant girls, poor kids who got into trouble, and poor people who were hard workers. Over time we see that poor kids, whether pregnant or not, became seen as more responsible for themselves (and in the case

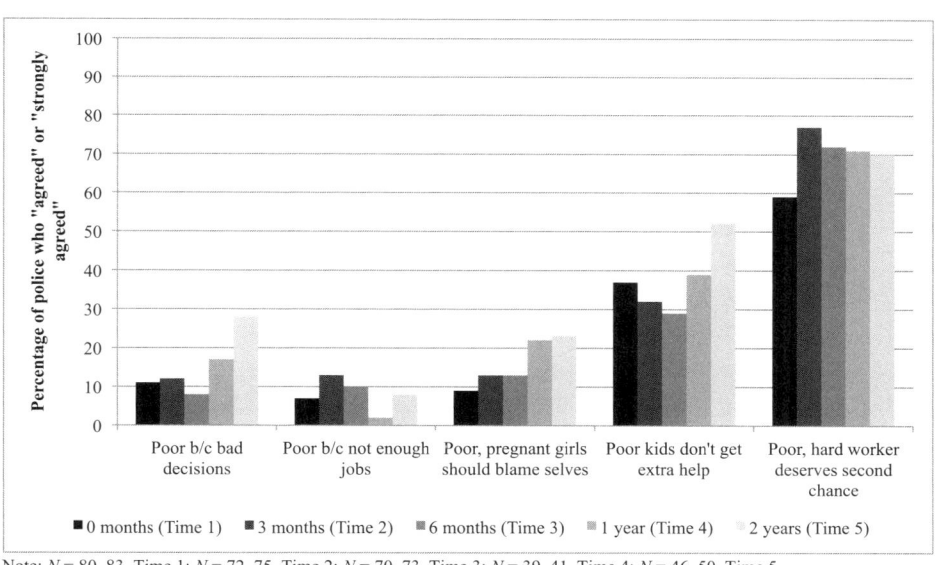

Figure 7.2. Police Attitudes About Poverty

of the kids question, less deserving of help). Hard workers were seen as deserving at the outset, and this perception appeared to increase over time.

In addition, it is important to consider the spread of officers' attitude responses throughout the study by examining the standard deviations of the population's responses to each attitude statement over time. This analysis revealed that in nine out of nine statements, there was an increase or no change in the standard deviation from Time 1 to Time 5. Therefore, we see little evidence that officers' attitudes became more similar during socialization as the institutional perspective would expect.

Thus far the survey data have been used to examine entrants' attitudes and make initial comments about change and continuity. Though useful for understanding population-wide trends, the above analysis is limited in explaining individual-level change.[1] As such, I sought to understand the extent to which individual newcomers altered their answers over the course of the project by calculating the absolute value of the difference between each officer's entering and subsequent attitudes. Figure 7.3 presents the average changes in officers' views about criminality and racism, and Figure 7.4 highlights changes in their views about poverty.[2]

These figures show no instances of radical change across the statements. However, across many outcomes we see gradual increases. By the end of their second year, the mean change for two statements was 25 percent or greater ("crime due to disadvantage" and "poor kids did not need extra help"). To provide one example, the mean response to the "crime due to disadvantage" statement at Time 1 was 3.1 (neutral) and at Time 5 was 2.7 (between neutral and disagree).[3] Compared to the change figures in Chapters 5 and 6, police entrants' attitudes appeared to change more than their motivations, but less than their bureaucratic identities.

Statistical Analysis

This section discusses the findings from a multivariate statistical analysis of officers' responses to attitude survey statements.[4] Since responses to statements are ordered, I used ordered probit to explore the relationship between dependent and independent variables. As discussed in prior chapters, probit coefficients are difficult to interpret on their own so the chapter presents odds ratios — the probability of a certain outcome based on variation in an independent variable. Initially, the analysis examined the "real-time" relationship between independent and dependent variables. Following that, it studied the likelihood that police

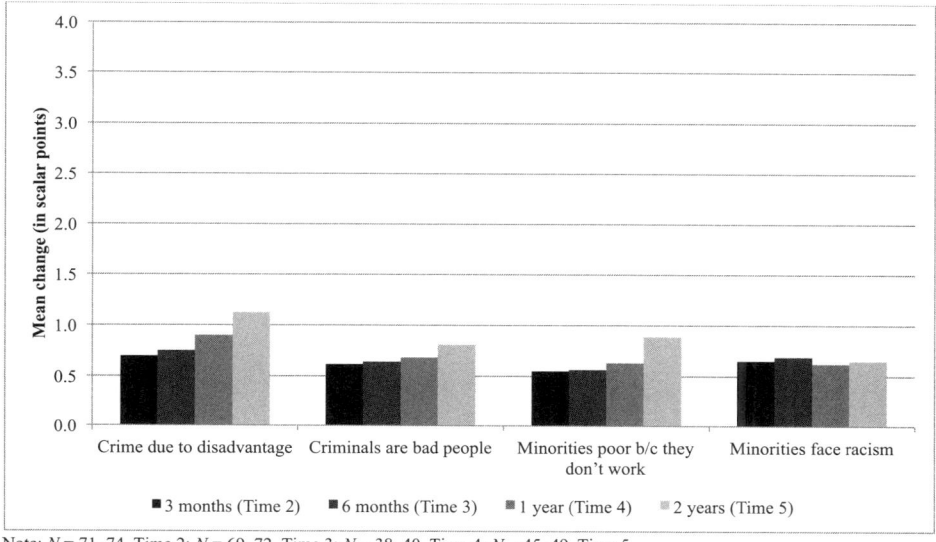

Note: $N = 71–74$, Time 2; $N = 69–72$, Time 3; $N = 38–40$, Time 4; $N = 45–49$, Time 5.

Figure 7.3. Police Attitudes About Crime and Racism: Mean Individual Change

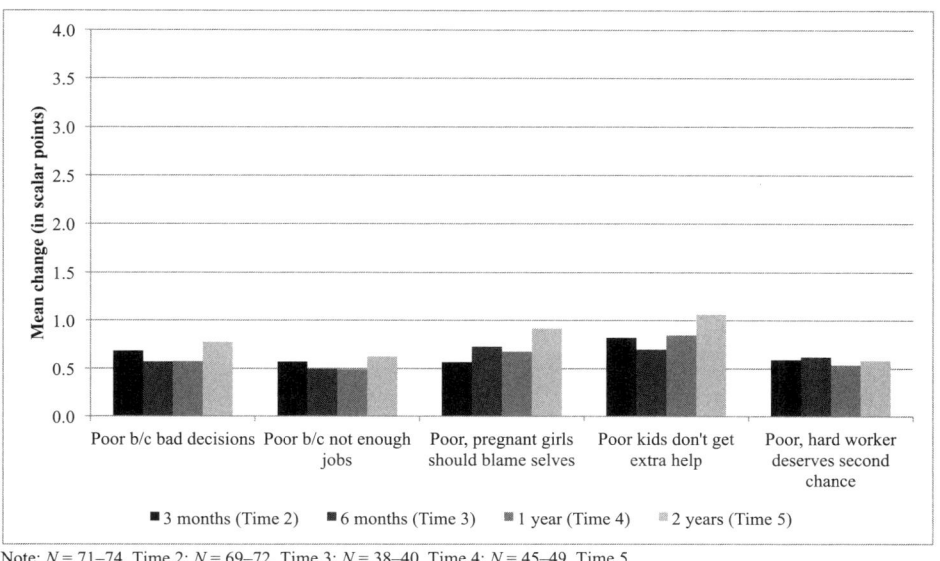

Note: $N = 71–74$, Time 2; $N = 69–72$, Time 3; $N = 38–40$, Time 4; $N = 45–49$, Time 5.

Figure 7.4. Police Attitudes About Poverty: Mean Individual Change

entrants would report different attitudes after entry. Several points emerged from this analysis.

As with police entrants' motivations (Chapter 5) and bureaucratic identities (Chapter 6), the strongest and most consistent predictors of entrants' subsequent attitudes were their entering attitudes. Figure 7.5 illustrates this trend. Though the size of the relationship changed in some cases, entering police remained anchored by their initial attitudes about the social world. For instance, entrants who initially indicated that people are poor due to bad decisions were 4.5 times more likely to articulate that viewpoint at Time 5. Cadets who articulated a more structural view of poverty on entry—agreeing that people were poor because there were not enough good jobs—were 2.3 times more likely to agree with this viewpoint at Time 5.

The strength of these relationships over time is somewhat ambiguous: in four of the nine statements, the size of the relationship appeared to grow through the end of the second year, and in five of the nine statements the size remained about the same or diminished. Buttressing findings from in-depth interviews, the

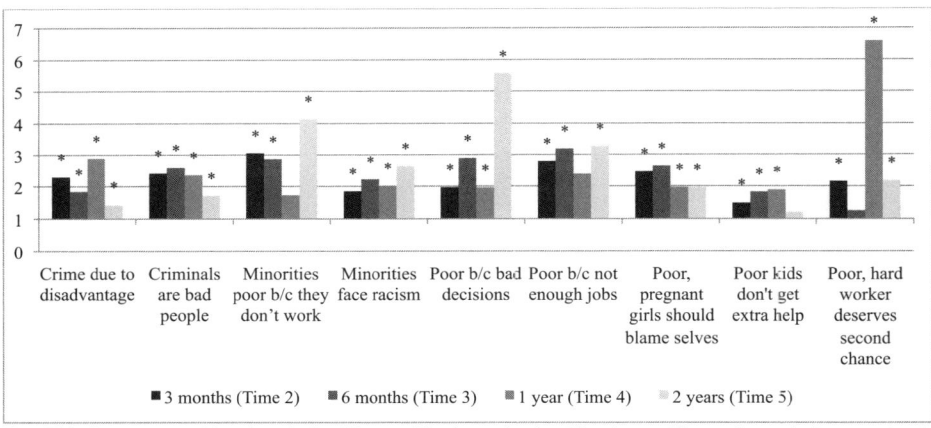

Note: This chart presents odds ratios calculated from multivariate ordered probit estimates. These ratios can be interpreted such that an increase of one unit of the independent variable (entering attitude) increases or decreases the chances of the dependent variable (subsequent attitude) by a certain amount, controlling for all other model variables (at Times 2 and 3 the model included education, age, pre-entry family income, welfare receipt, race, service in the armed forces, political ideology, academy instructors, culture, and academy peers; at Times 4 and 5 the model included education, age, pre-entry family income, welfare receipt, race, service in the armed forces, political ideology, academy training, department culture, supervisor, peers, veterans, amount of work, and monitoring). An odds ratio of 1 implies that the outcome is equally likely; an odds ratio of 1.25 indicates that the outcome is 0.25 times more likely due to an increase in the independent variable; an odds ratio of 0.75 indicates that the outcome is 0.25 times less likely due to an increase in the independent variable. An asterisk indicates that the underlying coefficient is statistically significant at the $p < .05$ level. $N = 58$–61, Time 2; $N = 56$–59, Time 3; $N = 32$–34, Time 4; $N = 37$–41, Time 5.

Figure 7.5. Predicting Police Attitudes: Entering Attitudes

association between past and present views of criminality dropped while the association between past and present explanations of poverty and views of race increased.

Another trend that emerged from the analysis of police entrants' attitudes was the importance of race. As in the interviews, white police tended to see the experiences and work ethics of minorities differently than minority police. White police also tended to explain poverty with reference to choices and to reject structural explanations. Figure 7.6 shows the predictive power of the racial identity of the officer with respect to four attitude statements. At the outset of training, whites were more likely to agree that minorities were poor because they didn't work hard. This relationship was evident even after six months of training (Time 3). However, after they graduated and began work, the relationship faded dramatically. In contrast, throughout the entire study, minorities were approximately 0.50 times more likely to agree that minorities have a tough time succeeding in society due to racism. There are also hints of a difference in how poverty is explained. Although the statistical significance of race as a predictor varied, whites were generally

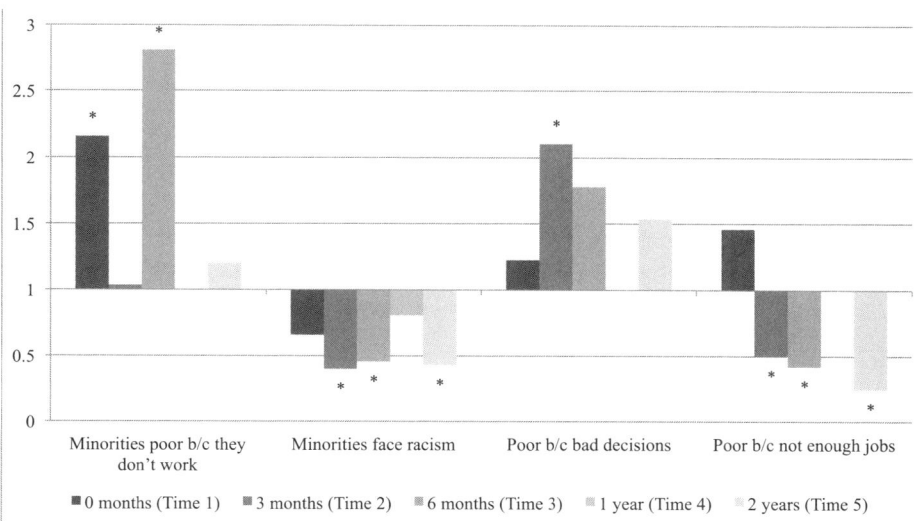

Note: This chart presents odds ratios calculated from multivariate ordered probit estimates. These ratios can be interpreted such that an increase of one unit of an independent variable—in this case moving from minority, which is coded as 0, to white, which is coded as 1—increases or decreases the chances of the dependent variable (subsequent attitude) by a certain amount, controlling for all other model variables (see the note to Figure 7.5 for a list of each model's variables and for further information about interpretation of odds ratios). An asterisk indicates that the underlying coefficient is statistically significant at the $p < .05$ level. $N = 58–61$, Time 2; $N = 56–59$, Time 3; $N = 32–34$, Time 4; $N = 37–41$, Time 5.

Figure 7.6. Predicting Police Attitudes: Race

more likely to agree that poverty resulted from bad individual decisions and less likely agree that poverty resulted from too few good jobs.

From the institutional perspective, there were few instances in which formal organizational influences were strong predictors of entrants' attitudes. For instance, at the three- and six-month points of the study (Times 2 and 3), cadets who saw training instructors as positive and important had similar views of criminality, poverty, and race as those who did not. Because the department had expended considerable effort to shape the views of police entrants, the lack of impact was somewhat surprising. In contrast, an informal organization influence, fellow rookies, appeared to play an important role. As cadets neared graduation, those who were influenced by fellow rookies were 0.35 times less likely to agree that crimes resulted from disadvantage and 0.27 times less likely to agree that minorities failed to succeed because of racism. However, the influence of cadets did not push uniformly toward individual-centered views: cadets influenced by other cadets were also less likely to agree that people were poor due to decisions that they had made. This paradoxical effect continued after graduation. At the end of their second year inside the department, officers who were influenced by fellow rookies were more likely to agree that criminals had bad character, that the poor were poor because of decisions that they made, and that poor kids did not deserve extra help. However, at this time they were also more likely to agree that racism was a problem.

The other informal influence that was associated with officers' views was veterans. Compared to the effect of rookies, veterans had a more uniform effect: it was associated with entrants articulating views about problems that emphasized individual control. For example, entrants who indicated being influenced by veterans were less likely to agree that crime resulted from disadvantage and that people were poor due to the lack of good jobs. They were also more likely to agree that minorities don't work hard.

Mirroring the change analyses in other chapters, there was no dominant predictor of changed attitudes. Unlike other chapters, there were no consistent relationships between institutional factors and entrants' likelihood of altering their attitudes. Rather, the two most consistent predictors of change were extraorganizational variables: age and race. Substantively, there were no distinct trends in the effect that age had on changes in entrants' attitudes. In other words, in some instances older entrants shifted toward seeing poverty and criminality as caused by individual-level factors; in other instances they shifted toward seeing these problems explained by macro forces. Also, it is interesting to note that age was significant, but it wasn't always younger people who altered their views. Age predicted the likelihood of change in many statements, but in some instances older entrants were more likely to change their views and in some instances they were less likely to do so.

Additionally, race was a significant predictor of the likelihood of changed attitudes. During the academy, minorities were more likely to shift their views about the relationship between poverty and the labor market; mirroring the group-level trends noted above, minorities shifted toward embracing the viewpoint that emphasized individual responsibility over structural factors. However, while at the academy, whites were more likely to shift their views about the deservingness of poor pregnant women; again, mirroring the group trend, they shifted toward seeing this group as undeserving. After graduation, minorities were again more likely to report altered views. Specifically, they embraced the view that criminality was linked to character and that poor pregnant women weren't deserving. At Time 5, whites were more likely to shift their views about the link between poverty and the job market (again, toward the direction of individual responsibility).

With this account complete, next we turn to considering the attitudes of entering welfare caseworkers during their first two years on the job.

Welfare Caseworkers' Attitudes

Interviews

At the outset of their careers, welfare caseworker entrants appeared to see poverty, in the abstract, differently from how they saw welfare recipients. In essence they saw poverty as caused by structural forces that individuals could not control, such as the economy and education system. However, they saw welfare receipt as caused by a mix of structural and individual forces. In this way, they saw some recipients as individually responsible for collecting welfare. For example, when I asked Karen, the black caseworker whose stressful experience with casework was described in Chapter 6, about the causes of poverty, she said,

> It goes back to your upbringing. Prime example. When black people were coming up years ago, we were not black people, were not taught how to save money. They weren't taught about the stock market, they weren't taught about mutual funds. So consequently they didn't know how to invest their money because they weren't taught. Because it was set up so that there would never be equality there. So consequently, since they weren't

taught they didn't invest. [They] didn't teach us. We don't teach our kids. So what happens is the cycle is that it keeps going on.

In her comments, we see a deflection of individual responsibility and an embracing of the view that patterns of money management, and therefore wealth accumulation, continue over time. However, when I asked Karen about welfare clients, she indicated that some people were content to manipulate the system and be lazy and others were really in need. When I asked her to estimate what percentage of welfare clients were manipulators, she said around 70 percent.

Over the two years of the study, interviewees maintained the view that poverty resulted from structural forces. However, their views did appear to evolve. Whereas initially entrants saw a sizable proportion of claimants as driven by forces out of their control, over time they tended to see more and more welfare clients as personally responsible for their situations. For example, at the outset of his career, Ralph indicated that he saw welfare receipt as caused by a mix of factors like limited education, which he indicated was not necessarily someone's fault, and bad decisions, which were. Later, when I asked him about recipients of the program most closely associated with the word "welfare"—Temporary Assistance for Needy Families—he pointed to bad decision making and a lack of personal motivation.

Another theme from the beginning of their careers was the linkage of attitude and deservingness. In particular, caseworkers saw shame and industriousness as characteristics that determined deservingness: those who didn't want welfare were the ones whom caseworkers perceived as most deserving of it. Since good, hardworking people would not want to be on welfare, caseworkers saw those who were ashamed of their status as welfare recipients as deserving of the benefits. Caseworkers, like police, also saw agreeable, passive recipients as "deserving." Clients who did not question their authority or talk back were more worthy of benefits. This may have resulted because applicants who were combative or ornery made caseworkers' jobs more difficult. In addition, "squeaky wheels" may have been seen as undeserving because of their willingness to go "uphill" and contact workers' superiors. Though caseworkers were clear that personal attributes or attitudes were key factors of deservingness, they also saw certain circumstances or categories of people as deserving. For example, recipients who were single mothers, disabled, elderly, victims of domestic violence, and clean (not drug users) were seen as deserving.

In addition, reflecting the messages sent to caseworkers during training, caseworkers tied deservingness to program usage. In other words, when I asked entrants about claimants in different programs, they tended to describe them as instructors had during training. For instance, Terrell commented that "[Medicaid] and Food Stamps are more on the positive side of welfare." When I asked Jasmine about how she generally saw welfare recipients, and whether their receipt was driven by choices that they made or circumstances that they did not control, she said,

> It depends on the [program]. TANF—a lot of it's decisions. You made some bad decisions and now you're here, but you don't have to stay here. You can correct those decisions, but a lot of them don't care to correct them. As for [Food Stamps] and [medical assistance], people I think it's just the jobs that they have at the time. You can go to college and get a degree in whatever, but in the meantime you still have to work and you still may not make that much and might need that little bit of help. Same with medical clients—you can't control that your boss doesn't offer medical.

When entrants commented on General Assistance (GA) recipients, typically single adults with a disability, there was considerable skepticism about their deservingness generally, and the injuries that they claimed particularly. They often saw these claimants as "flim-flammers" who feigned a disability in order to get a "crackpot" doctor to sign their disability form. These comments suggest that at least some workers articulated a hierarchical or tiered view of welfare programs and claimants.

Surprisingly, many black entrants appeared to shift their views about the causes of racial inequality. Initially, these entrants saw racial inequality as resulting from structural factors. For example, at Time 1, when asked about racial inequality, Janet commented, "Lack of resources, because a lot of white people they might have, most of the time it's not what you know but who you know so when you have that behind you you're like, 'Alright I can get this,' but the black person can't or the Hispanic can't." When I asked her if racism was still a problem for racial minorities, she answered affirmatively.

Over time, many shifted their views and came to see racial inequality as resulting from a mix of choices and structural factors. When I spoke to Janet at the two-year point, she struck a different chord: "Lack of knowledge, lack of the usage of resources. Because a lot of us don't read and including myself, we don't read a lot about you know what's available to us. We don't really look into it. It's just that if someone tells us we'll go after it but we don't seek it ourselves." When I asked her about racism, and whether it affected minorities' lives, she said, "I don't think it's a problem because, like I said, if we took the time to research, then we would have the same resources that white people have. So I don't think racism is a problem." Though not all entrants shifted their views so abruptly, there was a change for some from seeing racial inequality as a historical legacy to a matter of both history and choices.

Surveys

To provide a more systematic portrait of entrants' views, and the extent to which they evolved during entry, I asked them to respond to the following statements: "Most welfare recipients try to scam the system at some point"; "By and large welfare recipients are honest people"; "Generally welfare clients aren't personally responsible for being poor"; "The reason most welfare clients end up on welfare is because they make bad decisions"; "Families with children deserve public assistance even if the parents act irresponsibly"; "Healthy adults deserve public help even if they don't work hard"; "Poor pregnant girls that aren't married have no one to blame but themselves"; "Minorities have a tough time succeeding in our society because of racism"; and "A poor person who works hard deserves extra help to make it." Figure 7.7 charts entrants' views about welfare recipients throughout the course of the study.[5]

Initially, only a fifth of caseworkers agreed that welfare clients scam the system at some point—over the course of the study, this figure rose to half of all entrants. In contrast, at the outset relatively few entrants agreed that recipients were honest with the department. By the end of two years just under a third of entrants agreed that recipients were honest. This sets up a perplexing finding: as a group caseworkers shifted toward seeing welfare recipients as honest but more likely to scam. Moving to the right, we see that initially 40 percent of entrants agreed that welfare clients were not personally responsible for being poor; over time, this number dropped. Finally, on the far right side we see little agreement at the outset that clients were on welfare because of their bad decisions. Over time nearly a third agreed with this statement. Although the results for the honesty statement don't fit with the general trend, in sum this figure suggests that caseworker entrants developed more negative views about welfare clients.

Next, in Figure 7.8, we turn to examine entrants' views about deservingness and poverty. On the left side of the figure, we see that initially a strong majority agreed that families deserved welfare even if the parents in the family acted irresponsibly. Over time, the number who agreed with this statement dropped so that

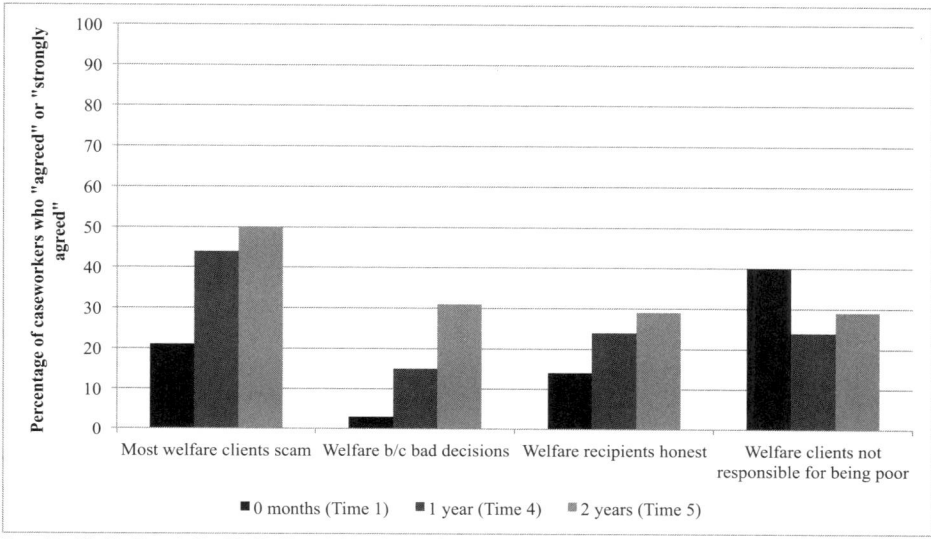

Note: $N = 28–33$, Time 1; $N = 17–20$, Time 4; $N = 13–16$, Time 5.

Figure 7.7. Caseworker Attitudes: Welfare Recipients

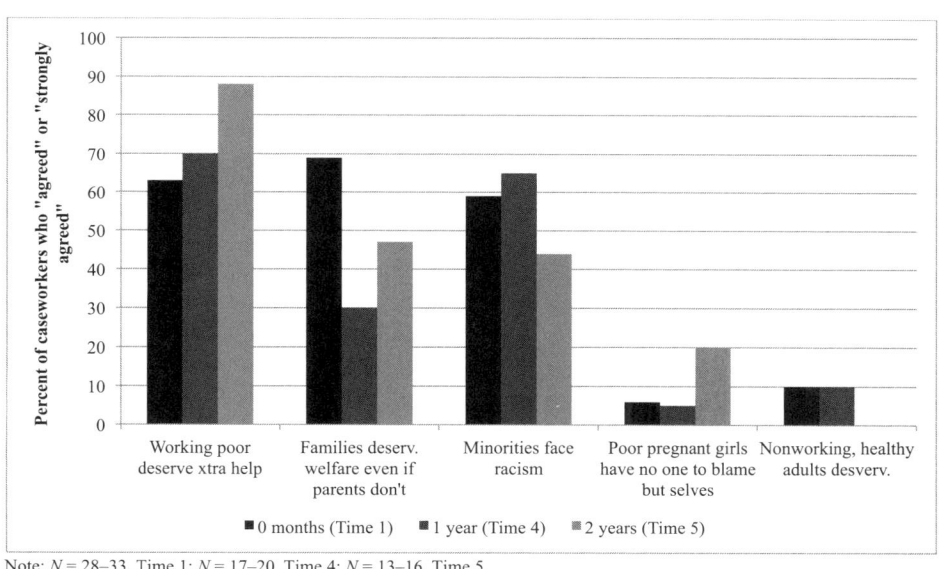

Note: $N = 28–33$, Time 1; $N = 17–20$, Time 4; $N = 13–16$, Time 5.

Figure 7.8. Caseworker Attitudes: Deservingness and Poverty

by the end fewer than half agreed. In contrast, we see relative continuity in entrants' views about nonworking healthy adults: few saw them as deserving at Time 1 or at subsequent times. Similarly, at the outset, nearly two-thirds of entrants saw the working poor as deserving of help; this figure rose so that by the end of the second year, nearly all workers agreed with this statement. Initially, few agreed that poor pregnant girls were responsible for their situation, but by Time 5 a fifth of workers agreed with it. Mirroring the discussion above, initially nearly two-thirds of entrants agreed that racism limited the chances of minorities. By Time 5 fewer than half of workers agreed with this statement.

At the one- and two-year points (Times 4 and 5), I asked entrants to rate the deservingness of claimants in the following welfare programs: GA, TANF (adults), TANF (children), Food Stamps, and medical assistance for the elderly. Prior to presenting entrants' views, it is useful to get a sense of how the American public generally views these programs. The most comprehensive source for this information comes from Cook and Barrett (1992). Although their study is somewhat dated, it is useful for two reasons. First, few public opinion studies use the same framing question to ask about a broad set of specific programs. Second, although there has been some movement in the public's views about these programs over time, there are also appears to be strong trends over time (Gilens 1999; Soss and Schram 2007). Cook and Barrett asked members of the public if they favored increasing, maintaining, or decreasing various programs. Although this question is somewhat different from asking about deservingness, both approaches probe respondents' underlying views about the people who get the program. Their results showed that 25 percent of respondents favored increasing Food Stamps, 33 percent favored increasing Aid to Families with Dependent Children (AFDC, the precursor to TANF), 47 percent favored increasing Medicaid, and 68 percent favored increasing Medicare.

Figure 7.9 highlights entrants' views about the deservingness of recipients of these particular welfare programs. As is evident in the figure, workers clearly made distinctions among these programs. Also, there are some overlaps with the public's views and some places where the two appeared to diverge. To begin, the figure shows that few entrants saw GA recipients as deserving. Also, fewer than half of caseworkers reported seeing TANF adults as deserving after just one year on the job. In contrast, nearly two-thirds of entrants saw Food Stamps recipients as deserving. This diverges from the data reported by Cook and Barrett. In addition, nearly all entrants saw child recipients of TANF and elderly recipients of a medical program (Medicaid) as deserving. Although Cook and Barrett do not provide evidence about the public's views about AFDC children, we see that entering

Attitudes

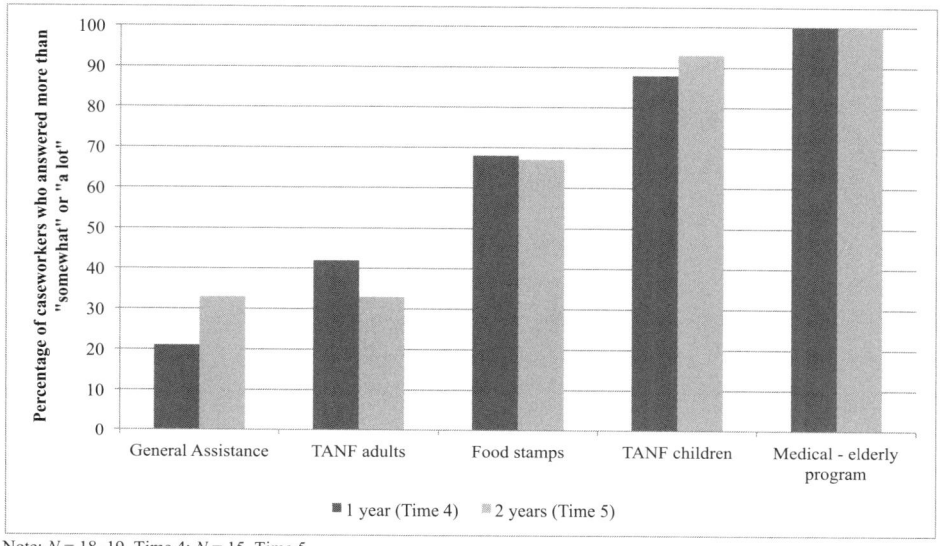

Note: $N = 18–19$, Time 4; $N = 15$, Time 5.

Figure 7.9. Caseworker Attitudes: Welfare Program Deservingness

caseworkers saw Medicaid much more favorably than the general public. Also, the data in Figure 7.9 match entrants' interview responses and the messages sent by instructors during training.

In addition to describing respondents' views, it is important to consider the spread of caseworkers' responses throughout the study to determine whether, at the population level, their attitudes moved closer together or diverged/remained static. To do this, I examined the standard deviations of the population's responses to each attitude statement over time. This analysis revealed that in five out of nine statements, the standard deviation decreased from Time 1 to Time 5. As such, we see mixed evidence about the convergence of newcomers' views.

In addition, I sought to understand the extent to which individual newcomers altered their answers over the course of the project by calculating the absolute value of the difference between each worker's entering and subsequent attitudes. Figure 7.10 charts the mean change of caseworkers' attitudes in scalar points. Since the figure shows absolute values, each bar indicates total change, not change toward a particular position.[6] There was substantial consistency throughout the study. By the end of the second year, there was only one statement in which workers shifted their views more than 25 percent (racism). In six of the nine statements,

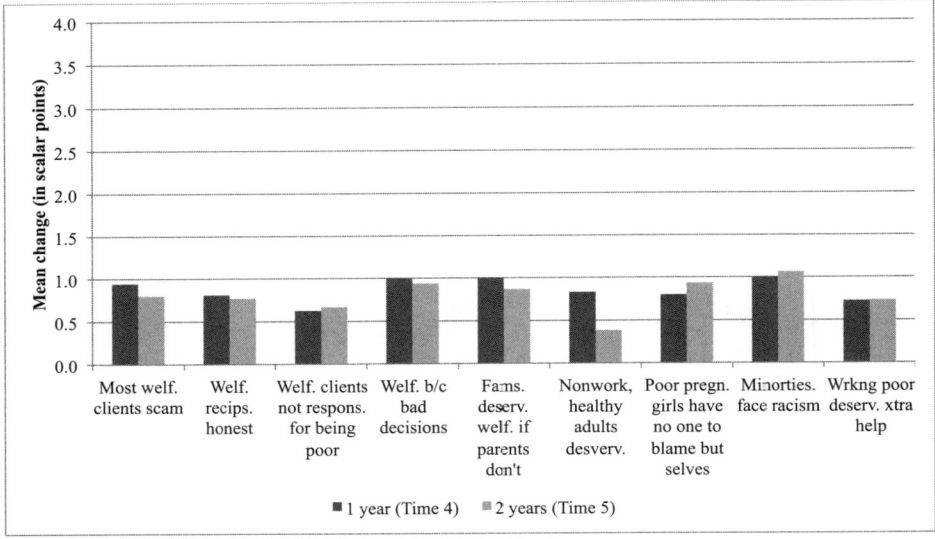

Figure 7.10. Caseworker Attitudes: Mean Individual Change

the level of change dropped or plateaued by the end of the second year. For example, the mean response to the statement about welfare recipient honesty was 3.1 (neutral) at Time 1 and 2.8 at Time 5 (between neutral and disagree).

Statistical Analysis

This section continues the inquiry by discussing the findings from a bivariate statistical analysis of caseworkers' responses to survey statements.[7] The statistical analysis was performed utilizing ordered probit as an estimation tool, and, for ease of interpretation, findings from odds ratio calculations are discussed. The analysis examined the "real-time" relationship between independent and dependent variables and the likelihood that caseworker entrants would give different responses to survey statements after entry.

As in other chapters, there is some evidence of continuity over time. For example, after spending a year inside the department (Time 4) and completing classroom training, entrants who initially saw welfare recipients as honest, and agreed that families deserved assistance even if the parents were not responsible, were more likely to articulate these views at Time 4. Similarly, there was some evidence of continuity after two years: caseworkers who believed that most welfare clients scam the system at some point at Time 1 were more likely to agree that this was true at Time 5. Despite these findings, the relationship between entering and subsequent views was considerably weaker than for police: at Time 4 in seven of the nine statements, caseworkers' entering attitudes were no longer strongly associated with their subsequent attitudes; at Time 5, entering attitudes were not a strong predictor in six of nine statements.

The analysis also showed that race was a predictor of entrants' attitudes midway through the study (at Time 4). Surprisingly, in contrast with the prior section which showed that white police tended to view issues of race and poverty in terms of personal responsibility, at Time 4 white welfare caseworkers articulated structural attitudes about welfare and poverty issues. For instance, whites were more likely to agree that single healthy adults deserved assistance and that racism was a factor that limited the life chances of minorities. Also, whites were less likely to agree that poor pregnant girls were to blame for their situations. Whites were also more likely to agree that GA recipients and TANF adults were deserving of assistance. It is not immediately clear why white police officers and white caseworkers initially held such different views about welfare and poverty issues. However, it seems likely that self-selection plays an important role: at the outset of the study, approximately 90 percent of the white caseworker entrants identified as liberals while only 25 percent of white police entrants identified this way. Despite the strong relationships between race and attitudes at Time 4, few relationships remained by the end of their second year inside the organization.

From the institutional perspective, the analysis generally showed few instances in which organizational influences were associated with entrants' attitudes. However, there were questions in which these influences appeared to matter. For example, at Time 4 entrants who indicated that training was important to them were more likely to agree that welfare clients were not personally responsible for being poor. However, they were less likely to agree that families with children deserve assistance even if their parents act irresponsibly. At Time 5 there were no instances in which training was a strong predictor of entrants' views.

The analysis also showed that two informal influences—peers and veterans—were associated with entrants' views at Time 4. Entrants who were influenced by their peers were 0.74 times more likely to agree that welfare clients were not personally responsible for being poor but 0.28 times less likely to agree that families deserved assistance even if the parents were irresponsible. Again, at Time 5 these associations diminished in strength and were no longer statistically significant.

Finally, there were few strong, consistent predictors of caseworkers' likelihood of altering their responses to attitude statements. This was true for extraorganizational, demographic characteristics such as age, race, and gender, which were generally expected to have a stabilizing effect on entrants' attitudes. For example, throughout the study younger caseworker entrants were just as likely to maintain their attitude responses as older entrants. At Times 4 and 5, some institutional variables were associated with the likelihood of change: in particular, variables capturing the effects of supervisors and entrants' units were associated with adopting new motives. However, the strength and consistency of these relationships varied and there were no coherent trends that emerged from the analysis.

Conclusion

This chapter has described and explained the attitudes held by entrants over their first two years on the job. These attitudes matter because, according the logic of appropriateness theory discussed in Chapter 1, organization members choose how to act in part based on how they understand the people with whom they are interacting. In comparing how police and caseworkers developed, we see a variety of similarities. For both groups, the demeanor of the person with whom they were interacting was a key indicator of that person's deservingness for assistance. Police saw cooperative, passive civilians who were honest and accepted their authority as worthy of a break; caseworkers saw polite recipients who were ashamed of being on welfare as deserving. Although one might expect that these views developed over time, based on these workers' needs to process their cases quickly and efficiently, this chapter shows that newcomers entered their organizations already holding many of these attitudes.

Another similarity was the continuity, throughout both groups' experiences, of the view that the working poor deserved help. Entrants' views remained consistent and matched the views expressed by many in the general public and experienced workers. In addition, both groups shifted their views, to at least some extent, from seeing social problems as caused by mostly structural factors, or a mix of structural and individual factors, to seeing them more as a result of individual choice or behavior. Police came to see some elements of criminality, racial inequality, and poverty as driven by individual actions; caseworkers came to see welfare claiming as resulting from an individual's bad decisions.

The chapter also analyzed entrants' views to explain why they held particular views. For both sets of entrants, there was some continuity throughout the project. Even after training, socialization, and beginning work, the best predictor of their views about social problems and deservingness were their entering views (this was particularly true of police). This is not to say that individuals did not adopt new views or that entrants, as a group, did not adopt new views. Rather, it means that even if workers shifted their views, they tended to remain anchored by the attitudes that they articulated prior to entering their organizations. Entrants' peers, in the form of fellow trainees, rookies, as well as organization veterans, were an important influence on the attitudes that they reported, especially throughout their first year. This finding suggests the importance of informal organization influences in shaping the development of these entrants.

Along with these similarities come important differences. Police showed more attitude change. For each group, I asked for responses to nine attitude statements at several points in time. For police, the mean response at Time 5 was statistically different from the mean response at Time 1 for five of the nine statements. For caseworkers, it was statistically different only for two of the nine statements.

The findings from this chapter combined with the findings from Chapters 5 and 6 give us a broad understanding of how these two groups developed during their first two years on the job. The next and final chapter brings all of this evidence together to draw conclusions and discuss the implications that these findings have for theory and practice.

CHAPTER 8

Change and Continuity at Government's Front Lines

Bureaucrats play an essential role in public policymaking because they decide what rules mean and how they are applied in practice. As they make choices about how to respond to people and situations, their behavior follows a logic of appropriateness — they think about who they are as members of an organization, what type of situation they are facing, and what people like themselves should do in such a situation (March 1994; March and Olsen 2006). Because the logic of appropriateness construct is a general decision-making theory, and does not put forward a holistic account of bureaucratic psychology, this book argues that bureaucrats' understandings of appropriateness are tied to their bureaucratic personalities. Though the term "bureaucratic personality" has a long and controversial history, this book breaks with a deterministic, one-dimensional view and defines it as the tendencies and structures that bureaucrats use to make sense of themselves and their work. In contrast to past conceptions of bureaucratic psychology, this framework allows for variation across workers, organizations, and time. The book's main goal is understanding how newcomers develop their bureaucratic personalities. To what extent are they shaped by the institutions that they enter? What is the role of self-selection?

To answer these questions, the book sets forth two competing explanations. The dispositional perspective argues that two key psychological characteristics — personality and habitus — are formed and, to some extent, set prior to entry. If entrants' bureaucratic personalities are tied to these underlying characteristics, we would not expect major changes in their bureaucratic personalities during entry. This perspective does not imply inertia. Rather, according the dispositional perspective, people develop psychological mechanisms and strategies early in life. When they encounter new situations, they draw upon these established strategies to make sense of their new surroundings. In essence, this perspective expects considerable continuity during bureaucratic socialization.

In contrast, the institutional perspective expects considerable change. Undergirding this expectation are the rational and natural systems perspectives on organizations. Though they point to different causes, both expect that the social forces that entrants encounter inside their organizations exert great influence on the bureaucratic personalities that they develop. Again, the institutional perspective should not be painted with too broad a brush: it doesn't argue that dispositions are unimportant, but that, in comparison with organizational influences, they are less important. From this perspective, entrants are expected to learn how to think and act mainly as a result of the formal and informal organizational influences that they encounter.

This book examines the utility of these perspectives by studying the development of two sets of street-level bureaucrats during their first two years on the job. Although the book's findings are limited in some ways,[1] longitudinal studies of bureaucratic socialization are exceedingly rare. When they have been conducted, they typically rely on either qualitative or quantitative data. As such, this book is useful because it presents a mixture of quantitative and qualitative data and provides a relatively holistic account of bureaucratic socialization.

Bureaucratic Personality Change

At the most general level, the book shows that both perspectives are needed to explain bureaucratic socialization. At the group and individual levels, entrants shifted in particular directions but remained tied to their entering perceptions, identities, and motivations. As such, the book joins other works that suggest that socialization is complex and influenced by dispositional and institutional factors. However, it distinguishes itself, and moves our understanding of bureaucratic socialization forward, by highlighting when, why, and how much entrants changed. To begin to summarize these findings, Figure 8.1 shows the mean individual change for entering police and caseworkers across each of the three areas of bureaucratic personality from Time 1 to Time 5. The bars in the figure represent the aggregated average individual-level change derived from absolute value calculations for all survey questions from Figures 5.1, 5.7, 6.1, 6.6, 7.1, 7.2, 7.7, and 7.8.[2]

The figure shows some change across each area: police shifted their attitudes the most, followed by their bureaucratic identities and motivations; caseworkers shifted their motivations the most followed by their attitudes and bureaucratic identities. When all three parts are aggregated, the data suggest that the typical police entrant altered his or her response to each bureaucratic personality

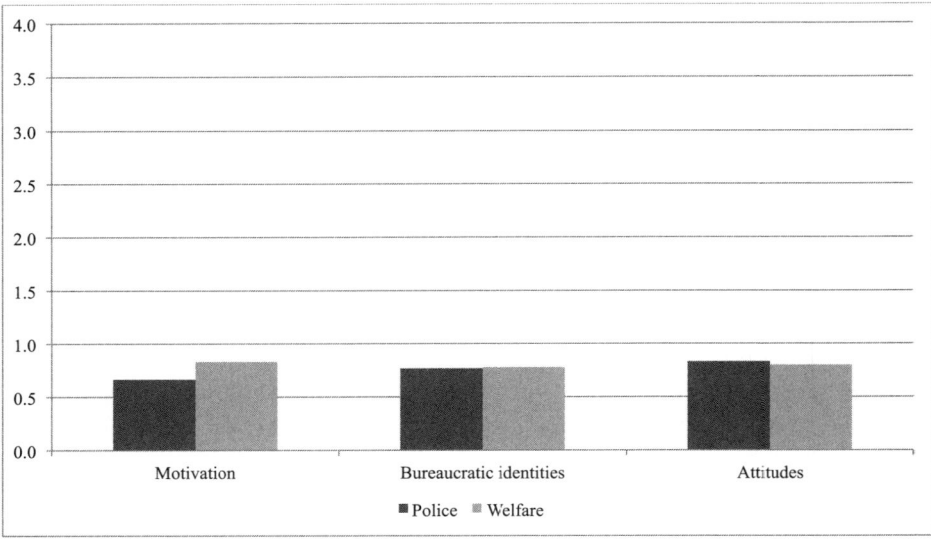

Note: Police: $N = 44-50$, Time 5; Welfare: $N = 12-16$, Time 5.

Figure 8.1. Comparing Police Officers and Welfare Caseworkers: Mean Individual Change at Two Years (Time 5)

question by an average of 0.75 points (out of a possible 4 points). The typical caseworker entrant altered his or her response to each question by an average of 0.80 points. This finding shows real change and supports the expectations drawn from the institutional perspective. However, it is also important to note that the figure shows no radical change. On average, neither group demonstrated change at the 25 percent level in any of the bureaucratic personality areas. As such, the evidence suggests that, even after two years inside their organizations, most entrants articulated mostly the same motivations, attitudes, and bureaucratic identities that they expressed at entry. Thus, there is evidence that supports both the dispositional and institutional perspectives, but, on the whole, there was more continuity than change.

This figure is also interesting because police socialization is often described as particularly strong (Chappell and Lanza-Kaduce 2010; Gallo 2001; Kappeler, Sluder, and Alpert 1998; Macvean and Cox 2012; Rubinstein 1973; Van Maanen 1974, 1975; Wilkins and Williams 2008), and the average police entrant age was ten years younger than the average caseworker entrant. Because younger people are typically more susceptible to psychological change, and police socialization is depicted as strong, it was expected that the police would exhibit greater change.

Nevertheless, there was essentially no difference between the two cases, in terms of average aggregate change, at the end of the second year of the study. Also, within each group, younger entrants were not more likely than their older colleagues to alter their responses to survey questions. As such, the findings here imply that age may not be a major factor in bureaucratic socialization.

In addition to comparing the cases to one another, it is important to look inside each case and ask when change took place and at what rate. Turning first to the police, Figure 8.2 shows the average aggregate change at each time (from Time 1) for each area of bureaucratic personality throughout the study (across all questions within an outcome area). This figure has three notable components. First, in each of the three outcome areas, a large majority of the change happened within the first three months (Time 2). In other words, the figure shows that development for police began with a "big bang": in each area of bureaucratic personality, approximately three-quarters of the total change that would be evident at Time 5 occurred by Time 2. As such, the findings here are somewhat consonant with other accounts that suggest police socialization happens quickly (Chappell and Lanza-Kaduce 2010; Conti 2009; Rubinstein 1973; Van Maanen 1974). However, as indicated above, the modest scope of change evident here is at odds with these prior studies.

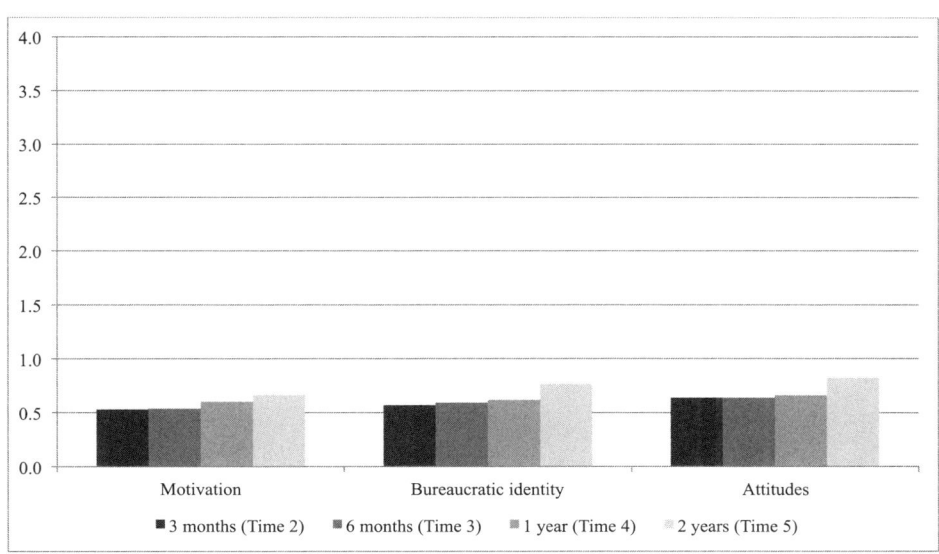

Note: $N = 64-75$, Time 2; $N = 61-73$, Time 3; $N = 37-41$, Time 4; $N = 44-50$, Time 5.

Figure 8.2. Police Bureaucratic Personality Change

Also, as readers will recall from Chapters 5 to 7, few organizational influences were strongly associated with entrants' views at that time.

Second, following this initial change, we see that police development mostly plateaued through the end of the second year (Time 4). For example, the average entrant changed his or her motivation responses by 0.01 points at Time 3 and another 0.06 points at Time 4. After the initial change, officers' bureaucratic personalities appeared to stabilize for the remainder of the first year. Third, at the end of the second year, we see an increase in bureaucratic identity and attitude change. For example, police officers' attitudes changed by 0.64 points from Time 1 to Time 2, stayed mostly stable at Times 3 and 4, then changed by another 0.17 points (from Time 1). Although this change is minor compared to the initial Time 2 change, it is considerable compared to Times 3 and 4.

Figure 8.3 directs our attention to caseworkers and highlights the average aggregate individual-level change for each area of bureaucratic personality throughout the study. This figure shows the development of welfare caseworkers was, in some ways, similar to the development of police entrants. Like police, most caseworker change occurred fairly early in development. This was especially true in regard to their motivations and attitudes. However, there are differences

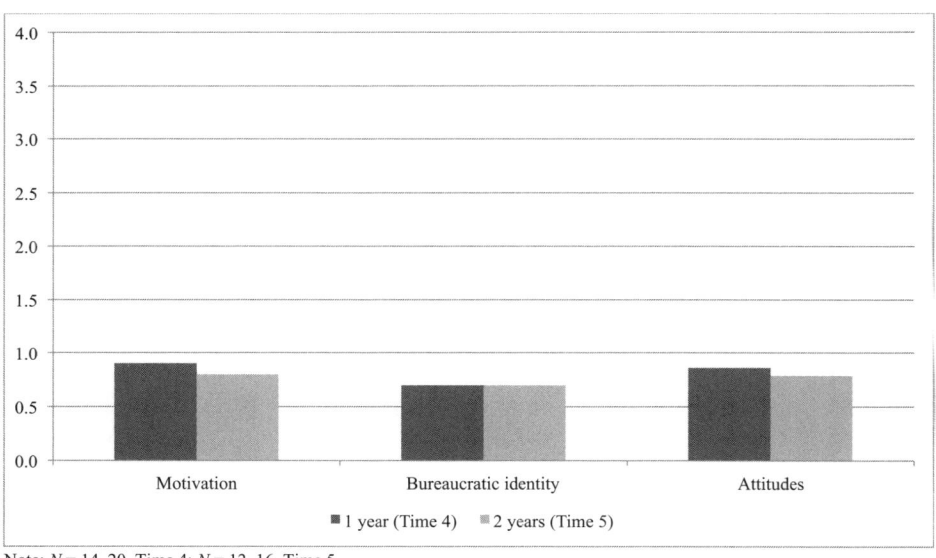

Note: $N = 14$–20, Time 4; $N = 12$–16, Time 5.

Figure 8.3. Caseworker Bureaucratic Personality Change

between figures 8.2 and 8.3 as well. Comparing aggregate change at the one-year point (Time 4), we see that caseworkers exhibited more change than did police. Also, unlike the police, the amount of individual-level change either plateaued or regressed between the one- and two-year marks. It isn't possible to say whether these trends continue beyond the two-year mark. However, the trend at the end of the study points to stability or a return back to entrants' initial views.

Differential Continuity

The evidence above shows modest change across each area of bureaucratic personality. Meanwhile, the statistical analysis described in Chapters 5 to 7 shows that, for the most part, entrants remained strongly connected to their entering bureaucratic personalities. To understand how these two findings fit together, it is important to recall that, as discussed in Chapter 2, there are different types of continuity. Absolute continuity refers to the stability of a particular trait or attribute, at the level of the individual, over time. Since the average entrant in each group shifted his or her response by around 20 percent, these two cases show relatively low levels of absolute continuity. However, both groups show high levels of differential continuity—even as the group shifted in a particular direction, individuals remained in a similar position, vis-à-vis the group, throughout the study.

An example helps to illustrate this general trend. Over the course of the study the police entrants, as a group, shifted away from agreeing that they would follow rules with which they disagreed: at Time 1, the mean response of the group was 4.3 (between agree and strongly agree); by Time 5 it had shifted to 3.8 (between neutral and agree).[3] Of the entrants who answered the question at those two times, 42 percent gave the exact same response, 44 percent shifted their response by one point, 12 percent shifted their response by two points, and 2 percent shifted their response by three points. Of those who gave different answers, only 8 percent moved against the general trend (toward disagreeing with the statement). Of those who moved with the general trend, 72 percent moved just one point on the scale. In other words, over half of the group shifted away from agreeing that they would follow rules with which they disagreed. However, most of those who reported new views changed very little. Thus, entrants were strongly influenced by where they started and remained roughly in the same spot, relative to the group, throughout the study.

One way of visualizing this phenomenon is to picture a roughly normal distribution for each of the bureaucratic personality questions at Time 1. Although the distribution for each question may have shifted in a particular direction over time, most entrants stayed in approximately the same place along the distribution throughout the study. If bureaucratic socialization is best understood as a process of differential continuity, the next logical question is: What explains this phenomenon? In other words, why do newcomers adopt slightly different bureaucratic personalities while remaining tethered to where they began?

Dispositional Explanations

One explanation for the stability of newcomers' bureaucratic personalities is that they are erected upon more fundamental psychological characteristics and processes, like personality and habitus. Because these characteristics remain largely constant throughout bureaucratic socialization, so would entrants' bureaucratic personalities. For example, one personality trait of particular interest to psychologists is openness to new experiences (John et al. 2008). One facet of this trait is liberalism—the stance that people have in regard to convention and authority. Some people are comfortable taking direction and obeying set protocols, while others chafe in such situations. Perhaps this underlying personality trait played an important role in shaping entrants' rule-following identities throughout the study. If so, newcomers began with differing levels of comfort with rule deviation and, though the group as a whole moved toward discretion usage, entrants remained psychologically tied to where they began. Although such an explanation seems compelling, unfortunately it was not possible to conduct a personality examination of all entrants prior to entry. As a result, it isn't possible to say whether or how personality played a role in entrant development. However, such tests might prove useful for future studies trying to understand bureaucratic socialization.

Another possible explanation for the patterns observed in this study is newcomers' extraorganizational experiences with, among other things, education, class, and gender. From this perspective, it isn't personality that accounts for stability as much as it is pre- and postentry social experiences with demographic characteristics. Although such an explanation is possible, as readers will recall from the empirical chapters, relatively few extraorganizational characteristics were strong predictors of entrants' responses. However, one demographic characteristic, race, appeared to be an important predictor of entrants' views. Chapters 5 and 7 showed that race was a strong predictor of police entrants' motivations and attitudes. Even after entry, minority police officers held significantly different motivations than their white colleagues (Chapter 5). In particular, minorities were more likely to be motivated by an array of altruistic outcomes like protecting people and treating them fairly. Chapter 7 also revealed important differences along the lines of officers' racial identities. In particular, minorities were more likely to explain social problems by referencing structural causes.

In some ways, it is not particularly surprising to see that race is an important predictor of entering police officers' views. Race has long been one of the fundamental cleavages in U.S. society (Dawson 1994; Myrdal 1944; R. Smith 1993). Internally, people use their racial identities to understand who they are and how they should act; externally, people categorize and treat one another, to some extent, based on perceptions of racial identity. Perhaps as a result, minorities and whites hold different views about a variety of social phenomena. Since race is such an important component of one's social experience prior to bureaucratic entry, it follows that one's racial identity might continue to matter after joining an organization. The findings here show that race remained an important factor shaping entrants' motivation and attitudes, although it was not a dominant explanation.

This finding has implications for the representative bureaucracy literature, which has tried to understand the role that descriptive representativeness plays in the interactions between government and citizens (Keiser et al. 2002). The literature has a diverse array of findings, but there is a general expectation that extraorganizational identities, like race and gender, shape the behavior of government actors, even after organization entry. Because the literature lacks an in-depth account of representativeness and socialization, this project may be helpful for guiding future work. In particular, it shows that, in at least some ways, entrants from different backgrounds, despite undergoing roughly similar organizational experiences, can emerge as different workers.

Despite this, it is important to note that race was not an important predictor in the bureaucratic identities that police developed or, generally speaking, an important predictor of caseworkers' bureaucratic personalities. Thus, what emerges here is a sense that race can matter, but may not always matter. In other words, newcomers' pre-entry experiences with race may have a stabilizing effect on some components of their bureaucratic personalities.

Institutional Explanations

The basic expectation of the institutional perspective, laid out in Chapter 2, is that newcomers are shaped by the formal and informal organizational influences that they encounter. The interviews and observant participation discussed in Chapter 4 show that these influences appeared to be salient for many entrants. Though there was less evidence in the statistical analysis showing that institutional influences were associated with the bureaucratic personalities that they developed, in total the data imply that organizations play an important role in explaining some features of bureaucratic development. As such, it is worth considering what the findings here suggest about how organizations shape entrants.

In comparing formal and informal influences, there was an interesting difference between the findings from interviews and those from surveys. In the interview data, entrants indicated that formal organizational influences early in their careers played an important role in shaping their approach to their work. For instance, during their time at the academy, police entrants gave high marks to their instructors (Chapter 4): they indicated that trainers were accessible and easy to communicate with, that they learned from their instructors, and that their instructors' stories were useful in prepping them for their work. Overall, they were confident that their academy training had prepared them for policing. Similarly, caseworker entrants indicated that their training supervisors played a crucial role in shaping them as caseworkers. In most cases, training supervisors taught them to bring a skeptical eye to encounters with applicants and manage their caseloads efficiently.

Despite these interview findings, statistical analysis of the survey data showed that there were few instances at Times 2 to 5 in which formal organizational influences were strong predictors of entrants' responses. Similarly, the change analysis showed few instances in which formal organizational variables predicted changed response. Thus, the effect of training on these entrants remains somewhat opaque.

In contrast, there was consistent support for the view that informal organizational influences shaped entrants. On the welfare side, entrants indicated that they worked closely with their fellow entrants and went to them frequently for advice about how to handle a case. Similarly, the police indicated that they learned how to do their jobs from the veterans whom they encountered on the force after graduation. The statistical analysis of police officers' surveys showed that veterans and peers were important predictors of entrants' motivations and attitudes. Furthermore, new police influenced by the department's culture appeared to adopt somewhat different bureaucratic identities than those who were not.

As such, this book reinforces the findings from prior studies that show the importance of the social dynamics among organization members (Brehm and Gates 1997). As entrants undergo institutional socialization, they are flooded with messages from department elites and trainers. After they complete their training, they move into work where they are monitored by superiors. Throughout it all, the evidence here shows, entrants are shaped more by the people with whom they interact on a daily basis—fellow rookie and veteran officers—than by formal influences. As a result, it appears that informal influences might be a more fruitful explanation for the modest change observed in this study.

Comparing Entrants and Veterans

The primacy of informal influences—including organization veterans—offers a nice segue into another goal of this chapter: comparing the bureaucratic personalities of entrants and veterans. Chapter 3 discussed the views held by veterans in these two organizations. The goal of that chapter was to provide a rough outline of the views of workers who had finished entry and become "insiders." Though it was not expected that all newcomers would come to share veterans' views, it is useful to understand how entrants compared to those who had been inside their organizations for a longer period of time. The evidence here suggests that congruence was relatively simple to achieve: in many ways entrants shared the views of experienced workers when they entered their organizations.

In regard to motivation, welfare caseworker veterans were mostly motivated by egoistic rewards like the job's benefits; as readers will recall from Chapter 5, caseworker entrants shared that primary motivation throughout the study. In contrast, there was more of a mixture of motivations among veteran police officers. Mirroring this trend, entrants also reported a mix of egoistic and altruistic motives throughout the study.

In terms of bureaucratic identity, police veterans saw themselves as versatile, powerful, and loyal to the department; they also saw themselves as rule followers but responsive to situations and people. Caseworker veterans saw themselves as going case by case, but having little real power or personal control to help or punish. There was very little loyalty in the welfare department. At the outset, both sets of entrants articulated a high regard for the rules that, over time, they moved away from (at least in part). As a result, it would seem that entrants had some lessons to learn about how to see themselves vis-à-vis the rules. However, they entered expecting to follow the approach articulated by most veterans: beginning encounters without bias and then responding based on the specifics of the encounter and individual. In regard to loyalty, police and welfare entrants matched veterans throughout the study.

Finally, with respect to attitudes, veteran police tended to see the world as bifurcated into good and bad and saw deservingness as linked to civilian characteristics such as work ethic and demeanor. There was not a consensus about the cause of social problems: veterans expressed structural and individual-centered views. Police entrants, throughout the study, also saw deservingness as linked to demeanor and characteristics; during entry they shifted toward a more individual-centered view of criminality. In the welfare department, veterans had more uniform views: they saw welfare clients as individually responsible for their situations but saw social problems as resulting from structural forces. Welfare entrants initially had somewhat mixed views of welfare recipients, but saw social problems in structural terms. Over time they shifted toward seeing welfare recipients as more individually responsible for being poor.

Overall, this section suggests broad consonance between the bureaucratic personalities held by veterans and entrants. Although entrants didn't perfectly mirror the views held by insiders prior to entry, the distance between insiders and outsiders wasn't far. As such, becoming an insider might more aptly be described as a subtle shift than a radical reconstruction.

Theorizing Bureaucracies and Bureaucratic Socialization

The implications of such an understanding of bureaucratic socialization are potentially profound. First, the extreme argument that bureaucracies "give birth to a new species of inhuman beings" (Hummel 1982, 3) would seem to bear little resemblance to reality. Additionally, the more nuanced and common view among scholars, that institutional factors are the most important influences on organizational thought and behavior, may also need rethinking. This is especially so since this book's findings echo those from military socialization studies (Bachman et al. 1987; Bachman et al. 2000; Jackson et al. 2012). Because military and police socialization are often referred to as cases in which organizations have a strong effect on entrants, much of this conventional wisdom may be suspect.

Rather, the findings here suggest that most of the work of organizational replication and maintenance depends upon recruitment and self-selection. In this way, the book's findings fit with Schneider's (1987) attraction-selection-attrition cycle. This theory suggests that organizations are largely a function of the people they attract, choose, and keep.[4] More colloquially, Schneider argues that "the people make the place." In many respects, the findings here support this proposition. However, focusing on the people in a particular place has the potential to obscure the deeper social patterns that lead people to particular organizations and drive organizations to select particular people. Thus, while recognizing the importance of "the people" it is important to see bureaucracies as porous and connected with their environments. In other words, the findings here suggest that understanding the character of a bureaucracy may best be understood using an open systems approach (Scott 2003). From this perspective, who is attracted to and sought out by a bureaucracy would depend on how the organization draws from and interacts with its environment. For example, recall Jacob's comments, quoted in Chapter 5, about why he wanted to be a police officer: "Um, I always wanted to be a cop. My dad's a cop, his dad's a cop, my dad's brother's a cop. I just grew up with that mentality, and you pay attention to it. And you say to yourself maybe it's something I'm interested in, and you check it out and you just realize that it's already a part of you, you already think like a cop because it's all you've known, is how to think like one."

As this officer's observation shows, it may be useful to think of a bureaucracy's human resources as including people who are not official members or formally affiliated with them. Rather, we might think of a bureaucracy as a coalition of like-minded people, some of whom are formally associated with it (insiders) and some of whom are not (outsiders). In fact, the findings here suggest that insiders may serve as recruiters and outsiders, including clients or customers, as a talent pool. For instance, recall that many welfare entrants were encouraged to apply for the job by the welfare caseworkers who were determining their eligibility. Similarly, like Jacob, many police entrants joined the force after hearing from police family members or friends that they could do the job.

This understanding of an organization's human capital has implications for how it functions and its capacity to change (Kaufman 1975; Kelman 2005; J. Wilson 1989). As members exit or retire from a bureaucracy, elites often seek out "new blood"—rookie workers who either are impressionable or will arrive with fresh perspectives—to push the organization in a new direction. However, the findings here suggest that unaffiliated members may share the sensibilities or habitus of existing or exiting members. As a result, new members may actually serve to maintain the organization's current trajectory.

If these findings are generally true, bringing change to an organization's personnel may require looking beyond the typical approaches to recruitment and hiring people who are not naturally drawn to the organization. Rather, organizations would want to develop fresh protocols to locate and attract workers from new sources. This could mean, counterintuitively, finding workers who have poor person-organization fits (O'Reilly, Chatman, and Caldwell 1991). The costs associated with hiring workers who don't neatly fold into the existing organization's patterns of thought and action may be the price to pay for achieving organizational change.

However, even if this approach is taken, change may prove elusive. And this leads to a final point about how this book's findings should be understood. Although the relative scope of change observed here was modest, that may be because there was a fairly good person-organization fit in both cases. In other words, there might have been little observable change because both bureaucracies recruited and selected entrants who were "preformed." But even if this is true, the findings here don't necessarily mean that bureaucracies *cannot* substantially change people. As outsiders enter organizations they have contact with insiders and, perhaps, begin to identify with new colleagues. As they develop a new peer group, social identity theory expects that they will, to some extent at least, adopt established sensibilities (Ashforth and Mael 1989). As a result, if researchers find a case study in which entrants don't share the outlook of insiders, they may discover that newcomers conform to the thinking and patterns of behavior of existing members. The amount of bureaucratic personality change observed, in other words, may depend on how close newcomers are to veterans when they begin their careers.

Thus, the book doesn't end arguing that bureaucracies are impotent or that situations don't matter. Rather, the argument is that government organizations are socially situated: citizens who aren't inside its formal confines may, nonetheless, understand and share its values and culture. Therefore, the traditional understanding that bureaucracies change people may be true but beside the point. More important, in this account, is how bureaucracies find people and how people find them.

Future Research

There are many interesting avenues available for future research. First, it is important to know how general the findings of this book are. To what extent does entry across a wide variety of government agencies conform to the patterns described here? Since there were key similarities and differences between the two cases here, there is clearly much to be learned by further study. Along these lines, this book set forth a general perspective of bureaucratic personality, but was able to study only particular elements of it. Working within the framework developed here, future work could investigate a variety of other types of outcomes. For instance, one identity outcome that is particularly relevant for public administration research is representativeness—the perception by bureaucrats about whom they represent. By studying representativeness from a developmental perspective, we can build a better understanding of when and why bureaucrats act as representatives.

Second, it is interesting to note that this book's statistical analysis did a better job of explaining variation in entrants' views at each point in time than in explaining the likelihood of change. Although some dispositional and institutional variables explained the likelihood of change, in general the analysis revealed no strong patterns across all three areas of bureaucratic personality and both cases. In other words, while the analysis shows a pattern of differential continuity, more research is needed to understand why some individuals changed while others remained static. Some of the classic explanations—like age, education, and training—were not consistent, powerful predictors of change and stability. Future research should explore which dispositional and institutional factors explain the likelihood of change at the individual level.

Finally, the book's findings show the complexity of the interactions between people and bureaucracies when examined temporally. In the various public affairs literatures—public administration, public management, and political science—it is typical to study people and bureaucracies using a cross-sectional research design. However, such an approach misses many of the important nuances about how bureaucracies change and remain the same; cross-sectional approaches also have a difficult time showing where and when public organizations exert influence on individuals. Thus, the book closes with a call for more bureaucratic socialization studies—we should pay close attention to how public employees enter their organizations, interact with management over time, and contribute to change and inertia. In doing so, we can gain a deeper appreciation for how bureaucracies shape entrants, how public policy is made, and whom citizens are likely to encounter when they interact with government.

APPENDIX A

Research Design

Case Choices

To examine the diverging expectations set forth in Chapters 1 and 2, this book outlines the findings from a comparative case study of entering police officers and welfare caseworkers. These two cases were selected because they have much in common but also differ in important ways. This section discusses the similarities and differences between these cases and why they are useful for understanding the process of bureaucratic socialization.

Similarities Between the Cases

Police officers and welfare caseworkers belong to the class of street-level bureaucrats—workers who have some discretion and interact face-to-face with the public (Lipsky 1980). Though they operate in different settings, they share much in common and have been referred to as the "archetypical" and "paradigmatic" street-level bureaucrats (Brehm and Gates 1997; Maynard-Moody and Portillo 2010). Both groups must process a large number of people on a regular basis (Hasenfeld 1972; Lipsky 1980; Prottas 1979). As they do their work, they assess and classify situations and people (Rubinstein 1973; Sandfort, Kalil, and Gottschalk 1999). This means both groups are charged with transforming messy human situations into neat "cases." This is a burden, but it is also a source of power: by deciding who goes into which categories these workers can affect people's material well-being, freedom, and social statuses. Processing and assessing people, prior studies suggest, pushes street-level bureaucrats toward skepticism: they are concerned with arriving at an accurate assessment of people's situations (getting "the real story") and, as a result, tend to bring a cynical or critical eye to interactions with the public (Sandfort, Kalil, and Gottschalk 1999; Twersky-Glasner 2005; Van Maanen 1974).

Another way that these bureaucrats are similar is that they both operate in highly formalized, "rule-saturated" environments (Maynard-Moody and Musheno 2003). Both have thick guidebooks filled with policies that are meant to guide their every action. Although rule saturation may provide workers with some amount of guidance, it is also presents a problem: the guidebooks are voluminous, constantly being updated, and, sometimes, contradictory. As a result, it is difficult for police and welfare caseworkers to know all the relevant policies and to keep up with changes. When two policies contradict, they must determine how to proceed. Therefore, although they operate in highly formalized environments, these workers are not necessarily "rule bound." Rather, rule saturation may actually enhance their power: since they cannot know everything, they, to some extent, pick and choose which rules to follow. This is not to suggest that these are rogue operators who are contemptuous of the rules. Rather, the rules are part constraint and part resource.

Police officers and welfare caseworkers are also similar cases because both sets of workers operate in organizations that have, to at least some extent, joined the performance management revolution (Moynihan 2008). Using this approach to management, organizations collect real-time information and monitor the actions of organization members. Managers then use this information to make relevant organizational decisions. In theory this type of management is supposed to lead to more effective public organizations. However, as critics have noted (Radin 2000; Soss, Fording, and Schram 2011b), in practice performance management can lead to perverse incentives and a distortion of how public organizations function. Though these two cases are linked in that both have adopted performance management, it is important to comment on how each has been implemented to illustrate their comparability.

Police officers have traditionally operated outside the view of superiors (D. Smith and Visher 1981). As part of the performance management movement, in recent years departments have adopted Compstat programs in an effort to track real-time crime developments and more effectively monitor officers (D. Smith and Bratton 2001). In particular, many departments have installed cameras in police vehicles to document automobile stops and use computers to document and track police behavior. Although this may reduce officer discretion in some ways, many interactions with civilians occur off camera in nonautomotive interactions. Also, more important, Compstat programs ultimately depend on the paperwork submitted by officers. As a result, though Compstat and technological changes have made it easier to monitor police, officers retain significant power over the information by which they will be judged. Also, the rising demand for police supervisors to monitor officer behavior and crime reporting may counterintuitively diminish their actual knowledge of what is happening on the streets. Some sergeants in departments that have adopted Compstat-like performance management reforms report feeling even more drowned in paperwork than before, spending less time on the streets and being unable to fully support officers (Butterfield, Edwards, and Woodall 2005). Therefore, despite the adoption of performance management, and the technological advances in monitoring over the past twenty years, police retain significant discretion (Novak, Smith, and Frank 2003). They can make an arrest, give a warning, choose a particular space for surveillance, and prioritize which law breaking to penalize.

In welfare offices performance management has manifested in similar ways. Many aspects of a caseworker's caseload are monitored remotely by supervisors and upper-level managers within the office. This ability means that managers can track how many cases a worker has and which cases are pending or require attention and action. As a result, in some ways managers have enhanced power over caseworkers who cannot ignore self-generated computer alerts or manager-generated emails. However, like with the police, caseworkers control the information that enters the performance management machine and, therefore, retain considerable power. For example, a caseworker is the point of contact when an applicant arrives at the office to apply for benefits. How quickly applications are entered into the system, and moved along after verifying certain requirements are met, is ultimately decided by caseworkers. Similarly, the blinking computer alerts that greet caseworkers each day are ultimately satisfied as they see fit. As a result, although an alert may disappear from a manager's computer, that does not mean that the problem was dealt with properly.

As this short description shows, performance management has altered the ways in which police officers and welfare caseworkers are monitored. However, in both cases it would be exaggerating to say that the reforms have given supervisors a perfect understanding of the behaviors of frontline workers. Also, it seems too soon to tell whether these changes have seriously altered the balance of power between frontline workers and supervisors. As such, these cases are similar and useful for comparison.

Moving away from performance management, police and welfare caseworkers are also similar because they both use powerful symbols to exercise their authority (Thompson 1961). Police wear uniforms and guns and invoke authority quite easily. Though they do not carry weapons, welfare caseworkers, with their computers, folders, and forms, also portray state power. In fact, the welfare application process—in which an applicant sits across the desk from a caseworker, who stares at a computer and enters information—quickly establishes the power of the caseworker: the computer screen, which is unseen by applicants, appears powerful and mystical. By controlling what goes into the computer, the caseworker shares in this mystification (Lurie 2006).

These cases are also comparable because, as with other street-level bureaucrats, both police and welfare caseworkers interact with low-income populations on a regular basis (Lipsky 1980). Police must attend to poor and rich neighborhoods, but they spend significant time and energy policing the poor (Rubenstein 1973). Welfare caseworkers, by definition, have repeated and sustained interactions with poor people who must come to them to preserve their economic well-being. As a result, both sets of workers play important roles in poor neighborhoods: police set the terms of the use of force and determine which people will enter the criminal justice system (D. Smith and Visher 1981); welfare caseworkers have the power to affect the material and physical well-being of poor families.

Finally, from a training and development standpoint, welfare caseworkers and police cadets have similar experiences. Both groups are typically trained institutionally (i.e., in groups) as opposed to individually (Jones 1986). As a result, they enter "classes" or "cohorts" that serve as networks for sensemaking. Also, in the research city at least, police and welfare training takes approximately six months. In addition, the two specific departments studied here also handled promotion similarly. In the welfare department, an entrant must have worked as a caseworker for two years prior to applying to become a supervisor. In the police department, an entrant must have worked as an officer for two years before applying to become a sergeant. Thus, entrants from both cases remained at the entry level throughout the study and are, in that way, comparable.

Differences Between the Cases

Since they come from the same class of bureaucrats, and their jobs are similar in some respects, these cases are useful to compare. However, it is also important to understand the ways that these cases differ. As discussed in Chapter 1, one important way that these cases differ is in *a priori* expectations about the strength of socialization into them. Police officer socialization is expected to be considerably stronger than welfare caseworker socialization. Additionally, these two cases have different histories. During different eras, welfare caseworkers have had varying levels of training and education. In the 1950s and 1960s, welfare was administered predominantly by white women who had degrees in social work and a strong normative commitment to activism and social justice (Leighninger 1999; Wagner 1990). The 1970s was a period of change for social work. First, the nation experienced a massive shift in workplace gender norms prodded by the feminist movement. As a result, educated women had more job opportunities outside the realm of social work (Wagner 1990). Simultaneously, as welfare policy shifted toward the twin goals of eligibility determination and work promotion, the role of a welfare caseworker became seen as unskilled, and potentially repressive (Leighninger 1999; Wagner 1990). As a result of these changes, welfare casework by the end of the 1970s was largely deprofessionalized, and trained social workers in modern times tend to be employed in sectors other than welfare provision (Gibelman and Schervish 1997; Leighninger 1999; Schram 2011; Specht and Courtney 1995; Watkins-Hayes 2009).

As a result, this is not an examination of social worker development. Although there are no national data about the racial and gender dynamics of welfare casework over time, there is evidence that welfare offices, around the time of the study, employed a significant number of female and minority caseworkers (Lurie, Riccucci, and Meyers 2001; Watkins-Hayes 2009). The entering caseworkers in this study reflected these general trends: 74 percent were racial minorities and 71 percent were women. Most racial minorities identified as black or African American; however, for ease of analysis this book dichotomizes race as "white" and "minority."

In the first decade of the twenty-first century, when the data for this project were collected, welfare caseworkers operated in a decentralized policy environment in which states and local governments had significant autonomy over welfare policy. Though welfare reform in the 1980s and 1990s pushed a greater emphasis on encouraging work, caseworkers were still primarily responsible for determining program eligibility and ensuring that work requirements were met (Lurie 2006; Riccucci 2005). In particular, they were responsible for administering the Temporary Assistance for Needy Families (the means-tested cash program that replaced Aid to Families with Dependent Children), Food Stamps, and Medicaid programs. Although the duties associated with this administration were somewhat rote, welfare caseworkers retained significant discretion (Brodkin 2007; Lurie 2006; Riccucci 2005; Sandfort 2000). They could speed up or slow down the time it took to process a case, influence the sanctioning process (whereby individuals or whole families have their cash grant reduced or ended), deter clients from applying for welfare, challenge or accept the validity of documents, and grant "good cause" for exceptions to program guidelines. Though they worked in close proximity to other workers, with towering caseloads and distant supervisors, they retained significant autonomy.

Police work began as a way for societies to regulate violations of moral and religious law. Over time, this shifted and police became responsible for regulating secular conduct and enforcing democratically enacted laws (Rubinstein 1973). Though the particulars of enforcement have changed, police have long been understood as agents of social control: they monitor community behavior and respond to and investigate disturbances. Unsurprisingly, this role has often led to conflict between police and the communities that they monitor. In the United States, there has been a long history of strife between minority communities and police departments (Nelson 2001). In contrast to welfare casework, police officer jobs have tended to attract recruits with less education; however, due to the position's power and prestige, police work has typically been a relatively high-status, middle-class job. Demographically, though there were some changes at the end of the twentieth century, policing in the United States remains a primarily white, male occupation (Gould and Volbrecht 1999; Weisburd et al. 2001). The entering police officers in this study reflected these general trends: 67 percent of police entrants were white and 87 percent were men. Most racial minorities identified as black or African American; however, for ease of analysis this book dichotomizes race as "white" and "minority."

In terms of day-to-day work, at the time of the study police patrol officers spent most of their time mediating interpersonal disputes (domestic calls), patrolling, and enforcing traffic violations. Although there have been efforts to reform police behavior—in particular, many departments have introduced "community policing"—most police departments today are tasked with two traditional goals: keeping the peace and enforcing the law. To accomplish these goals, police have a vast array of tools at their disposal, including, among others, handcuffs, billy clubs, firearms, stun guns, and pepper spray. In comparison with the tools used by welfare caseworkers, which involve paperwork, verification, and data entry, police have a great many options for how to deal with situations.

In addition to having different jobs and histories, the two organizations studied here also had different age recruitment regulations. The police required that entering cadets be at least nineteen years old but younger than forty on their first day of their appointment; the welfare department had no established age requirements. Perhaps as a result of these differences, the police entrants studied in this project were younger (mean age of twenty-six) than the entering welfare caseworkers (mean age of thirty-six).

Gaining Access to the Police and Welfare Departments

Police

Gaining access to the workers in each of the subject groups required different tactics. To gain access to the police academy's recruits I arranged a meeting with some members of the academy training staff. At the meeting I informed them about my research interests, and they indicated that they were willing to assist me if I received approval from the commissioner's office. I sent a letter to the commissioner, and after several meetings with the commissioner's legal counsel, we signed a research agreement.

With the agreement signed, I met with the commissioner's legal counsel, the academy chief, and other high-ranking academy instructors. The chief was briefed on my research plan and offered his assistance with the project. Though my initial plan was to collect data at three times, the chief suggested that significant changes occur at the academy and that I should survey the cadets at the halfway point of the academy and at its completion to observe those changes. I accepted the chief's suggestion and refer to those surveys as Times 2 and 3. Unfortunately, as described below, it wasn't possible to survey welfare caseworker entrants at those times.

I asked to have access to the cadets on their first day at the academy, and the chief agreed but indicated that they were unlikely to participate without his assistance. He said that he would introduce me to them and ask them to participate in the project. I had initially hoped to bring some food item to encourage the cadets to participate. However, the chief indicated that the academy was quite strict about food during the first few months and that I should consider having something made up with the department's name and the academy's class. After some deliberation, the chief suggested handing out pens inscribed with the academy's name and the cadets' class number. As I describe below (in the "Surveys" section), I followed his suggestion.

Welfare

To gain access to the welfare department, I decided to become a welfare caseworker in the city. To begin, I scheduled an appointment and took the state's civil service exam. After receiving my score, I was contacted for an interview with the human resources department. The interview went well and soon thereafter I received an offer to start work as a welfare caseworker for the state. Shortly after beginning my employment, I met with the head of the human resources department and signed a research agreement. He also provided me with the names and addresses of all trainees who were undergoing training at the same time that I was. On the first day of training I was in a room with about twenty-five other trainees. When we went around the room to introduce ourselves, I announced that I was a graduate student completing a dissertation in political science. As part of my project, I informed them, I would be asking to speak with them about their experiences in the welfare department.

Method

As discussed in Chapter 1, I used two main research methods to gather data for this book: in-depth interviews and pen-and-paper surveys. In addition, I underwent a period of "observant participation" (Wacquant 2004)—during the first year of the study I trained and was employed as a welfare caseworker. This section provides further details about each of these methods.

Surveys
Police: Administration and Concurrence

To collect population-wide data I surveyed all police entrants at five times: at the beginning of their training period (Time 1), after three months of training (Time 2), at the completion of training (Time 3), at the end of their first year on the job (Time 4), and at the end of their second year on the job (Time 5). Time 1 police surveys refer to cadets' first day at the academy. On that day, the cadets were assembled in a large auditorium and were seated alphabetically. I brought gift pens that I had ordered, as the chief suggested. The chief introduced me and my project. His introduction highlighted my interest in police work and indicated to them that participation was voluntary. I addressed the cadets from a podium and told them a little bit about myself and the project; in particular, I told them that the surveys were confidential and no one in the department would ever see their answers. Since all of the police cadets had the chance to take their Time 1 survey at the exact same time, the data gathered at that time are strongly concurrent.

Following the chief's suggestion, I returned to administer surveys at the academy to the same cadets two more times (Times 2 and 3). Since the academy lasted

6 months, I returned at the halfway point and in the final days before graduation. In these situations the cadets were divided into four platoons, and I visited each of their classrooms to administer the surveys. Again, cadets were told that participation was voluntary and that all information would be kept confidential. At these times the rules on food had been relaxed. To encourage their participation I provided candy bars and gum to all participants. Again all cadets had the chance to take the Time 2 and Time 3 surveys at the exact same time, so these data are strongly concurrent.

A year from their entrance into the department (Time 4), police had graduated from the academy and had been on the streets for six months. Since they had been deployed to districts around the city, surveys were sent to the officers by U.S. or electronic mail. Participants were again rewarded with an engraved pen, which I sent to them after receiving their returned survey. This process was repeated again a year later (Time 5). Although all entrants received surveys on approximately the same day, some took longer than others to complete and return the survey. As a result, the survey data from Times 4 and 5 are reasonably concurrent: I estimate that all survey data at this time were collected within a two-month period. Responses that were received after this period were not included in the analysis.

Police: Response Rates, Nonresponse, and Attrition

Of the ninety entering police cadets, eighty-four chose to participate at Time 1—a response rate of 93 percent. Due to resignation, termination, and other reasons, four cadets left the academy. Of the eighty-six remaining, seventy-seven cadets chose to participate at Time 2, for a response rate of 89 percent; seventy-three chose to participate at Time 3, for a response rate of 85 percent. The fourth time that I surveyed the group, due to resignations, transfers, and terminations, seventy-two remained employed with the department. Of the officers remaining on the force, forty-one returned surveys, for a response rate of 57 percent. By the end of their second year in the department, sixty-eight officers remained on the force; of those remaining, fifty returned surveys, for a response rate of 74 percent.

Since all entering police employed by the department had the chance to complete a survey at each time, this was a population-wide survey free of sampling problems. However, after police graduated from the academy the response rate dropped. In an effort to detect response bias at Times 4 and 5, I predicted police officers' likelihood of responding using a multivariate model that included a variety of demographic and attitudinal predictors. At Time 4 there were no statistically significant predictors of responding. At Time 5 the responses were generally unbiased, but men were more likely to respond than women. The cause of this pattern is unclear as I made equal efforts to reach out to all officers. Due to this finding, the book's statistical analysis of police officers' survey responses does not use sex in its model.

In addition to response bias, longitudinal research projects must reckon with concerns about attrition bias: perhaps those who dropped out of the study, in this case by leaving their jobs, held different views from those who stayed. If true, the appearance of change or continuity at the group level could mask actual individual-level change. To examine this possibility, I estimated police officers' likelihood of dropping out at Times 4 and 5 based on a model that included various demographic and attitudinal characteristics. This analysis showed that, by and large, attrition was not related to the variables that I examined. However, at Time 4 older cadets were more likely to drop out of the academy; by Time 5 this relationship had diminished and there were no strong predictors of attrition. In addition, I compared the responses of the sixteen officers who left the department prior to the end of the second year to those of their peers who remained in the department. This analysis showed that the officers who dropped out of the department did not hold significantly different views than those who stayed. Finally, I compared officers' group-level responses in total and after dropping the Time 1 responses of officers who departed. This analysis also revealed no major differences.

Welfare: Administration and Concurrence

In the welfare department there were seventy-six caseworkers undergoing training when the project began. Although we were all at the training facility at the same time, one class was ahead of mine by a number of days, and another was behind my class by a number of days. Since these differences were not major, and entrants were at roughly the same place in their development, I treat all entrants as a single cohort. (Below, in the "Project Limitations" section, I discuss this decision further as well as tests to determine whether this was a reasonable decision.) I administered surveys to those entrants from my classroom on a break during the first days of training. Since I didn't have direct contact with the other two classes, I mailed surveys to them at their home addresses. I incentivized participation by providing participants with a candy bar (my class) or five dollars (other classes). Due to the differences in when they completed their first survey, the data gathered at that time are reasonably concurrent: they were collected within the same month.

At Times 4 and 5, caseworker entrants had graduated from training and begun working as caseworkers. Since they were dispersed around the city, I sent them surveys via U.S. or electronic mail. All participants were given five dollars for returning their surveys. As at Time 1, these survey data were not all collected at the exact same moment; nonetheless, the survey data at these times are reasonably concurrent since they were all collected within the same two-month period. Responses that were received after this period were not included in the analysis.

Welfare: Response Rates, Nonresponse, and Attrition

Thirty-four caseworkers returned surveys at Time 1, for a response rate of 45 percent. After Time 1, there was considerable attrition among caseworker entrants. Unfortunately, no official human resource information was made available to me, so it was impossible to know how many of the entering seventy-six caseworkers had exited the department. However, I learned through word of mouth that eight of the thirty-four workers who had participated at Time 1 had resigned. I applied this attrition rate to the group as a whole and estimate that fifty-eight of the entering seventy-six caseworkers remained at Time 4. Of this group, twenty returned surveys at Time 4, for an estimated response rate of 34 percent. By the end of their second year on the job (Time 5), I learned through word of mouth that thirteen caseworkers of the initial thirty-four had exited. I applied this new rate to the group and estimate that forty-seven of the entering seventy-six caseworkers remained at Time 5; of this total, sixteen returned surveys, for a response rate of 34 percent.

To determine whether there was any bias in caseworker response patterns at Times 4 and 5, I examined their likelihood of responding using multivariate probit estimates. Since I had no data on the seventy-six entrants, I used the initial thirty-four respondents as my baseline. I found that there were no statistically significant response patterns at Times 4 and 5. Also, as I did with the police, I sought to explore caseworkers' surveys to determine if the data suffered from attrition bias: perhaps those who exited the department held different views from those who stayed. To examine this possibility, I predicted caseworkers' likelihood of exiting the welfare agency based on a variety of demographic and attitudinal characteristics. Again I used the initial thirty-four respondents as the baseline since I had no information on nonrespondents from Time 1. This analysis showed that there were no statistically significant predictors of workers' likelihood of dropping out of the welfare department. In addition to these estimates, I compared the responses of the caseworkers who left the department prior to the end of the second year with those of their peers who remained in the department. This analysis showed that the caseworkers who dropped out of the department did not hold different views than those who stayed. Finally, I compared caseworkers' group-level responses in total and after dropping the Time 1 responses of caseworkers who departed. This analysis also revealed no major differences.

Interviews

Since it was not feasible to conduct in-depth interviews with all entrants, I selected a sample of fifteen police officers and fourteen welfare caseworkers from among those who were willing to participate. In addition, I interviewed an entering caseworker who was employed in a private welfare-to-work agency at the same intervals. In essence, my goal was to get a sense of how private welfare entry differed from public welfare entry. However, there were significant differences between the two agencies in terms of how entrants were socialized and had contact with welfare clients. Specifically, public entrants were socialized as a group and did not become full organization members until after six months of training; private entrants were socialized individually and were full-time staff after a two-week training process. Due to these differences, interview data from my conversations with the private entrant are not included in this book. I interviewed members of these subgroups at three times: at the outset of training (Time 1), at the completion of one year in their organizations (Time 4), and at the end of their second year (Time 5). I conducted these interviews in person or over the phone; with the subjects' consent, I recorded all interviews and transcribed them for analysis. The interviews typically lasted about thirty to forty-five minutes. In return for their participation, I typically bought the interviewee a small meal or beverage. Since I could not conduct interviews simultaneously, I scheduled them around the two-month period when I administered surveys. Thus, although they were not all conducted at the exact same time, the interview data for this project are reasonably concurrent. All told, I conducted seventy-seven in-depth interviews with entrants over the course of the study.

Since the interviewee groups were samples, it is important to discuss how they were selected and how they compared to the broader pool of entrants. For the police, I asked for volunteers on the Time 1 survey. To examine the potential bias of volunteers I analyzed their likelihood of volunteering based on a variety of demographic and attitudinal predictors. The analysis showed that there were no strong predictors of cadets' willingness to participate in project interviews. As I chose police interviewees from those who were willing, I sought variation on key demographic characteristics like race, gender, income, age, political ideology, education, and prior government work. However, I balanced the desire for variation with the recognition that the project's interviewees needed to reflect the class as a whole. In an effort to compare interviewees with the general population of police entrants, I examined the average demographic summary statistics for the two groups. This analysis showed that, by and large, the interviewee pool had similar demographic characteristics as the cadet population.

I selected welfare interviewees by asking for their participation in person. No workers whom I asked for an interview turned down my request. Like with the police, in seeking interviewees I sought variation as well as a group that represented the population as a whole. To understand the extent to which the two groups were similar, I compared the welfare interviewees with the population as a whole. This analysis showed that the welfare interviewee pool was very similar to the trainee population as a whole. Of the initial fourteen caseworker interviewees, one resigned during training and two resigned around Time 4. These latter two workers were interviewed since they had gone through significant work in their district offices since Time 1. I was not able to reach the worker who resigned during training at Time 4. In all, thirteen of the original fourteen workers were interviewed at Time 4. By Time 5 another four workers had quit or were on maternity leave; unfortunately, at that time it wasn't possible to interview those caseworkers. However, I did interview all of the remaining seven caseworkers who were still employed by the department and working on a daily basis.

Substantively, interviews enabled me to get a more thorough understanding of workers' views. For instance, if a worker described herself as "by the book," I was able to ask what she meant by that. Interviews also offered the advantage of being more flexible than surveys. Though I followed an interview protocol in each session, interviews enabled me to ask relevant follow-up questions of workers and to hear stories in their own words. Interviews also allowed for greater interaction between me and the workers. This interaction enabled me to build trust and rapport with entrants, which, I hope, permitted more candor and comfort during the session. Interviews also had the advantage of removing the workers from their normal social milieu, which may have encouraged them to talk more freely about their views and experiences.

Observant Participation

In addition to the two main research methods, I also underwent training and worked in a welfare office for a year. As a result, I was able to experience much of the process that I wanted to observe. Borrowing Wacquant's (2004) term, I refer to this experience as "observant participation." This experience differs from an ethnography or participant observation since I was tracking my own experience as opposed to observing others' experiences. To document my experiences I maintained a field notes journal. Reflecting on the day's events in my journal helped me document key developments. In addition, experiencing what I was studying improved the project by helping me develop more meaningful research instruments and make sense of the data.

Though I did not have a comparable experience in the police department, there are a number of police academy and socialization ethnographies in the literature that were helpful for understanding police socialization (Chappell and Lanza-Kaduce 2010; Conlon 2004; Conti 2009; Rubinstein 1973; Van Maanen 1974). Also, I did spend many days at the police academy talking with instructors and observing some aspects of the training process. In addition, after cadets graduated and were working in the field, I visited many of the precincts in which they worked. Also, I engaged in a ride-along with one police entrant. Thus, although I did not have a comparable observant participation experience in the police department, I spent significant time observing the organization.

Project Limitations

Although this book's methodology is useful for answering its questions, it is important to note and discuss its limitations.

Generalization

First, as with most case studies, the book's empirical claims are limited. Although these two cases have been called "paradigmatic" and "archetypal" street-level bureaucracies (Brehm and Gates 1997; Maynard-Moody and Musheno 2003), they are not necessarily representative of other street-level bureaucracies or other bureaucracies. In addition, the research took place in a particular setting. As such, some of the findings may be location-specific. (But see the general discussion of the city's characteristics in Chapter 1.) It is also important to consider the timing of the study: the data were gathered from February/March 2006 to February/March 2008. The latter part of this period, of course, coincides with the beginning of a serious recession (Isidore 2010) and may have had an effect on entrants' views.

As a result of these particularities, this project does not seek to generalize empirically to all other street-level bureaucrats, the general class of bureaucrats, all U.S. police and caseworkers, or workers from different eras. Rather, the process described and explained here is best understood as an effort to refine our understanding of bureaucratic socialization at the level of theory. In other words, this book can be understood as an effort in theory building: its goal is to provide an empirical account that clarifies future expectations about the process of bureaucratic socialization.

Case and Temporal Unevenness

Another limitation of this study is that there was some unevenness between the cases. First, I had access to police cadets within hours of their arrival at the academy. As a result, my first survey of cadets (Time 1) came very close to capturing the cadets prior to entry. However, I did not have the opportunity to administer surveys to welfare entrants on their first day of training (though, as discussed above, I administered surveys within the first few days). Second, the welfare department's entry and training process was less cut-and-dry—some of the trainees in my class (including me) spent up to a month in the district office before officially beginning training. During this time we mostly completed clerical assignments, surfed the Internet, and chatted. Though we had no interactions with clients during that time, all around us were veteran caseworkers who found us interesting and would stop by to talk. Also, we were in the welfare office: the loudspeaker called out client names and appointments, workers rushed around busily or lollygagged; we saw that most workers' desks were disorderly and piled with papers; we saw the clients waiting in lines that sometimes snaked out the front door; and we began entering through the staff door, which required us to enter a code and which was affixed with a sign saying "Employees ONLY." The police did not have a comparable pretraining experience. Although this distinction is potentially problematic, as recounted in Chapter 4, many entrants in both organizations had contact with their organizations prior to becoming insiders. As such, this pretraining interlude in the welfare office may not have had much of an effect.

To determine the extent of this problem, in our first interview I asked entrants about their initial impressions of their organizations. In response, many welfare caseworkers indicated that they felt like outsiders at their offices—they described the district offices as alien places where they felt dismayed by the other workers, the conditions, and the way the clients were treated. For instance, when asked about her month at the district, Janet responded, "I think I want to quit because these people are saying, 'Girl, you better enjoy the training,' and everyone was just saying that and it's like wow that's a lot of work and everyone was complaining about the work and the changes. I understood them but then again from my perspective ok we're here to work and I already know it's gonna be a lot of work so that's what we're here for so what are you complaining about?" Similarly, when asked about her district, Jasmine responded, "They're weird. I think that honestly the people that have been there forever versus the people that are newer. The old people are always complaining and everything's bad the whole world's coming to an end type of people. The rules change everyday. Duh duh duh. And the people that haven't been there long are the laid back and quiet ones saying if you do the job you'll be ok." If the office felt "weird" and welfare trainees wanted to quit after their month in the district office, it seems clear that they continued to see themselves as organizational outsiders.

To develop a more systematic assessment of the degree to which pre-entry shaped caseworker entrants' views, I compared the amount of change on survey questions by caseworkers and police (see Chapter 8). This analysis shows that, over the two years, the average entrant in each group changed his or her survey responses by approximately the same amount. Thus, although it is impossible to know for sure, being inside the department before training may not have had a major effect on caseworker entrants.

In addition, there were temporal differences among the research methods: the surveys were administered very close to the first day of training for caseworkers and on the first day of training for police. However, the interviews were conducted during entrants' first two months in their organizations. As such, by the time that I interviewed them they may have internalized some organizational messages. This reality is both a strength and a limitation. It is a strength because it enabled me to ask entrants about their experiences in training thus far. As a result, I am able to see entrants in real time as they were making sense of life in their organizations. However, it can also be a limitation if, by dint of being in their organization, they had already altered their views, making Time 1 a less useful baseline. To assess this potential problem, I compared the responses given by entrants in Time 1 interviews and surveys. This analysis revealed few indications that Time

1 interview data were unaligned with Time 1 survey data. Nonetheless, since surveys provide a more accurate baseline snapshot of Time 1, the book's empirical chapters rely more on survey data to evaluate change and stability.

Finally, another potential temporal issue with welfare entrants is that, though all entrants were training concurrently, their start dates were not perfectly aligned. Unfortunately, although the human resources office provided me with entrants' home addresses, they didn't indicate which class entrants were in or by how many days entrants were separated. Thus, although all surveys from caseworker entrants who were in training at the same time are treated as concurrent, not all were at the exact same place in training. To examine the extent to which this was a substantive problem, I conducted a statistical analysis that separated members of my training class from other entrants who were in training at the same time, and compared their responses to survey questions. The analysis revealed that, among the book's major independent and dependent variables, there were no statistically significant differences between the groups at each time of the study.

Response Biases

One potential criticism of this project is that it suffers from social desirability bias—subjects may have consciously presented themselves to me in ways that they thought I would view more favorably (Podsakoff et al. 2003). If so, workers may have portrayed themselves as politically correct or might have been willing to reveal only instances when they used their discretion in a flattering or law-abiding way. Similarly, it could suffer from recollection bias if individuals mainly remembered positive experiences and subconsciously forgot about instances that were negative or that cast them in an unfavorable light (Walker, Skowronski, and Thompson 2003). These problems are difficult to diagnose and, therefore, address. However, during interviews, my general sense was that workers answered honestly and fully. This belief was buttressed when, on a number of occasions, workers recounted stories that cast themselves in unflattering lights and/or mentioned borderline illegal behavior. It's probably safe to assume that some workers felt more comfortable being honest with me than others, but it is difficult to know who felt what.

Another potential problem with the data is consistency bias, or the "practice effect" (Litwin 1995). This may have occurred if entrants became familiar with questions on the surveys and sought to achieve some measure of consistency in the views that they articulated. Since people do not want to seem like they are equivocating, respondents may have reported the same views as they did earlier in the project even if they no longer held them. This could be particularly true with the police who answered survey questions at five times during the study (compared with welfare caseworkers, who answered questions at three times). Unfortunately, there are no easy fixes for this problem and there are no ways to systematically check for it. However, in my interviews with workers I detected only one instance of a subject trying to remember his earlier answer. Despite his effort, this officer's answer was not consistent with his Time 1 answer.

Another potential problem is contamination: perhaps entrants discussed aspects of the study with one another and coordinated responses. If true, the research findings would be skewed. For a study that focuses on two groups of entering workers that are to some extent secluded from the rest of their future organizations, this is a potentially serious problem. In general I expect that any contamination effects will bias the research findings toward uniformity as opposed to heterogeneity. Though one might argue that this problem could be detected by examining the spread of workers' answers—a narrowing of the spread could be taken as indicating contamination—there are alternative explanations for such a development. In particular, socialization may cause workers to adopt similar views. As such, contamination is another difficult problem for this project to diagnose and remedy.

Despite this, there are two reasons to think that this project had little contamination. First, with the interview data I generally did not detect canned or "party-line" answers to my questions. There were definitely themes, based on training and supervision, but I never got the sense that workers were deliberately or subconsciously feeding each other answers. Second, the method in which I distributed surveys acted as a minor prevention against contamination. While the police completed their surveys at the academy I was able to administer them and ensure that there was minimal talking and communicating. After they graduated from the academy I sent surveys to their houses. Though they may have gotten together to fill out their surveys, sending them to their home addresses minimized contamination relative to sending the surveys to their workplaces. The same argument holds for welfare caseworkers. As a result, though I cannot be sure that the data that I gathered for this project are uncontaminated, I took various steps to prevent this problem.

Omitted Variable Bias

In the empirical chapters I conduct a statistical analysis of entrants' survey responses. As discussed in Appendix C, I made an effort to include as many possible influences (demographic and organizational) on entrants as possible. However, as with any model of the social world, there are inevitably variables that could not be or were not included (Oberfield 2012). In particular, it is important to note that the analysis does not include variables that measure the subjective experience that entrants had with the public (positive, negative, etc.), the objective crime or poverty rates of the district offices in which they worked, or how much work they were assigned from their superiors. Since each of these factors, as well as others that aren't on that list, could have played a role in shaping entrants' bureaucratic personalities, the book's analysis may suffer from omitted variable bias.

With that said, the statistical analysis includes variables that measure the key theoretical components of the dispositional and institutional perspectives (demographic characteristics, formal organizational influences, and informal organizational influences). In addition, the multivariate models include a lagged dependent variable. These variables are theorized as capturing a variety of time invariant influences on respondents' answers (Keele and Kelly 2006) and, as such, reduce concerns about omitted variable bias. As such, the findings are useful for assessing the utility of dispositional and institutional perspectives for explaining bureaucratic socialization.

Sample Size

As noted in the figures throughout the empirical chapters, the number of respondents at each time of the survey was relatively small. In part this was due to my resources during the project and my inability to track successive groups of entrants. As discussed above, the survey data suffer from little response or attrition bias. Nonetheless, attrition was a serious problem in the welfare case, so that by the end of the study (Time 5) approximately 40 percent of the class had quit or been terminated. With only 34 percent of the remaining caseworkers participating in the survey, it wasn't possible to utilize a multivariate statistical analysis for that case. As such, the power of the statistical analysis is limited and the population-wide descriptive statistics may be shaped by outliers. Despite this, bureaucratic socialization studies are exceedingly rare. As such, even if the number of participants in this study is relatively small, the book provides a useful account of development.

Behavior

Finally, it is important to acknowledge that this book theorizes that a connection exists between how bureaucrats think and act. This assumption has been made by many generations of organization theorists (Lipsky 1980; Maynard-Moody and Musheno 1993; Merton 1940; Simon 1997) and is central to the logic of appropriateness framework articulated in Chapter 1 (March and Olsen 2006). However, the book's data do not in fact chart bureaucratic behavior. As a result, it is not possible to empirically examine this theorized relationship. Thus, it is possible that the portrait of bureaucratic psychological development detailed here diverges from how a behavioral portrait would unfold. For instance, perhaps throughout the study an entrant articulated altruistic motivations for his service. However, analysis of administrative data, or the observations of an outside observer, suggests that his actions were mostly egoistic. Due to this possibility, the book should not be understood as studying bureaucratic behavioral development. Rather, readers should understand that, as laid out in Chapter 1, the book studies bureaucratic psychological development which is theorized to have behavioral implications.

Conclusion

This section has outlined a number of potential problems or limitations of the empirical data presented in this book. Where possible, I have sought to demonstrate that potential limitations weren't realized. Although it was not possible to do this with each concern, most of the potential problems are common to longitudinal studies. As such, though this analysis isn't perfect, the book's data are useful for answering its main question.

APPENDIX B

Recruitment and Job Requirements

Chapter 4 provides an in-depth portrait of the experiences that these two sets of workers had when they entered their organizations. Although the first day of training was an important milestone for newcomers, it is important to describe the recruitment tactics used by each of these organizations as well as the job requirements that entrants had to meet.

Recruitment

The first way that entrants had official, work-related contact with their organizations was via recruitment—the efforts made by the organization to attract new workers (Wanous 1992). Though entry into these organizations was ultimately determined by the individuals, and therefore shaped by self-selection, it is important to understand how the organizations presented themselves to attract candidates. Both agencies posted advertisements on their respective websites, and the police department advertised on billboards around the city. Both jobs were advertised with their pay levels, job duties, and requirements. The pay level for the police was approximately $40,000, while the pay level for welfare caseworkers was advertised as approximately $35,000.

The advertised job duties for being a police officer included patrolling, preventing and discovering crime, gathering evidence, making arrests, appearing in court, responding to complaints, and conducting investigations. Being a welfare caseworker was described as determining eligibility for various public assistance programs, interviewing applicants, establishing a contract with applicants that specified their rights and responsibilities, making referrals, and helping clients overcome employment barriers. In addition to these formal recruitment appeals, in both cases recruitment also occurred through more informal channels. Many police reported learning about the job from family and friends. Similarly, many welfare caseworkers reported learning about the job from family members or from their welfare caseworkers (see Chapter 5).

Requirements

The advertised requirements for being a police officer included being a city resident and U.S. citizen, having a high school education (or passing an equivalency exam), being at least nineteen years old, having the ability to learn and apply police procedures and the law, having the ability to cope with situations courteously, being able to analyze and make decisions quickly, writing and speaking effectively, using and caring for firearms effectively, being generally intelligent and emotionally stable, and being in acceptable physical and medical condition. In addition police recruits were informed that they would need to pass a written examination that tested police strategies, a reading test, a physical fitness test, a background investigation, a medical evaluation, a psychological evaluation, a drug test, as well as academy and on-the-job training. As in most U.S. police departments, candidates were not graded evenly on their written examinations: military veterans were given a set number of bonus points on the exam to reflect the department's hiring preference.

The requirements for being a welfare caseworker, a job described as stressful and demanding in the job advertisement, included being a state resident, having good moral character, having interviewing and analysis experience or a college degree, passing a civil service examination meant to gauge caseworker ability, passing an in-person interview, completing training, being able to manage a large caseload, being able to gather information by telephone or in person, and using a computer. Recruits who felt that they were able to meet the stated requirements and who took the civil service examinations were then put on waiting lists based on their scores. As positions became available, the department would take the top names off of the list. I had the good fortune of beginning this project in the winter of 2006 when both organizations were hiring; after the recession began, both agencies slowed or stopped hiring.

APPENDIX C

Measurement and Analysis

Modeling

To analyze entry, Chapters 5 to 7 rely on bivariate (welfare) and multivariate (police) statistical analysis of entrants' responses to survey questions. Since the two cases differ, and the theorized influences on entrants vary depending on where they were in their development, the book uses a variety of models (discussed below). The majority of the survey questions asked entrants to respond on a scale of 1 to 5. As such, I used ordered probit for the statistical analysis. Unfortunately, probit coefficients are difficult to interpret on their own. Therefore, the chapters present odds ratios—the probability of a certain outcome based on variation in an independent variable. An odds ratio of 1 implies that, due to an increase in an independent variable, the outcome is equally likely; an odds ratio greater than 1 implies that the outcome is more likely; an odds ratio less than 1 implies that the outcome is less likely.

Police

Participation by the entering police class was considerably higher than the entering welfare caseworker class. Over the course of entry, the police experienced considerably less attrition than the welfare agency. As a result, there were enough police observations at each time to permit multivariate statistical analysis. At entry police cadets had not yet entered their organizations, and thus the primary purpose of the analysis was to tease out differences in bureaucratic personality based on extraorganizational characteristics. The model that was used to analyze their views at entry included entrants' age, education, family income, receipt of welfare, race (coded as white or minority), experience in the armed services, and political ideology (a 7-point scale from liberal to conservative). While cadets were at the academy, at Times 2 and 3, the model included these extraorganizational variables, their Time 1 response to the relevant question (an autoregressive variable), and three organizational influences: training instructors, culture, and rookies. (All questions and statements used to create organizational variables are presented below in the section titled "Operationalization of Variables.") At Times 4 and 5, when cadets had graduated from the academy and begun work on the streets, the model included the extraorganizational variables, their Time 1 response to the relevant question (an autoregressive variable), as well as variables measuring the effect of training, culture, supervision, rookies, veterans, amount of work, and monitoring.

Welfare

Due to a lower response rate, and considerable attrition during entry, multivariate statistical analysis of caseworkers' bureaucratic personalities was not possible. Thus, at each time I analyzed their survey answers using bivariate analysis. This limits the power of the conclusions that can be drawn from this analysis—since any relationships do not control for other important factors—but permits a basic understanding of how independent and dependent variables were related. Like for the police, the variables that were used to analyze caseworkers' views at entry included entrants' age, education, family income, receipt of welfare, race (coded as non-Hispanic white or minority), experience in government work, and political ideology (a 7-point scale from liberal to conservative). At Times 4 and 5, after they had been inside the organization for a year and two years, respectively, the variables used to analyze caseworkers' views included the extraorganizational variables used at entry, their Time 1 response to the relevant question (an autoregressive variable), and organizational variables that sought to explore the influence of training, culture, supervision, rookies, veterans, the amount of work, and monitoring.

Operationalization of Variables

This section presents the survey questions used to operationalize the independent and dependent variables for the statistical analyses in Chapters 5 to 7. It also includes summary statistics of independent variables and a discussion of the validity and reliability of these questions.

Independent Variables
Police

- Training instructors: Times 2 and 3; an index variable composed of the following statements (Cronbach's α for the index at Time 2 = .80; at Time 3 = .79):
  - In general I don't feel like our training has been sufficient. (reversed)
  - Communication between the cadets and the trainers is pretty good.
  - Academy instructors pay close attention to our development.
  - The instructors' stories are an important aspect of learning this job.
  - It is easy to ask instructors questions when I feel confused.
- Training: Times 4 and 5; an index variable composed of the following statement and question (Cronbach's α for the index at Time 4 = .69; at Time 5 = .69):
  - In general I don't feel like our training was sufficient. (reversed)
  - Thinking about how you do your job, how much [does what you learned at the Academy] influence you?
- Monitoring: Times 4 and 5; an index variable composed of the following question (Cronbach's α for the index at Time 4 = .83; at Time 5 = .86):
  - How closely are you monitored on the following actions?
    - Making arrests
    - Writing tickets
    - Walking or driving a beat
    - Keeping up with paperwork/reports
    - Interacting with civilians face-to-face
    - Using a weapon
    - Issuing warnings
- Culture: Times 2 and 3:
  - Just being around the Academy environment has had an effect on me.

- Culture: Times 4 and 5:
    - The district environment has had an effect on me.
- Veterans: Times 4 and 5:
    - When you think about how you do your job, how much [do veteran officers in your district] influence you?
- Supervisors: Times 4 and 5:
    - When you think about how you do your job, how much [does your superior officer] influence you?
- Rookies: Times 2 and 3:
    - I haven't learned much from other cadets. (reversed)
- Rookies: Times 4 and 5:
    - When you think about how you do your job, how much [other rookies in your district] influence you?
- Amount of work: Times 4 and 5:
    - When you think about how you do your job, how much [the amount of work you have] influence you?

Welfare

- Training: Time 4:
    - When you think about how you do your job, how much [does what you learned in training] influence you?
- Training: Time 5:
    - When you think about how you do your job, how much [does training] influence you?
- Monitoring: Time 4; an index variable composed of the following question (Cronbach's α for the index = .81):
    - How closely are you monitored on the following actions?
        - Processing reapplications
        - Processing [reporting forms]
        - Processing child care
        - Maintaining [computer databases]
        - Interviewing clients face-to-face
        - Interacting with clients on the phone
        - Explaining how a client is managing
- Monitoring: Time 5; an index variable composed of the following question (Cronbach's α for the index = .76):

- How closely are you monitored on the following actions?
  - Processing reapplications
  - Processing [reporting forms]
  - Maintaining [computer databases]
  - Interviewing clients face-to-face
  - Interacting with clients on the phone
  - Explaining how a client is managing
- Culture: Times 4 and 5:
  - When you think about how you do your job, how much [does the district culture] influence you?
- Veterans: Times 4 and 5:
  - When you think about how you do your job, how much [do veteran workers] influence you?
- Supervisors: Times 4 and 5:
  - When you think about how you do your job, how much [does your supervisor] influence you?
- Rookies: Times 4 and 5:
  - When you think about how you do your job, how much [do other rookies in your unit (Time 4) and (workers you trained with (Time 5)] influence you?
- Amount of work: Times 4 and 5:
  - When you think about how you do your job, how much [does the amount of work you have] influence you?

Summary Statistics
Police officer entrants

	N	Mean	Std. Dev.	Min	Max
Education	83	2.00	0.96	1	4
Age	74	26.39	4.81	19	39
Family income	82	4.87	1.68	1	7
Welfare receipt	80	0.25	0.44	0	1
Race	81	0.67	0.47	0	1
Armed forces	84	0.35	0.48	0	1
Political ideology	81	4.06	1.29	1	7
Time 2: Training instructors	75	22.16	2.28	16	25
Time 2: Culture	74	4.30	0.70	2	5
Time 2: Rookies	74	3.88	0.91	1	5
Time 3: Training instructors	72	21.00	2.95	12	25
Time 3: Culture	73	4.00	0.90	1	5

Summary Statistics
Police officer entrants

	N	Mean	Std. Dev.	Min	Max
Time 3: Rookies	72	3.83	0.93	1	5
Time 4: Culture	41	3.37	0.94	1	5
Time 4: Supervisor	40	3.50	1.20	1	5
Time 4: Rookies	40	2.53	1.22	1	5
Time 4: Veteran officers	40	3.88	1.02	1	5
Time 4: Amount of work	39	3.59	1.16	1	5
Time 4: Monitoring	41	24.15	5.17	11	35
Time 5: Training	48	6.33	1.94	2	10
Time 5: Culture	49	3.65	1.01	1	5
Time 5: Supervisor	49	3.18	1.09	1	5
Time 5: Rookies	50	2.20	1.20	1	5
Time 5: Veteran officers	50	3.16	1.20	1	5
Time 5: Amount of work	49	3.27	1.19	1	5
Time 5: Monitoring	50	23.26	6.64	10	35

Welfare caseworker entrants

	N	Mean	Std. Dev.	Min	Max
Education	34	3.74	1.08	2	6
Age	27	35.96	11.23	22	56
Family income	34	4.15	2.40	1	8
Welfare receipt	33	0.79	0.42	0	1
Female	34	0.71	0.46	0	1
Race	34	0.26	0.45	0	1
Prior government work	34	0.38	0.49	0	1
Political ideology	33	3.36	1.41	1	6
Time 4: Training	20	10.10	2.25	5	13
Time 4: Monitoring	19	15.74	5.17	9	26
Time 4: Culture	18	2.78	1.40	1	5
Time 4: Amount of work	19	4.32	0.75	3	5
Time 4: Supervisors	20	4.15	0.88	3	5
Time 4: Rookies	20	3.00	1.38	1	5
Time 4: Veterans	19	2.37	1.07	1	4
Time 5: Training	16	3.25	1.06	1	5
Time 5: Monitoring	13	16.38	5.91	6	28
Time 5: Culture	15	2.53	1.30	1	5
Time 5: Amount of work	16	4.38	0.89	3	5
Time 5: Supervisors	16	2.88	1.26	1	5
Time 5: Rookies	16	1.94	1.00	1	4
Time 5: Veterans	16	1.75	0.93	1	4

Dependent Variables

This section summarizes the questions used to measure the book's dependent variables.

Motivation

To measure motivation at Time 1, police were asked, "When you think back to why you wanted to join the force, how important was each of the following?" They were then given the list of motivations presented in Chapter 5. Respondents indicated how much they were motivated by each on a 5-point scale from "not at all" to "a lot" (they were also given the option of having no opinion). At the conclusion of that section of the survey, police were then asked, "Of the above reasons (1–8), which one was most important to you? ___ (indicate the #)." At Times 2 and 3 they were asked, "What is your motivation for completing the Academy and becoming a police officer?" They were given the same list of motivations and the same 5-point scale. Again they were asked which of the reasons was most important to them. At Times 4 and 5 they were asked, "What is your motivation for being a police officer?" They were given the same list of motivations and the same 5-point scale. Again they were asked which of the reasons was most important to them.

To measure motivation at Time 1, caseworkers were asked, "Thinking back to why you wanted to work in welfare, how important was each of the following?" They were then given the list of motivations presented in Chapter 5. Respondents indicated how much they were motivated by each on a 5-point scale from "not at all" to "a lot" (they were also given the option of having no opinion). At the conclusion of that section of the survey, they were then asked, "Of the above reasons (1–6), which one was most important to you? ___ (indicate the #)." At Times 4 and 5 they were asked, "How important [is] each of the following in explaining why you continue to work as an [caseworker]?" They were given the same list of motivations and the same 5-point scale. Again they were asked which of the reasons was most important to them.

Identities and Attitudes

For survey questions used for dependent variables in Chapters 6 and 7, respondents were asked to "please indicate how much you agree or disagree with the following statements." They then chose an answer on a 5-point scale from "strongly disagree" to "strongly agree" (they were also given the option of having no opinion). The full list of specific statements can be found in the relevant chapter.

Reliability and Validity

In addition to presenting the survey questions used to create the variables for this book's statistical analysis, it is important to discuss the survey instrument's reliability and validity. Reliability measures the extent to which data collected on a survey instrument are reproducible (Litwin 1995). The most common way to test for reliability is the test-retest approach, in which the same group is given a survey at two different times and researchers aim to understand the stability of their responses (using correlation coefficients). Though entrants were asked the same questions repeatedly in this study, comparing present and past answers will not measure reliability because it is theorized that they were undergoing a process that included some amount of change.

Although it wasn't possible to assess the instrument's reliability over time, I did make efforts to assess its internal reliability using alternate form questions (reversed). For example, as readers can see in Chapter 6, the questions about entrants' rule-following identities are reversed so that for some questions a higher score indicates greater rule following and for others a higher score indicates greater discretion use. As readers will recall from the discussion of survey results in Chapter 6, these questions resulted in similar trends over time suggesting that the questions were reliable. Another nontemporal way of assessing reliability is through use of an internal consistency reliability measure (like Cronbach's alpha). This measure compares the statistical relationship between respondents' answers to similarly worded questions. Unfortunately, due to an interest in asking a broad array of questions, there was little substantive overlap in many areas of the instrument. For example, each of the motivation questions points to a distinct motivation. Although they can be roughly classified as altruistic or egoistic, they are not measuring the exact same motivation. Therefore, internal reliability scores were not useful for assessing reliability.

Validity refers to the extent to which a survey instrument faithfully measures what it sets out to measure (Adcock and Collier 2001; Litwin 1995). Assessing validity is a lengthy, iterative process whereby measures are created, tested and refined. In each interaction, there are three main ways of assessing validity: face, content, and construct. Face validity is the most casual and refers to the process of distributing the survey instrument to a group of untrained people. These people are asked to make a general assessment of the extent to which the survey instrument measures what it claims to measure. To assess the face validity of the survey instruments used in this research project, I gave the survey to fifteen fellow graduate students and acquaintances prior to my administering it to a pretest group of caseworkers. This group recommended changing some of the wording and ordering of the questions, but, in general, they agreed that the instrument was valid.

Content validity is a subjective assessment made by a set of reviewers with expertise in related areas of research (Litwin 1995). In essence, experts are asked to assess the extent to which indicators accurately and fully measure a concept. To assess the survey instrument's content validity I asked members of my dissertation committee, experts in the areas of welfare policy, public opinion, and political psychology, and welfare managers (government employees working in welfare offices above the caseworker position) to examine the survey. (Unfortunately it was not possible to share the police instrument with a police chief or supervisor.) Again these outside experts made recommendations for changes in question terminology and order, but, in general, they agreed the instrument was valid.

There are different views about how to evaluate construct validity. Litwin (1995) argues that assessments of construct validity are determined by how meaningful a survey is in practice. Taking this approach requires a relatively long period of time during which a survey is in the field and being used by researchers and practitioners. Since this project's timeline did not allow for multiple periods of entrance, and the results of the survey are only now being published, it is difficult to assess construct validity in this way. Another approach to evaluating construct validity uses statistical tools – like confirmatory factor analysis – to evaluate the extent to which composite measures in a multivariate analysis are different from other composite measures and internally related. This approach asks, in essence, whether composite measures have sufficient discriminant and convergent validity (Adcock and Collier 2001). In this project, multivariate analysis was only used to measure police survey items.

At Times 2 and 3, only one composite variable was employed (training instructors) so there was no way to formally determine discriminant/convergent validity. However, above I showed that the composite variables had acceptable levels of internal reliability (Cronbach's α) which is similar to examining convergent validity. Additionally, a correlation analysis, which is not presented here due to space limitations, revealed that no independent variables were correlated above the $r = 0.60$ level. Again, this is not a formal way to evaluate discriminant validity but it offers some perspective on the extent to which different variables were related to one another.

At Times 4 and 5, the police model included two composite variables (training and monitoring). Above I showed that the composite variables had acceptable levels of internal reliability. Additionally, a correlation analysis revealed that none of the model's independent variables were correlated above the level of $r = 0.60$. A confirmatory factor analysis examining these two variables at each time revealed mixed evidence of convergent/discriminant validity. At Time 4 the fit indices used to measure this type of validity were borderline: the CFI, which should be above 0.90, was 0.50 and the RMSEA, which should be below 0.08, was 0.14. At Time 5, the fit indices indicated more acceptable levels of convergent/discriminant validity: the CFI was 0.81 and the RMSEA was 0.07.

In summary, the measures used in this project have relatively high levels of face and content validity. The levels of construct validity are somewhat lower but, on the whole, still acceptable.

NOTES

Chapter 1. Bureaucratic Socialization

1. The term "bureaucrat" refers to an employee of a bureaucracy—an administrative agency of government (Plano and Greenberg 1985; Safire 1978; Smith and Zurcher 1949). The term need not apply solely to government agencies; however, that is how it is generally understood.

2. This definition borrows from Wanberg (2012a, 17) and others in the organizational socialization (OS) literature. The main difference is that the OS literature focuses on the general process of organizational entry, whereas this book focuses exclusively on entry into public organizations. Though this distinction is one of degree and not kind, it is important because public and private organizations are subject to different types of political and economic pressures (Bozeman 2004; Meier and O'Toole 2011; Perry and Rainey 1988). At times, the term "bureaucratic development" will be used synonymously with "bureaucratic socialization."

3. As discussed below, there are a variety of studies in the organizational socialization literature that take a longitudinal approach to development. Although these studies are informative, they tend to focus on private-sector workers, a narrow range of outcomes (like satisfaction and productivity), and short periods of time. There are also a few recent works that have tried to understand bureaucratic motivation over time (see, for example, Kjeldsen and Jacobsen 2012).

4. There is some overlap between this term and "professional identity" (Watkins-Hayes 2009). However, "bureaucratic identity" is preferable for this study since it directs attention more precisely to the organization in which workers operate rather than their broader set of professional commitments.

5. Arguing that bureaucrats use their attitudes to understand situations and decide how to respond does not imply that their attitudes are deterministically linked to behavior. Rather, as per the LOA, attitudes should be understood as one important psychological factor that has the potential to influence how bureaucrats behave.

6. For exceptions, see Fielding (1988), Rubinstein (1973), Teahan (1975), and Van Maanen (1974, 1975).

7. As discussed in Appendix A, at the time of the study, few welfare caseworkers were

trained social workers. As such, readers should understand that the term "caseworker" is not used as a synonym for "social worker."

8. Though these workers differ in obvious and important ways, they share much in common and have been referred to as "paradigmatic" and "archetypal" street-level bureaucrats (Brehm and Gates 1997; Maynard-Moody and Portillo 2010). See Appendix A for an overview of the similarities and differences between these two cases.

9. See Appendix A for an overview of how these research methods were used to gather the data analyzed in this book. In addition, Appendix A contains a description of how I gained access to these two populations. All personal names used in connection with interviews that I conducted for this book are pseudonyms.

10. See Appendix A for a discussion of the limitations of this research design.

Chapter 2. Dispositions and Institutions

1. Van Maanen is quoting from Ahern (1972).

2. Although impressionability may reemerge in advanced age, such concerns are beyond the scope of this book since few bureaucratic entrants are elderly.

3. Although training need not refer only to the period in which entrants encounter their organizations for the first time, this is the type of training discussed here. These types of training are sometimes referred to as "orientation programs" in the organizational socialization literature (Saks and Gruman 2012).

4. Subsequent studies have depicted a more positive view of institutionalized tactics: they may be associated with less role ambiguity, role conflict, and turnover intent and better job satisfaction and performance (Saks and Gruman 2012).

5. For information about modeling, see Appendix C.

6. For information about operationalization of institutional variables, see Appendix C.

Chapter 3. The Long View

1. This survey was fielded in 2001 and was funded by the Rockefeller Institute for Government; it analyzed welfare systems in four states: Michigan, New York, Georgia, and Texas. The survey mainly focused on public welfare caseworkers but also included nonpublic welfare-to-work workers. Since my study focuses on public welfare caseworkers, all data presented focus only on public workers.

2. Sanctioning is an act in which part or all of an individual's welfare grant is reduced as a penalty for not following agency rules.

3. Many of the questions set up five-point Likert-type responses ranging from "strongly disagree" to "strongly agree." For the purposes of this analysis I collapsed the "agree" and "strongly agree" categories as well as the "disagree" and "strongly disagree" categories.

4. This question asked, "When you think about TANF clients, including both recipients and applicants, approximately how many: receive welfare due to circumstances beyond their control?" For the purposes of the above discussion I reversed the question.

Chapter 4. Entry

1. See Appendix B for a description of the experiences that recruits had with their organizations prior to entry as well as a description of the requirements for getting a job in each of these organizations.

2. One of the goals of welfare reform in the 1990s was to make welfare provision seem more like a service and less like an entitlement. As part of this goal, welfare departments around the nation rejected the term "welfare recipients" and began referring to recipients as "customers" or "clients." Although the reality of this language is somewhat suspect—dissatisfied welfare recipients could not go elsewhere if they were unhappy with the treatment they received—this book sometimes borrows this language.

3. See Appendix C for the full text of these questions.

4. Each program received roughly a week of training sessions.

5. The Food Stamps program is now called the Supplemental Nutrition Assistance Program (SNAP).

6. Poverty ethnographies suggest that there are a variety of informal sources from which low-income women can receive support, including the father of a child, a parent, and under-the-table work (DeParle 2005; Stack 1975; Venkatesh 2006).

7. One of the classic examples of suspicious management, trainees were told, was when a claimant indicated that her rent and utility bills exceeded her monthly income. How then, trainees were instructed to ask, was she "managing"?

8. This statement was given as "I haven't learned much from other cadets," but it is reversed here for ease of presentation.

9. For a full description of caseworker monitoring, see Appendix A.

10. In my experience there was some truth to what these workers said: I often did not have a good sense of when I was being lied to and, much to the consternation of my supervisors, sometimes accepted applicants' dubious claims about their lives and cases.

Chapter 5. In the Service of Others?

1. The full questions asked at each time can be found in Appendix C.

2. Though family influences do not fit neatly into the altruistic/egoistic framework, it was important to include nonetheless.

3. Since the family motive could not be classified as altruistic or egoistic, it was excluded from the altruistic-egoistic analysis of entrants' primary motives.

4. Although the population of respondents at each time varied somewhat, Appendix A shows that the data were generally free of attrition and response bias throughout the study.

5. The maximum of the y-axis is 4 because that would represent the largest possible change from one time to another.

6. These figures include only entrants who answered this question at entry and Time 5.

7. Information about modeling and operationalization can be found in Appendix C.

8. As a reminder, an odds ratio of 1 indicates that, due to an increase in an independent

variable, the outcome is equally likely. Therefore, an odds ratio of 4.5, as seen in Figure 5.4 (for fair treatment), is interpreted as indicating that respondents are 3.5 times more likely to be so motivated.

9. Twenty-seven entering police indicated that they were racial minorities. Of this group, 75 percent identified as black or African American, 15 percent identified as Hispanic, and 11 percent identified as Asian.

10. Due to space constraints, it was not possible to include odds ratio figures to analyze the relationship between each variable and motivation. As such, this sentence refers to findings from an unreported analysis of the relationship between informal influences and motivation.

11. The full questions asked at each time can be found in Appendix C.

12. Although fraud prevention may not accord with some readers' understanding of altruism, I define it as such because the primary beneficiary is the collective (the agency or the state's taxpayers), not the caseworker.

13. Because the number of respondents at each time was fairly small, readers should interpret descriptive and explanatory statistics with some caution.

14. The maximum of the y-axis is 4 because that would represent the largest possible change from one time to another.

15. Due to a lower response rate, and considerable attrition during entry, multivariate statistical analysis of caseworkers' motivations was not possible. Thus, at each time I analyzed their survey answers using bivariate analysis. This limits the power of the conclusions that can be drawn from this analysis—since any relationships do not control for other important factors—but permits a basic understanding of how independent and dependent variables were related. Information about operationalization can be found in Appendix C.

Chapter 6. Bureaucratic Identity

1. The only question in which the spread narrowed over time was the question about whether situations and people should be dealt with on a "case-by-case" basis.

2. Although the population of respondents at each time varied somewhat, Appendix A shows that the data were generally free of attrition and response bias throughout the study.

3. The maximum of the y-axis is 4 because that would represent the largest possible change from one time to another.

4. Information about modeling and operationalization can be found in Appendix C.

5. See Appendix A for a more detailed discussion of this topic.

6. Aspects of this caseworker's biography have been changed to protect her anonymity.

7. Because the number of respondents at each time was fairly small, readers should interpret descriptive and explanatory statistics with some caution.

8. Although the population of respondents at each time varied somewhat, Appendix A shows that the data were generally free of attrition and response bias throughout the study.

9. The maximum of the y-axis is 4 because that would represent the largest possible change from one time to another.

10. These figures include only entrants who answered this question at entry and Time 5.

11. Information about operationalization can be found in Appendix C.

Chapter 7. Attitudes

1. Although the population of respondents at each time varied somewhat, Appendix A shows that the data were generally free of attrition and response bias throughout the study.

2. The figures depict the mean change of officers' attitudes in scalar points; since the figures show absolute values, each bar indicates total change, not change toward a particular position. The maximum of the y-axis is 4 because that would represent the largest possible change from one time to another.

3. These figures include only entrants who answered this question at entry and Time 5.

4. Information about modeling and operationalization can be found in Appendix C.

5. Because the number of respondents at each time was fairly small, readers should interpret descriptive and explanatory statistics with some caution.

6. The maximum of the y-axis is 4 because that would represent the largest possible change from one time to another.

7. Information about operationalization can be found in Appendix C.

Chapter 8. Change and Continuity at Government's Front Lines

1. For a discussion of the project's limitations, see Appendix A.

2. The maximum of the y-axis is 4 because that would represent the largest possible change from Time 1 to Time 5.

3. These figures include only entrants who answered this question at entry and Time 5.

4. The major difference between Schneider's account and this one is the role of attrition. Appendix A shows that there were few measurable differences between the entrants who left and those who remained.

BIBLIOGRAPHY

Abdelal, R., Y. Herrera, A. Johnston, and R. McDermott. 2009. *Measuring Identity: A Guide for Social Scientists*. New York: Cambridge University Press.

Aberbach, J., and B. Rockman. 2000. *In the Web of Politics: Three Decades of the US Federal Executive*. Washington, D.C.: Brookings Institution Press.

Adcock, R., and D. Collier. 2001. "Measurement Validity: A Shared Standard for Qualitative and Quantitative Research." *American Political Science Review* 95 (3): 529–46.

Ahern, J. 1972. *Police in Trouble: Our Frightening Crisis in Law Enforcement*. New York: Hawthorn Books.

Ajzen, I. 2001. "Nature and Operation of Attitudes." *Annual Review of Psychology* 52 (1): 27–58.

Allinson, C. 1984. *Bureaucratic Personality and Organization Structure*. London: Gower.

Alpert, G., and R. Dunham. 2004. *Understanding Police Use of Force: Officers, Suspects, and Reciprocity*. New York: Cambridge University Press.

Arendt, H. 1963. *Eichmann in Jerusalem: A Report on the Banality of Evil*. New York: Penguin.

Argyris, C. 1957. *Personality and Organization: The Conflict Between System and the Individual*. New York: Harper.

———. 1993. *Integrating the Individual and the Organization*. New York: John Wiley.

Ashforth, B., and F. Mael. 1989. "Social Identity Theory and the Organization." *Academy of Management Review* 14 (1): 20–39.

Bachman, J., P. Freedman-Doan, D. Segal, and P. O'Malley. 2000. "Distinctive Military Attitudes Among U.S. Enlistees, 1976–1997: Self-Selection Versus Socialization." *Armed Forces and Society* 26 (4): 561–85.

Bachman, J., L. Sigelman, and G. Diamond. 1987. "Self-Selection, Socialization, and Distinctive Military Values: Attitudes of High School Seniors." *Armed Forces and Society* 13 (2): 169–87.

Bakker, A., and E. Heuven. 2006. "Emotional Dissonance, Burnout, and In-Role Performance Among Nurses and Police Officers." *International Journal of Stress Management* 13 (4): 423–40.

Balch, R. 1972. "The Police Personality: Fact or Fiction?" *Journal of Criminal Law, Criminology, and Police Science* 63 (1): 106–19.

Bardach, E. 1977. *The Implementation Game: What Happens When a Bill Becomes Law*. Cambridge, Mass.: MIT Press.
Bardach, E., and R. Kagan. 1982. *Going by the Book: The Problem of Regulatory Unreasonableness*. Philadelphia: Temple University Press.
Barnard, C. 1938. *The Functions of the Executive*. Cambridge, Mass.: Harvard University Press.
Barnett, M. 1999. *Eyewitness to a Genocide: The United Nations and Rwanda*. Ithaca, N.Y.: Cornell University Press.
Bass, B., and B. Avolio. 1994. "Transformational Leadership and Organizational Culture." *International Journal of Public Administration* 17 (3): 541–54.
Becker, B., and P. Connor. 2005. "Self-Selection or Socialization of Public-and Private-Sector Managers? A Cross-Cultural Values Analysis." *Journal of Business Research* 58 (1): 111–13.
Blau, P. 1955. *The Dynamics of Bureaucracy*. Chicago: University of Chicago Press.
Bourdieu, P. 1990. *The Logic of Practice*. Stanford, Calif.: Stanford University Press.
Bozeman, B. 2004. *All Organizations Are Public: Bridging Public and Private Organizational Theories*. Washington, D.C.: Beard Books.
Bozeman, B., and H. Rainey. 1998. "Organizational Rules and the 'Bureaucratic Personality.'" *American Journal of Political Science* 42 (1): 163–89.
Brehm, J., and S. Gates. 1997. *Working, Shirking, and Sabotage: Bureaucratic Response to a Democratic Public*. Ann Arbor: University of Michigan Press.
Brewer, G., and S. Selden. 1998. "Whistle Blowers in the Federal Civil Service: New Evidence of the Public Service Ethic." *Journal of Public Administration Research and Theory* 8 (3): 413–40.
Brewer, G., S. Selden, and R. Facer. 2000. "Individual Conceptions of Public Service Motivation." *Public Administration Review* 60 (3): 254–64.
Brodkin, E. 2007. "Bureaucracy Redux: Management Reformism and the Welfare State." *Journal of Public Administration Research and Theory* 17 (1): 1–17.
Brown, M. 1988. *Working the Street: Police Discretion and the Dilemmas of Reform*. New York: Russell Sage Foundation.
Brubaker, R., and F. Cooper. 2000. "Beyond 'Identity.'" *Theory and Society* 29 (1): 1–47.
Bruch, S., M. Ferree, and J. Soss. 2010. "From Policy to Polity: Democracy, Paternalism, and the Incorporation of Disadvantaged Citizens." *American Sociological Review* 75 (2): 205–26.
Butterfield, R., C. Edwards, and J. Woodall. 2005. "The New Public Management and Managerial Roles: The Case of the Police Sergeant." *British Journal of Management* 16 (4): 329–41.
Caro, R. 1975. *The Power Broker: Robert Moses and the Fall of New York*. New York: Vintage.
Carpenter, D. 2001. *The Forging of Bureaucratic Autonomy: Reputations, Networks, and Policy Innovation in Executive Agencies, 1862–1928*. Princeton, N.J.: Princeton University Press.

Caspi, A., and B. Roberts. 2001. "Personality Development Across the Life Course: The Argument for Change and Continuity." *Psychological Inquiry* 12 (2): 49–66.

Center for Budget and Policy Priorities. 2013. "What Is Medicaid?" Washington, D.C.: Center for Budget and Policy Priorities. http://www.cbpp.org/cms/index.cfm?fa=view&id=2223.

Chappell, A., and L. Lanza-Kaduce. 2010. "Police Academy Socialization: Understanding the Lessons Learned in a Paramilitary-Bureaucratic Organization." *Journal of Contemporary Ethnography* 39 (2): 187–214.

Cheek, C., and K. Piercy. 2001. "The Other Side of the Desk: Former Welfare Recipients Who Now Work for 'The System.'" *Journal of Sociology and Social Welfare* 28 (3): 139–56.

Chemerinsky, E. 2000. "An Independent Analysis of the Los Angeles Police Department's Board of Inquiry Report on the Rampart Scandal." *Loyola of Los Angeles Law Review* 34: 545–656.

Chetkovich, C. A. 1997. *Real Heat: Gender and Race in the Urban Fire Service*. New Brunswick, N.J.: Rutgers University Press.

Conlon, E. 2004. *Blue Blood*. New York: Riverhead Books.

Conti, N. 2009. "A Visigoth System: Shame, Honor, and Police Socialization." *Journal of Contemporary Ethnography* 38 (3): 409–32.

Cook, F., and E. Barrett. 1992. *Support for the American Welfare State: The Views of Congress and the Public*. New York: Columbia University Press.

Cooper-Thomas, H., and N. Anderson. 2006. "Organizational Socialization: A New Theoretical Model and Recommendations for Future Research and HRM Practices in Organizations." *Journal of Managerial Psychology* 21 (5): 492–516.

Costa, P., and R. McCrae. 1994. "Set Like Plaster? Evidence for the Stability of Adult Personality." In *Can Personality Change?* edited by T. Heatherton and J. Weinberger. 21–40. Washington, D.C.: American Psychological Association.

Crewson, P. 1997. "Public-Service Motivation: Building Empirical Evidence of Incidence and Effect." *Journal of Public Administration Research and Theory* 7 (4): 499–518.

Crozier, M. 1964. *The Bureaucratic Phenomena*. Chicago: University of Chicago Press.

Dawson, M. 1994. *Behind the Mule: Race and Class in African-American Politics*. Princeton, N.J.: Princeton University Press.

De Fruyt, F., M. Bartels, K. G. Van Leeuwen, B. De Clercq, M. Decuyper, and I. Mervielde. 2006. "Five Types of Personality Continuity in Childhood and Adolescence." *Journal of Personality and Social Psychology* 91 (3): 538–52.

DeHart-Davis, L. 2007. "The Unbureaucratic Personality." *Public Administration Review* 67 (5): 892–903.

DeParle, J. 2005. *American Dream: Three Women, Ten Kids, and a Nation's Drive to End Welfare*. New York: Penguin.

Desmond, M. 2006. "Becoming a Firefighter." *Ethnography* 7 (4): 387–421.

———. 2007. *On the Fireline: Living and Dying with Wildland Firefighters*. Chicago: University of Chicago Press.

Dessler, G. 1999. "How to Earn Your Employees' Commitment." *Academy of Management Executive* 13 (2): 58–67.

Downs, A. 1967. *Inside Bureaucracy*. Boston: Little, Brown.

Elder, G. 1998. *Children of the Great Depression: Social Change in Life Experience*. Boulder, Colo.: Westview.

Ellemers, N., R. Spears, and B. Doosje. 2002. "Self and Social Identity." *Annual Review of Psychology*: 53: 161–87.

Ellwanger, S. 2010. "How Police Officers Learn Ethics." In *Justice, Crime and Ethics*, edited by M. Braswell, B. McCarthy, and B. McCarthy, 45–70. New York: Elsevier.

Evan, W. 1963. "Peer-Group Interaction and Organizational Socialization: A Study of Employee Turnover." *American Sociological Review* 28 (3): 436–40.

Evans, T., and J. Harris. 2004. "Street-Level Bureaucracy, Social Work and the (Exaggerated) Death of Discretion." *British Journal of Social Work* 34 (6): 871–95.

Falk, G., and R. Aussenberg. 2012. "The Supplemental Nutrition Assistance Program: Categorical Eligibility." Washington, D.C.: Congressional Research Service.

Fielding, N. 1988. *Joining Forces: Police Training, Socialization, and Occupational Competence*. New York: Routledge.

Gaines, L., N. Van Tubergen, and M. Paiva. 1984. "Police Officer Perceptions of Promotion as a Source of Motivation." *Journal of Criminal Justice* 12 (3): 265–75.

Gallo, G. 2001. *Armed and Dangerous: Memoirs of a Chicago Policewoman*. New York: Forge Books.

Gibelman, M., and P. Schervish. 1997. *Who We Are: A Second Look*. Washington, D.C.: NASW Press.

Gilens, M. 1999. *Why Americans Hate Welfare: Race, Media, and the Politics of Antipoverty Policy*. Chicago: University of Chicago Press.

Glaser, M. A, and J. Denhardt. 2010. "Community Policing and Community Building." *The American Review of Public Administration* 40 (3): 309.

Goffman, E. 1959. *The Presentation of Self in Everyday Life*. New York: Doubleday.

Golden, M. 2000. *What Motivates Bureaucrats? Politics and Administration During the Reagan Years*. New York: Columbia University Press.

Gordon, L. 1994. *Pitied but Not Entitled: Single Mothers and the History of Welfare, 1890–1935*. New York: Free Press.

Goodsell, C. 1984. "Welfare Waiting Rooms." *Journal of Contemporary Ethnography* 12 (4): 467–77.

———. 2004. *The Case for Bureaucracy: A Public Administration Polemic*. Washington, D.C.: CQ Press.

Gould, L., and M. Volbrecht. 1999. "Personality Differences Between Women Police Recruits, Their Male Counterparts, and the General Female Population." *Journal of Police and Criminal Psychology* 14 (1): 1–18.

Gourevitch, P., and E. Morris. 2008. "Exposure: The Woman Behind the Camera at Abu Ghraib." *New Yorker*. http://www.newyorker.com/reporting/2008/03/24/080324fa_fact_gourevitch.

Griffin, C., and J. Ruiz. 1999. "The Sociopathic Police Personality: Is It a Product of the 'Rotten Apple' or the 'Rotten Barrel?'" *Journal of Police and Criminal Psychology* 14 (1): 28–37.

Grissom, J., and L. Keiser. 2011. "A Supervisor Like Me: Race, Representation, and the Satisfaction and Turnover Decisions of Public Sector Employees." *Journal of Policy Analysis and Management* 30 (3): 557–80.

Hall, R. 1977. *Organizations: Structure and Process*. 2nd ed. Englewood Cliffs, N.J.: Prentice Hall.

Hall, R., N. Johnson, and J. Haas. 1967. "Organizational Size, Complexity, and Formalization." *American Sociological Review* 32 (6): 903–12.

Hampson, S., and L. Goldberg. 2006. "A First Large-Cohort Study of Personality-Trait Stability over the 40 Years Between Elementary School and Midlife." *Journal of Personality and Social Psychology* 91 (4): 763–69.

Hasenfeld, Y. 1972. "People Processing Organizations: An Exchange Approach." *American Sociological Review* 37 (3): 256–63.

Heatherton, T., and J. Weinberger. 1994. "Conceptual Issues in Assessing Whether Personality Can Change." In *Can Personality Change?* edited by T. Heatherton and J. Weinberger. 3–18. Washington, D.C.: American Psychological Association.

Hersh, S. 2004. "Torture at Abu Ghraib." *New Yorker* 10: 42–47.

Herzfeld, M. 1993. *The Social Production of Indifference: Exploring the Symbolic Roots of Western Bureaucracy*. Chicago: University of Chicago Press.

Heumann, M. 1981. *Plea Bargaining: The Experiences of Prosecutors, Judges, and Defense Attorneys*. Chicago: University of Chicago Press.

Houston, D. 2000. "Public-Service Motivation: A Multivariate Test." *Journal of Public Administration Research and Theory* 10 (4): 713–28.

Huber, G. 2007. *The Craft of Bureaucratic Neutrality: Interests and Influence in Governmental Regulation of Occupational Safety*. New York: Cambridge University Press.

Huber, J., and C. Shipan. 2002. *Deliberate Discretion: The Institutional Foundations of Bureaucratic Autonomy*. New York: Cambridge University Press.

Hummel, R. 1982. *The Bureaucratic Experience: A Critique of Life in the Modern Organization*. 2nd ed. New York: St. Martin's.

Inglehart, R. 1981. "Post-Materialism in an Environment of Insecurity." *American Political Science Review* 75 (4): 880–900.

Ingraham, P., P. Joyce, and A. Donahue. 2003. *Government Performance: Why Management Matters*. Baltimore: Johns Hopkins University Press.

Isidore, C. 2010. "Recession Officially Ended in June 2009." *CNN.com*. http://money.cnn.com/2010/09/20/news/economy/recession_over/index.htm.

Jackson, J., F. Thoemmes, K. Jonkmann, O. Lüdtke, and U. Trautwein. 2012. "Military Training and Personality Trait Development: Does the Military Make the Man, or Does the Man Make the Military?" *Psychological Science* 23 (3): 270–77.

Jennings, M. 1990. "The Crystallization of Orientations." In *Continuities in Political*

Action: A Longitudinal Study of Political Orientations in Three Western Democracies, edited by M. Jennings. 313–48. Berlin: Walter de Gruyter.

John, O., L. Naumann, and C. Soto. 2008. "Paradigm Shift to the Integrative Big Five Trait Taxonomy." In *Handbook of Personality: Theory and Research,* 3rd ed., edited by O. John, R. Robins, and L. Pervin, 114–58. New York: Guilford Press.

Jones, G. 1986. "Socialization Tactics, Self-Efficacy, and Newcomers' Adjustments to Organizations." *Academy of Management Journal* 29 (2): 262–79.

Kappeler, V., R. Sluder, and G. Alpert. 1998. *Forces of Deviance: Understanding the Dark Side of Policing*. Prospect Heights, Ill.: Waveland. http://works.bepress.com/vic_kappeler/10/.

Katz, D., and R. Kahn. 1966. *The Social Psychology of Organizations*. New York: John Wiley.

Katz, M. 2008. *The Price of Citizenship: Redefining the American Welfare State*. Philadelphia: University of Pennsylvania Press.

Kaufman, H. 1960. *The Forest Ranger: A Study in Administrative Behavior*. Washington, D.C.: Resources for the Future.

——. 1975. *The Limits of Organizational Change*. Tuscaloosa: University of Alabama Press.

Keele, L., and N. Kelly. 2006. "Dynamic Models for Dynamic Theories: The Ins and Outs of Lagged Dependent Variables." *Political Analysis* 14 (2): 186–205.

Keiser, L., V. Wilkins, K. Meier, and C. Holland. 2002. "Lipstick and Logarithms: Gender, Institutional Context, and Representative Bureaucracy." *American Political Science Review* 96 (3): 553–64.

Kelman, H., and V. Hamilton. 1990. *Crimes of Obedience: Toward a Social Psychology of Authority and Responsibility*. New Haven, Conn.: Yale University Press.

Kelman, S. 2005. *Unleashing Change a Study of Organizational Renewal in Government*. Washington, D.C.: Brookings Institution Press.

Kettl, D. 2002. *The Transformation of Governance: Public Administration for Twenty-First Century America*. Baltimore: Johns Hopkins University Press.

Kjeldsen, A., and C. Jacobsen. 2012. "Public Service Motivation and Employment Sector: Attraction or Socialization?" *Journal of Public Administration Research and Theory*. doi:10.1093/jopart/mus039. http://jpart.oxfordjournals.org/content/early/2012/10/26/jopart.mus039.

Koehler, M., and H. Rainey. 2008. "Interdisciplinary Foundations of Public Service Motivation." In *Motivation in Public Management: The Call of Public Service*, edited by J. Perry and A. Hondeghem. 33–55. New York: Oxford University Press.

Kohn, M. 1971. "Bureaucratic Man: A Portrait and an Interpretation." *American Sociological Review* 36 (3): 461–74.

Kornbluh, F. 2007. *The Battle for Welfare Rights: Politics and Poverty in Modern America*. Philadelphia: University of Pennsylvania Press.

Kuhlman, E. 1976. "Dogmatism and Deference: The Relationship Between Bureaucratic Orientation and Personality Type." *Alberta Journal of Educational Research* 22 (2): 179–86.

Lee, S., and D. Olshfski. 2002. "Employee Commitment and Firefighters: It's My Job." *Public Administration Review* 62: 108–14.

Lee, T. 2009. "Between Social Theory and Social Science Practice." In *Measuring Identity: A Guide for Social Scientists*, edited by R. Abdelal, Y. Herrera, A. Johnston, and R. McDermott. 113–44. New York: Cambridge University Press.

Leighninger, L. 1999. "The Service Trap: Social Work and Public Welfare." In *The Professionalization of Poverty: Social Work and the Poor in the Twentieth Century*, edited by G. Lowe and P. Reid. 63–88. Hawthorne, N.Y.: Aldine de Gruyter.

Lipsky, M. 1980. *Street-Level Bureaucracy: Dilemmas of the Individual in Public Service*. New York: Russell Sage Foundation.

Litwin, M. 1995. *How to Measure Survey Reliability and Validity*. Thousand Oaks, Calif.: Sage.

Louis, M. 1980. "Surprise and Sense-Making: What Newcomers Experience and How They Cope in Unfamiliar Organizational Settings." *Administrative Science Quarterly* 25: 226–51.

Lowe, K., K. Kroeck, and N. Sivasubramaniam. 1996. "Effectiveness Correlates of Transformational and Transactional Leadership: A Meta-Analytic Review of the MLQ Literature." *Leadership Quarterly* 7 (3): 385–425.

Lurie, I. 2006. *At the Front Lines of the Welfare System: A Perspective on the Decline in Welfare Caseloads*. Albany: State University of New York Press.

Lurie, I., N. Riccucci, and M. Meyers. 2001. "Survey of Front Line TANF Practices." Albany, N.Y.: Rockefeller Institute of Government.

Macvean, A., and C. Cox. 2012. "Police Education in a University Setting: Emerging Cultures and Attitudes." *Policing* 6 (1): 16–25.

March, J. 1994. *A Primer on Decision Making: How Decisions Happen*. New York: Free Press.

March, J., and J. Olsen. 2006. "The Logic of Appropriateness." In *The Oxford Handbook of Public Policy*, edited by M. Moran, M. Rein, and R. Goodin. 689–708. New York: Oxford University Press.

Martin, S. 1999. "Police Force or Police Service? Gender and Emotional Labor." *Annals of the American Academy of Political and Social Science* 561 (1): 111–26.

Maynard-Moody, S., and M. Musheno. 2003. *Cops, Teachers, Counselors: Stories from the Front Lines of Public Service*. Ann Arbor: University of Michigan Press.

Maynard-Moody, S., and S. Portillo. 2010. "Street-Level Bureaucracy Theory." In *The Oxford Handbook of Bureaucracy*, edited by R. Durant. 252–77. New York: Oxford University Press.

McElroy, J., P. Morrow, and T. Wardlow. 1999. "A Career Stage Analysis of Police Officer Work Commitment." *Journal of Criminal Justice* 27 (6): 507–16.

Meier, K. 1993. "Latinos and Representative Bureaucracy Testing the Thompson and Henderson Hypotheses." *Journal of Public Administration Research and Theory* 3 (4): 393–414.

Meier, K., and L. O'Toole. 2011. "Comparing Public and Private Management: Theoretical

Expectations." *Journal of Public Administration Research and Theory* 21 (suppl. 3): i283–99.
Merton, R. 1940. "Bureaucratic Structure and Personality." *Social Forces* 18 (4): 560–68.
Mettler, S. 1998. *Dividing Citizens: Gender and Federalism in New Deal Public Policy*. Ithaca, N.Y.: Cornell University Press.
Morrison, E. 2002. "Newcomers' Relationships: The Role of Social Network Ties During Socialization." *Academy of Management Journal* 45 (6): 1149–60.
Moynihan, D. 2007. "The Reality of Results: Managing for Results in State and Local Government." In *In Pursuit of Performance: Management Systems in State and Local Government*, edited by P. Ingraham. 151–77. Baltimore: Johns Hopkins University Press.
———. 2008. *The Dynamics of Performance Management: Constructing Information and Reform*. Washington, D.C.: Georgetown University Press.
Moynihan, D., and S. Pandey. 2007. "The Role of Organizations in Fostering Public Service Motivation." *Public Administration Review* 67 (1): 40–53.
Muir, W. 1977. *Police: Streetcorner Politicians*. Chicago: University of Chicago Press.
Myrdal, G. 1944. *An American Dilemma: The Negro Problem and Modern Democracy*. New York: Harper.
Nelson, J. 2001. *Police Brutality: An Anthology*. New York: Norton.
Novak, K., B. Smith, and J. Frank. 2003. "Strange Bedfellows: Civil Liability and Aggressive Policing." *Policing: An International Journal of Police Strategies and Management* 26 (2): 352–68.
Oberfield, Z. 2012. "Public Management in Time: A Longitudinal Examination of the Full Range of Leadership Theory." *Journal of Public Administration Research and Theory*. doi:10.1093/jopart/mus060.
O'Leary, R. 2010. "Guerrilla Employees: Should Managers Nurture, Tolerate, or Terminate Them?" *Public Administration Review* 70 (1): 8–19.
O'Reilly, C., J. Chatman, and D. Caldwell. 1991. "People and Organizational Culture: A Profile Comparison Approach to Assessing Person-Organization Fit." *Academy of Management Journal* 34 (3): 487–516.
Ostroff, C., and S. Kozlowski. 1992. "Organizational Socialization as a Learning Process: The Role of Information Acquisition." *Personnel Psychology* 45 (4): 849–74.
Perry, J. 1996. "Measuring Public Service Motivation: An Assessment of Construct Reliability and Validity." *Journal of Public Administration Research and Theory* 6 (1): 5–22.
———. 1997. "Antecedents of Public Service Motivation." *Journal of Public Administration Research and Theory* 7 (2): 181–97.
———. 2000. "Bringing Society In: Toward a Theory of Public-Service Motivation." *Journal of Public Administration Research and Theory* 10 (2): 471–88.
Perry, J., J. Brudney, D. Coursey, and L. Littlepage. 2008. "What Drives Morally Committed Citizens? A Study of the Antecedents of Public Service Motivation." *Public Administration Review* 68 (3): 445–58.

Perry, J., and A. Hondeghem. 2008. "Editors' Introduction." In *Motivation in Public Management: The Call of Public Service*, edited by J. Perry and A. Hondeghem. 1–14. New York: Oxford University Press.

Perry, J., and H. Rainey. 1988. "The Public-Private Distinction in Organization Theory: A Critique and Research Strategy." *Academy of Management Review* 13 (2): 182–201.

Perry, J., and W. Vandenabeele. 2008. "Behavioral Dynamics: Institutions, Identities, and Self-Regulation." In *Motivation in Public Management: The Call of Public Service*, edited by J. Perry and A. Hondeghem. 56–79. New York: Oxford University Press.

Perry, J., and L. Wise. 1990. "The Motivational Bases of Public Service." *Public Administration Review* 50 (3): 367–73.

Piliavin, J., and H. Charng. 1990. "Altruism: A Review of Recent Theory and Research." *Annual Review of Sociology* 16: 27–65.

Piven, F., and R. Cloward. 1979. *Poor People's Movements: Why They Succeed, How They Fail*. New York: Vintage.

Plano, J., and M. Greenberg. 1985. *The American Political Dictionary*. 7th ed. New York: Holt, Rinehart, and Winston.

Podsakoff, P., S. MacKenzie, J. Lee, and N. Podsakoff. 2003. "Common Method Biases in Behavioral Research: A Critical Review of the Literature and Recommended Remedies." *Journal of Applied Psychology* 88 (5): 879–903.

Portillo, S. 2008. "The Face of the State: The Role of Social Status and Official Position in the Mobilization of Authority." Lawrence: University of Kansas.

———. 2012. "The Paradox of Rules: Rules as Resources and Constraints." *Administration and Society* 44 (1): 87–108.

Portillo, S., and L. DeHart-Davis. 2009. "Gender and Organizational Rule Abidance." *Public Administration Review* 69 (2): 339–47.

Pressman, J., and A. Wildavsky. 1984. *Implementation: How Great Expectations in Washington Are Dashed in Oakland; Or, Why It's Amazing That Federal Programs Work at All, This Being a Saga of the Economic Development Administration as Told by Two Sympathetic Observers Who Seek to Build Morals on a Foundation*. Berkeley: University of California Press.

Prottas, J. 1979. *People-Processing: The Street-Level Bureaucrat in Public Service Bureaucracies*. Lexington, Mass.: Lexington Books.

Radin, B. 2000. "The Government Performance and Results Act and the Tradition of Federal Management Reform: Square Pegs in Round Holes?" *Journal of Public Administration Research and Theory* 10 (1): 111–35.

Raganella, A., and M. White. 2004. "Race, Gender, and Motivation for Becoming a Police Officer: Implications for Building a Representative Police Department." *Journal of Criminal Justice* 32 (6): 501–13.

Rainey, H. 2003. *Understanding and Managing Public Organizations*. 3rd ed. New York: Jossey-Bass.

Rainey, H., and P. Steinbauer. 1999. "Galloping Elephants: Developing Elements of a

Theory of Effective Government Organizations." *Journal of Public Administration Research and Theory* 9 (1): 1–32.

Reid, T. 2009. "'Abu Ghraib US Prison Guards Were Scapegoats for Bush' Lawyers Claim." *Sunday Times*. http://www.timesonline.co.uk/tol/news/world/iraq/article6207484.ece.

Reingold, D., and H. Liu. 2009. "Do Poverty Attitudes of Social Service Agency Directors Influence Organizational Behavior?" *Nonprofit and Voluntary Sector Quarterly* 38 (2): 307–32.

Riccucci, N. 2005. *How Management Matters: Street-Level Bureaucrats and Welfare Reform*. Washington, D.C.: Georgetown University Press.

Riccucci, N., M. Meyers, I. Lurie, and J. Han. 2004. "The Implementation of Welfare Reform Policy: The Role of Public Managers in Front-Line Practices." *Public Administration Review* 64 (4): 438–48.

Riemann, R., A. Angleitner, and J. Strelau. 1997. "Genetic and Environmental Influences on Personality: A Study of Twins Reared Together Using the Self- and Peer Report NEO-FFI Scales." *Journal of Personality* 65 (3): 449–75. doi:10.1111/j.1467-6494.1997.tb00324.x.

Roberts, B., K. Walton, and W. Viechtbauer. 2006. "Patterns of Mean-Level Change in Personality Traits Across the Life Course: A Meta-Analysis of Longitudinal Studies." *Psychological Bulletin* 132 (1): 1–25.

Rubinstein, J. 1973. *City Police*. New York: Hill and Wang.

Safire, W. 1978. *Safire's Political Dictionary*. New York: Random House.

Saks, A. 1996. "The Relationship Between the Amount and Helpfulness of Entry Training and Work Outcomes." *Human Relations* 49 (4): 429–51.

Saks, A., and B. Ashforth. 1997. "Organizational Socialization: Making Sense of the Past and Present as a Prologue for the Future." *Journal of Vocational Behavior* 51 (2): 234–79.

Saks, A., and J. Gruman. 2012. "Getting Newcomers On Board: A Review of Socialization Practices and Introduction to Socialization Resources Theory." In *The Oxford Handbook of Organizational Socialization*, edited by C. Wanberg, 27–55. New York: Oxford University Press.

Saks, A., K. Uggerslev, and N. Fassina. 2007. "Socialization Tactics and Newcomer Adjustment: A Meta-Analytic Review and Test of a Model." *Journal of Vocational Behavior* 70 (3): 413–46.

Sandfort, J. 2000. "Moving Beyond Discretion and Outcomes: Examining Public Management from the Front Lines of the Welfare System." *Journal of Public Administration Research and Theory* 10 (4): 729–56.

Sandfort, J., A. Kalil, and J. Gottschalk. 1999. "The Mirror Has Two Faces." *Journal of Poverty* 3 (3): 71–91.

Schneider, B. 1987. "The People Make the Place." *Personnel Psychology* 40 (3): 437–53.

Schneider, B., D. Smith, S. Taylor, and J. Fleenor. 1998. "Personality and Organizations: A Test of the Homogeneity of Personality Hypothesis." *Journal of Applied Psychology* 83 (3): 462–70.

Schott, L. 2012. "Policy Basics: An Introduction to TANF." Center for Budget and Policy Priorities. http://www.cbpp.org/cms/?fa=view&id=936.

Schram, S. 2011. "Welfare Professionals and Street-Level Bureaucrats." In *Social Work Handbook*, edited by M. Gray, J. Midgley, and S. Webb, 67–80. London: Sage.

Schram, S., J. Soss, R. Fording, and L. Houser. 2009. "Deciding to Discipline: Race, Choice, and Punishment at the Frontlines of Welfare Reform." *American Sociological Review* 74 (3): 398–422.

Scott, W. 2003. *Organizations: Rational, Natural, and Open Systems*. Upper Saddle River, N.J.: Prentice-Hall.

Selden, S., J. Brudney, and J. Kellough. 1998. "Bureaucracy as a Representative Institution: Toward a Reconciliation of Bureaucratic Government and Democratic Theory." *American Journal of Political Science* 42 (3): 717–44.

Shermer, Michael. 2007. "Bad Apples and Bad Barrels: Scientific American." *Scientific American*. http://www.scientificamerican.com/article.cfm?id=bad-apples-and-bad-barrels.

Shonkoff, J., and D. Phillips. 2000. *From Neurons to Neighborhoods: The Science of Early Childhood Development*. Washington, D.C.: National Academies Press.

Simon, D. 1993. *Homicide: A Year on the Killing Streets*. New York: Ballantine.

Simon, H. 1947. *Administrative Behavior: A Study of Decision-Making Processes in Administrative Organizations*. New York: Macmillan.

———. 1997. *Administrative Behavior: A Study of Decision-Making Processes in Administrative Organizations*. 4th ed. New York: Free Press.

Skolnick, J. 1966. *Justice Without Trial*. New York: John Wiley.

———. 2002. "Corruption and the Blue Code of Silence." *Police Practice and Research: An International Journal* 3 (1): 7–19.

Skowronek, S. 1982. *Building a New American State: The Expansion of National Administrative Capacities, 1877–1920*. New York: Cambridge University Press.

Small, D., and J. Lerner. 2008. "Emotional Policy: Personal Sadness and Anger Shape Judgments About a Welfare Case." *Political Psychology* 29 (2): 149–68.

Smith, D., and W. Bratton. 2001. "Performance Management in New York City: Compstat and the Revolution in Police Management." In *Quicker Better Cheaper? Managing Performance in American Government*, edited by D. Forsythe, 453–82. Albany, N.Y.: Rockefeller Institute Press.

Smith, D., and C. Visher. 1981. "Street-Level Justice: Situational Determinants of Police Arrest Decisions." *Social Problems* 29: 167–77.

Smith, E., and A. Zurcher. 1949. *New Dictionary of American Politics*. New York: Barnes & Noble.

Smith, R. 1993. "Beyond Tocqueville, Myrdal, and Hartz: The Multiple Traditions in America." *American Political Science Review* 87 (3): 549–66.

Soss, J. 2000. *Unwanted Claims: The Politics of Participation in the U.S. Welfare System*. Ann Arbor: University of Michigan Press.

Soss, J., R. Fording, and S. Schram. 2011a. *Disciplining the Poor: Neoliberal Paternalism and the Persistent Power of Race*. Chicago: University of Chicago Press.

———. 2011b. "The Organization of Discipline: From Performance Management to Perversity and Punishment." *Journal of Public Administration Research and Theory* 21 (suppl. 2): i203–32.

Soss, J., and S. Schram. 2007. "A Public Transformed? Welfare Reform as Policy Feedback." *American Political Science Review* 101 (1): 111–27.

Specht, H., and M. Courtney. 1995. *Unfaithful Angels: How Social Work Has Abandoned Its Mission*. New York: Free Press.

Stack, C. 1975. *All Our Kin: Strategies for Survival in a Black Community*. New York: Basic Books.

Steinhaus, C., and J. Perry. 1996. "Organizational Commitment: Does Sector Matter?" *Public Productivity and Management Review* 19 (3): 278–88.

Sun, I. 2003. "Police Officers' Attitudes Toward Their Role and Work: A Comparison of Black and White Officers." *American Journal of Criminal Justice* 28 (1): 89–108.

Sun, I., and B. Payne. 2004. "Racial Differences in Resolving Conflicts: A Comparison Between Black and White Police Officers." *Crime and Delinquency* 50 (4): 516–41.

Taylor, J. 1983. "Bureaucratic Structure and Personality: The Merton Model Revisited." In *Bureaucracy as a Social Problem*, edited by G. Sjoberg and L. Zurcher, 151–71. Greenwich, Conn.: JAI.

Teahan, J. 1975. "A Longitudinal Study of Attitude Shifts Among Black and White Police Officers." *Journal of Social Issues* 31 (1): 47–56.

Terrill, W., and S. D. Mastrofski. 2002. "Situational and Officer-Based Determinants of Police Coercion." *Justice Quarterly* 19 (2): 215–48.

Terrill, W., and M. Reisig. 2003. "Neighborhood Context and Police Use of Force." *Journal of Research in Crime and Delinquency* 40 (3): 291–321.

Theobald, N., and D. Haider-Markel. 2009. "Race, Bureaucracy, and Symbolic Representation: Interactions Between Citizens and Police." *Journal of Public Administration Research and Theory* 19 (2): 409–26.

Thompson, V. 1961. *Modern Organization*. New York: Knopf.

Thompson, V., and L. Bobo. 2011. "Thinking About Crime: Race and Lay Accounts of Lawbreaking Behavior." *Annals of the American Academy of Political and Social Science* 634 (1): 16–38.

Twersky-Glasner, A. 2005. "Police Personality: What Is It and Why Are They Like That?" *Journal of Police and Criminal Psychology* 20 (1): 56–67.

UCLA: Statistical Consulting Group. 2013. "Stata Annotated Output: Probit Regression." http://www.ats.ucla.edu/stat/stata/output/Stata_Probit.htm.

Van Maanen, J. 1974. "Working the Street: A Developmental View of Police Behavior." In *The Potential for Reform of Criminal Justice*, edited by H. Jacob, 83–130. Thousand Oaks, Calif.: Sage.

———. 1975. "Police Socialization: A Longitudinal Examination of Job Attitudes in an Urban Police Department." *Administrative Science Quarterly* 20 (2): 207–28.

Van Maanen, J., and E. Schein. 1979. "Toward a Theory of Organizational Socialization." *Research in Organizational Behavior* 1: 209–64.

Vandenabeele, W. 2007. "Toward a Public Administration Theory of Public Service Motivation." *Public Management Review* 9 (4): 545–56.
Venkatesh, S. 2006. *Off the Books: The Underground Economy of the Urban Poor*. Cambridge, Mass.: Harvard University Press.
Visser, P., and J. Krosnick. 1998. "Development of Attitude Strength Over the Life Cycle: Surge and Decline." *Journal of Personality and Social Psychology* 75: 1389–1410.
Wacquant, L. 2004. *Body and Soul: Notebooks of an Apprentice Boxer*. New York: Oxford University Press.
———. 2009. *Punishing the Poor: The Neoliberal Government of Social Insecurity*. Durham, N.C.: Duke University Press.
Wagner, D. 1990. *The Quest for a Radical Profession: Social Service Careers and Political Ideology*. Lanham, Md.: University Press of America.
Walker, W., J. Skowronski, and C. Thompson. 2003. "Life Is Pleasant—and Memory Helps to Keep It That Way!" *Review of General Psychology* 7 (2): 203–10.
Wanberg, C. 2012a. "Facilitating Organizational Socialization: An Introduction." In *The Oxford Handbook of Organizational Socialization*, edited by C. Wanberg. 17–21. New York: Oxford University Press.
———, ed. 2012b. *The Oxford Handbook of Organizational Socialization*. New York: Oxford University Press.
Wanous, J. 1992. *Organizational Entry: Recruitment, Selection, and Socialization of Newcomers*. Reading, Pa.: Addison-Wesley.
Warner, W. 1963. *The American Federal Executive: A Study of the Social and Personal Characteristics of the Civilian and Military Leaders of the United States Federal Government*. New Haven, Conn.: Yale University Press.
Watkins-Hayes, C. 2009. *The New Welfare Bureaucrats: Entanglements of Race, Class, and Policy Reform*. Chicago: University of Chicago Press.
Weaver, V., and A. Lerman. 2010. "Political Consequences of the Carceral State." *American Political Science Review* 104 (4): 817–33.
Weber, M. 1947. *The Theory of Social and Economic Organization*. Translated by T. Parsons. New York: Free Press.
Weick, K. 1995. *Sensemaking in Organizations*. Thousand Oaks, Calif.: Sage.
Weisburd, D., R. Greenspan, E. Hamilton, K. Bryant, and H. Williams. 2001. *The Abuse of Police Authority: A National Study of Police Officers' Attitudes*. Washington, D.C.: Police Foundation.
Whyte, W. 1956. *The Organization Man*. New York: Simon & Schuster.
Wilkins, V., and B. Williams. 2008. "Black or Blue: Racial Profiling and Representative Bureaucracy." *Public Administration Review* 68 (4): 654–64.
Wilson, G., and A. Nielsen. 2011. "'Color Coding' and Support for Social Policy Spending: Assessing the Parameters Among Whites." *Annals of the American Academy of Political and Social Science* 634 (1): 174–89.
Wilson, J. 1989. *Bureaucracy: What Government Agencies Do and Why They Do It*. New York: Basic Books.

Wilson, W. 1996. *When Work Disappears: The World of the New Urban Poor*. New York: Vintage.
Wood, W. 2000. "Attitude Change: Persuasion and Social Influence." *Annual Review of Psychology* 51 (1): 539–70.
Woodward, S. 1995. *Balkan Tragedy: Chaos and Dissolution After the Cold War*. Washington, D.C.: Brookings Institution Press.
Worden, R. 1989. "Situational and Attitudinal Explanations of Police Behavior: A Theoretical Reappraisal and Empirical Assessment." *Law and Society Review* 23 (4): 667–711.
——. 1995. "Police Officers' Belief Systems: A Framework for Analysis." *American Journal of Police* 14 (1): 49–81.
Wright, B., D. Moynihan, and S. Pandey. 2012. "Pulling the Levers: Transformational Leadership, Public Service Motivation, and Mission Valence." *Public Administration Review* 72 (2): 206–15.
Wright, B., and S. Pandey. 2008. "Public Service Motivation and the Assumption of Person—Organization Fit Testing the Mediating Effect of Value Congruence." *Administration and Society* 40 (5): 502–21.
Zhang, L., and M. Gowan. 2012. "Corporate Social Responsibility, Applicants' Individual Traits, and Organizational Attraction: A Person–Organization Fit Perspective." *Journal of Business and Psychology* 27 (3): 345–62.
Zimbardo, Philip. 2004. "A Situationist Perspective on the Psychology of Evil: Understanding How Good People Are Transformed into Perpetrators." In *The Social Psychology of Good and Evil*, 21–50. New York: Guilford.

INDEX

Abu Ghraib prison scandal, 2–3
African Americans, 17; among police officers, 89–90, 184, 214n9; police profiling of, 115, 143–44; welfare caseworkers' views of, 81, 130–31, 155–56, 159–60, 183. *See also* race
Aid to Families with Dependent Children (AFDC), 64, 158, 183. *See also* Temporary Assistance for Needy Families
allegiance. *See* loyalty
altruism, 11–12, 43–44, 50–51, 55, 87–88; fraud prevention as, 110, 214n12; volunteerism and, 29. *See also* motivation and public service motivation
appropriateness. *See* logic of appropriateness
Argyris, C., 7
Asian Americans, 47, 214n9. *See also* race
at-risk youth, 40, 45–46, 89
attitudes, 13–14, 140–41; of police officers, 44–47, 101, 141–53, 165–76; policymaking and, 164; of welfare caseworkers, 52–53, 140, 153–63, 165–76

Barnard, Charles, 11, 31
Barnett, Michael, 3, 30, 31
Barrett, E., 158–59
Bourdieu, Pierre, 6, 25–26
Brehm, J., 12
Brown, M., 42
Brubacker, R., 9
bureaucratic identities, 9–14, 20, 113–14, 137–39, 165–76; of police officers, 58, 114–27, 138–39, 165–69; of veteran police officers, 40–47, 54–55; of veteran welfare caseworkers, 48–50, 54–55; of welfare caseworkers, 57, 58, 66, 127–39, 165–69
bureaucratic personality, 6–15, 24–29, 37–40, 55, 164–65; changes in, 19–21, 165–76; components of, 9–10; criticisms of, 8–9

bureaucrats, 6–7, 115–16; burn-out among, 87; definition of, 211n1; representativeness of, 27–28, 171, 177; socialization of, 14–16, 34–35, 39–40, 165–76, 211n2
Bush, George W., 2–3

caseworkers. *See* welfare caseworkers
categorization of people, 13–14, 44, 57, 83
Chappell, A., 18
Chemerinsky, E., 80
community policing, 18, 89, 184
competence: bureaucratic inertia and, 30; among forest rangers, 22. *See also* professionalism
Compstat reforms, 75
Cook, F., 158–59
Cooper, F., 9
crime, 17; police views of, 13–14, 114, 143, 145–53

decision-making theory, 5–6, 31, 48, 54, 164
Desmond, M., 22, 26
differential continuity, 21, 23, 169–70
discretionary judgment: of police officers, 13, 33, 41–46, 58–62, 76, 113–18, 141–45, 152; of welfare caseworkers, 48–50, 53, 62–69, 132–35, 153–63. *See also* rule-following
dispositional perspective, 22–29, 38, 164, 165, 170–71; on bureaucracy, 27–28; on habitus, 25–27, 29; on personality, 2, 24–25, 29; on public service motivation, 28–29; scholarly literature on, 34–35; on training programs, 57, 85–86
drug abuse, 46, 113, 145

education, 29, 32, 127; ethnic representativeness in, 27–28; poverty and, 53

"efficiency engineers" (Watkins-Hayes), 48, 55, 66
egoism, 11–12, 87–88. *See also* motivation
elderly: Medicaid programs for, 64–65, 67; police officers' views of, 40, 45; socialization of, 212n2; welfare caseworkers' views of, 53, 63
emotional detachment: among police officers, 41, 59, 116–18; among welfare caseworkers, 48, 51, 57, 69–70, 130–31, 134
English proficiency, 67
entrants, 2–5, 22–27, 31–32, 38; motivations of, 88–92; socialization of, 14–21, 34–35, 39–40, 56–57; veterans' interaction with, 36, 58, 75–80, 101, 173–74; workplace influences on, 71–85. *See also* training programs

Farmers Home Administration, 5
firefighters, 22, 32
First Amendment rights, 115
Food Stamps, 49, 63–67; successor program of, 213n5; welfare caseworker views of, 155, 158, 159
forest rangers, 3, 8–9, 22
formalism, 6–7, 115–16
formalization, 5, 7, 32–34, 180
fraud, welfare, 51, 68, 105–10, 129, 156–58, 214n12

Gallo, G., 18
Gates, S., 12
General Assistance, 63, 65–67; successor program of, 155; welfare caseworkers' views of, 155, 158, 159, 161
genetics, 24, 29
Golden, M., 5
graffiti, 33

habitus, 6, 25–27, 29
Herzfeld, Michael, 4
Hispanics, 42, 47; in education, 27–28; as police officers, 89–90, 184, 214n9
Holocaust, 30
Hummel, Ralph, 4, 174
Hussein, Saddam, 2

identities, 9–13; in-group, 31; professional, 22–23, 48, 211n4; racial/ethnic, 38, 214n9. *See also* bureaucratic identities
indifference. *See* emotional detachment

institutional perspective, 22–23, 30–38, 164, 171–73; scholarly literature on, 34–36; on training programs, 57, 85
Internal Revenue Service auditors, 32
interviews, 37, 70; with police officers, 40–46, 58–62, 88–92, 114–19, 141–45; with welfare caseworkers, 48–52, 101–4, 127–31, 153–56
Iraq War, 2–3

James, William, 25
Jones, G., 34–35
judgment calls. *See* discretionary judgment

Kappeler, V., 18
Kaufman, H., 3

Lanza-Kaduce, L., 18
Latinos. *See* Hispanics
Lipsky, Michael, 16, 49, 51
logic of appropriateness (LOA) theory, 4–6; attitudes and, 13, 140–41, 164; discretionary calls and, 113; habitus and, 26; identities and, 31, 113, 137–38; personality and, 9–10; welfare caseworker training and, 66
loyalty, 13, 20, 113–14; among police officers, 42–43, 83–85, 119–26; among welfare caseworkers, 50, 82–83, 132–36

March, James, 5–6, 9–10, 113, 137, 140. *See also* logic of appropriateness theory
Medicaid, 49, 63, 155, 183; for elderly, 64–65, 67, 158–59; handbooks on, 66–67
Meier, K., 27–28
Merton, R., 7, 8
methodology, research, 17–19, 37–38
military experience, police officers with, 71–72, 77, 90, 124, 127, 141, 200
motivation, 10–12, 87–88; altruistic vs. egoistic, 11–12, 43–44, 50–51, 54, 87–88, 91, 106–7; bureaucratic personality and, 165–76; family influence on, 25, 29, 90, 175, 213nn3–4; organizational influences on, 31–32, 99; of police officers, 41, 88–101, 110–12, 121–22, 165–74; public service, 11, 28–29, 87–88; of veteran police officers, 43–44, 101; of veteran welfare caseworkers, 50–51, 54; of welfare caseworkers, 87–88, 101–12, 165–74
Muir, W., 44

Native Americans, 144
natural systems (NS) perspective, 31, 33–38
Nazi Germany, 30
new recruits. *See* entrants

odds ratio calculations: definition of, 214n8; of police attitudes, 148–53; of police bureaucratic identities, 122–27; of police motivations, 96–101; of welfare caseworker attitudes, 153–56, 160–62; of welfare caseworker identities, 108–10; of welfare caseworker motivations, 108–10
Olsen, Johan, 5–6, 9–10, 113, 137, 140. *See also* logic of appropriateness theory
open systems approach, 32, 175
organizational culture, 18, 35–36, 58, 80–85; Internal Revenue Service and, 32; police motivations and, 101; United Nations and, 30–31; welfare caseworker motivations and, 110
organizational socialization (OS), 15, 34–35, 39–40, 211n2. *See also* socialization
orientation programs, 212n3. *See also* training programs
out-group identity, 31

peer influences, 35–36, 57, 70–71, 80. *See also* socialization
personality, 9–10; definitions of, 9, 24; dispositional perspective of, 24–25; habitus and, 25–27, 29; twin studies on, 24. *See also* bureaucratic personality
police officers, 8–9, 18; attitudes of, 13, 44–47, 141–53, 162–63, 165–76; bureaucratic identities of, 114–27, 138–39, 165–76; categorization of people by, 13–14, 44, 83; code of silence among, 43, 232; community relations and, 18, 89, 184; corruption among, 16–17; discretionary calls by, 13, 33, 41–46, 58–62, 113–18, 141–45, 152; emotional detachment of, 41, 59, 116–18; family members as, 25, 90–91, 93, 213nn3–4; interviews with, 40–49, 58–62, 88–92, 114–19, 141–45; loyalty among, 42–43, 83–85, 119–26; with military experience, 71–72, 77, 90, 124, 127, 141, 200; minority, 89–90, 98–99, 184, 214n9; motivations of, 43–44, 88–101, 110–12, 121–22, 165–76; overtime pay for, 91–92; profiling by, 115, 143–44; training of, 56–62, 70–71, 75–78, 99–101; use of force by, 41, 61, 114–15, 182; workplace influences on, 71–72, 75–78, 83–85. *See also* veteran police officers
police sergeants, 33, 75–76
poverty, 17; police views of, 45–47, 143–53; welfare caseworkers' views of, 52–54, 104–7, 153–63
probit coefficients, 96, 107–8, 122, 135, 148, 160–62
professionalism, 28–29; identity and, 22–23, 48, 211n4; norms of, 7
public service motivation (PSM), 11, 28–29, 87–88. *See also* motivation and altruism

race, 17, 38; of police officers, 89–90, 98–99, 184, 214n9; police profiling by, 115, 143–44; police views of, 46–47, 143–53, 171; welfare caseworkers' views of, 81, 155–56, 159–62, 183
rational systems (RS) perspective, 31–35, 37–38
Reagan, Ronald, 5
religion, 28–29, 184
research methodology, 17–19, 37–38
rookies. *See* entrants
Rubenstein, J., 42, 75
rule-following, 12, 16, 20–21; by police officers, 41–42, 49–50, 59, 115–22; rational systems perspective on, 32; by welfare caseworkers, 49–50, 66–67, 127–28, 132–36. *See also* discretionary judgment
Rwanda genocide, 30

sanctions, by welfare caseworkers, 49, 132–35, 183–84, 212n2
Schneider, B., 174
self-concept, 9, 113. *See also* identities
silence, code of, 43, 232
Simon, Herbert, 3–4, 31
social identity theory, 31
social workers, 48, 50, 55, 70, 73, 211n7.
socialization, 14–19, 34–35, 39–40; changes during, 25, 61, 165–76; definitions of, 211n2; of elderly, 212n2; entrants' motivations and, 28–29, 96–99; environment and, 25, 31–32, 71–85; habitus and, 26–27; military, 174; organizational, 15, 34–35, 39–40, 211n2; peer influence on, 35–36, 57, 70–71, 80

"Song for Employees Suffering Mistreatment," 82
standardization of practices, 12, 59, 60; rational systems perspective of, 32
statistical analysis, 37–38; of police attitudes, 148–53; of police bureaucratic identities, 122–27; of police motivations, 96–101, 121–22; of welfare caseworker attitudes, 160–62; of welfare caseworker bureaucratic identities, 135–37; of welfare caseworker motivation, 107–10
street-level bureaucrats, 16–17, 85; categorization of people by, 13–14, 83; natural systems perspective on, 35–36; "paradigmatic," 212n8
substance abuse, 46, 61, 113, 145
Supplemental Nutrition Assistance Program (SNAP). See Food Stamps
surveys, 37–38; of police attitudes, 146–48; of police bureaucratic identities, 119–22; of police motivations, 92–96, 121–22; of welfare caseworker attitudes, 156–60; of welfare caseworker bureaucratic identities, 131–35; of welfare caseworker motivations, 104–7

teachers, Hispanic, 27–28
Temporary Assistance for Needy Families (TANF), 52; forerunner of, 64, 158, 183; training for, 63–68; welfare caseworker views of, 154, 155, 158, 159, 161
Thompson, V., 7
totalizing institutions, 30, 31
training programs, 56–86; first day of, 56–58; individual vs. group, 34–36; orientation programs and, 212n3; for police cadets, 56–62, 70–71, 75–78, 99–101; for welfare caseworkers, 56–58, 62–74, 78–80, 109–10, 154–55; workplace influences on, 71–85. See also entrants
twin studies, of personality, 24

United Nations, 30
use of force, by police officers, 41, 61, 114–15, 182

Van Maanen, J., 22
veteran police officers, 40–47, 54–55, 58; attitudes of, 44–47, 145; bureaucratic identities of, 40–47, 54–55; cadets' interaction with, 36, 58, 76–78; motivations of, 43–44, 101. See also police officers
veteran welfare caseworkers, 47–55, 78–80. See also welfare caseworkers
veteran workers, 39–55, 76–80; attitudes of, 44–47, 52–53; bureaucratic identities of, 40–55; entrants' interactions with, 36, 58, 75–80, 173–74; motivations of, 43–44, 51–52, 101
volunteerism, 29. See also altruism

Wanberg, C., 211n2
Watkins-Hayes, C., 48, 55, 66
Weber, Max, 6–7, 11, 31, 115–16
welfare caseworkers: attitudes of, 52–53, 140, 153–63, 165–76; bureaucratic identities of, 48–50, 58, 127–39, 165–69; categorization of people by, 13–14, 57, 83; client investigations by, 68–69; discretionary calls by, 48–50, 53, 62–69, 132–36, 153–63; emotional detachment of, 48, 51, 57, 69–70, 130–31, 134; as former welfare recipients, 102, 110–11, 127; interviews of, 48–52, 101–4, 127–31, 140, 153–56; loyalty among, 50, 82–83, 132–36; motivations of, 50–51, 54, 87–88, 101–12, 165–74; sanctions by, 49, 132–35, 183–84, 212n2; social workers and, 48, 50, 73, 211n7; training of, 56–58, 62–74, 78–80, 109–10, 154–55; veteran, 47–55, 58, 78–80; violence against, 57; workload management by, 70, 73, 130–31; workplace influences on, 71–74, 79–83
welfare reform policies, 109, 213n2
whistle-blowing, 43, 232
Whyte, William H., 7
Wilson, James, 8, 13, 80
Worden, R., 13
work ethic, 14, 44, 46, 53, 62, 143, 147, 151, 154, 174
workplace influences, 25, 71–85; on police officers, 71–72, 75–78, 83–85; rational systems perspective on, 31–32; on welfare caseworkers, 71–74, 79–83

youth, at-risk, 40, 45–46, 80

ACKNOWLEDGMENTS

During the writing of this book, I had the good fortune to be a member of four terrific scholarly communities. First, at the University of Wisconsin–Madison I was part of a political science department in which people generously shared their ideas and time. In particular I would like to thank John Coleman, Kathy Cramer Walsh, Graham Wilson, and John Witte for all the time, energy, and care they invested in me and this work. Also, special thanks to Joe Soss whose research helped to inspire my interest in the front lines of government and who, even after he left Madison, was a tremendous help with all aspects of this book. I would also like to acknowledge and thank Debbie Bakke, Barry Burden, Paul Hutchcroft, Deb McFarlane, Joe Stathus, Tammi Simpson, and Daun Wheeler. While in Madison I was associated with the Institute for Research on Poverty (IRP) which provided generous financial support for this project. In particular, I would like to thank Maria Cancian, Carolyn Heinrich, and Bill Wambach. Finally, Jon and Kathryn Wiens began as part of my UW family and now, many years later, are just family.

After Madison, I found a superb group of colleagues at the Department of Health and Human Services in the Office of Planning, Research, and Evaluation. In particular, I am grateful for the openness and collegiality of Naomi Goldstein, Mark Fucello, Nancye Campbell, Steve Hanmer, John Tambornino, and Brendan Kelly. And thanks to Mike Fitzpatrick and Allison Billings for their amazing kindness and hospitality during my year in D.C. I would also like to acknowledge my friends and colleagues at the City College of New York where I worked as a postdoctoral research fellow from 2009 to 2010. In particular, thanks to Mark Musell, Brett Silverstein, Lamar Bennett, Alisha Godette, Meghna Sabharwal, and Hawai Kwok. Finally, I am grateful to Haverford College. It is a remarkable place to work and I feel privileged to interact with such curious students and devoted colleagues. In particular, I would like to thank Cristina Beltran, Steve McGovern, Anita Isaacs, Craig Borowiak, Barak Mendelsohn, and P.J. Brendese.

Additionally, thank you to the welfare caseworkers and police officers who participated in this study and made this book possible. They had busy work and home lives and I thank them for taking the time to talk with me about their experiences. Thanks also to the legal counsel and academy staff of the police department for their enthusiasm and support from conception to completion. Though I was warned about the "blue wall of silence" I never encountered it. Thanks also to the welfare department for approving and supporting this project.

I also received excellent advice about this book from a variety of colleagues. In particular thank you to John Brehm, Steven Maynard-Moody, Michael Lipsky, Don Moynihan, Stephane Lavertu, Alejandro Rettig-y-Martinez, and Leisha DeHart-Davis. I am also indebted to Norma Riccucci, Irene Lurie, and Marcia Meyers for their willingness to share the data from the Rockefeller Institute of Government survey of welfare caseworkers in four states. In addition, earlier versions of portions of this book were previously published in: "Rule-Following and Discretion at Government's Frontlines: Continuity and Change During Organization Socialization," *Journal of Public Administration Research and Theory* 20 (4): 735–755, © 2010 Oxford University Press; "Socialization and Self-Selection: How Police Officers Develop Their Views About Using Force," *Administration & Society* 44 (6): 702–730, © 2012 Sage Publications; and "Motivation, Change, and Stability: Findings from an Urban Police Department," *American Review of Public Administration* doi: 10.1177/0275074012461297, © 2012 Sage Publications. I am grateful to the three journals for permission to reprint published work.

Thanks also to the editors of the American Governance Series at the University of Pennsylvania Press and, in particular, to Chris Howard for his insightful, detailed comments on my manuscript. Working with Peter Agree, my editor at Penn Press, could not have been better. I appreciate his enthusiasm, kindness and flexibility, and the fact that he is the fastest email responder I've ever met. Thanks also to Noreen O'Connor-Abel for her careful attention and thoughtful suggestions throughout the editing of the manuscript.

Finally, thank you to my dear family. My parents, Bill and Lynn Oberfield, have given me a lifetime of support and love. I am thankful to have them as role models, friends, and co-conspirators. Thanks also for the company and counsel of my siblings and in-laws Josh and Annie Oberfield, Jillian Oberfield and Ben Fenwick, and Amy Lin and Brett Sedgewick, and Sarah and Tom Lin. My biggest thanks go to Felicia Lin. Over the last 13 years, each stop along our way has been home because you were there. I treasure your humor, intelligence, and kindness. Caring for our sweet Theo has been my life's greatest joy. I dedicate this book to the two of them.